Perspectives in Law, Business and Innovation

Series Editor

Toshiyuki Kono, Faculty of Law, Kyushu University, Fukuoka, Japan

Over the last three decades, interconnected processes of globalization and rapid technological change—particularly, the emergence of networked technologies—have profoundly disrupted traditional models of business organization. This economic transformation has created multiple new opportunities for the emergence of alternate business forms, and disruptive innovation has become one of the major driving forces in the contemporary economy. Moreover, in the context of globalization, the innovation space increasingly takes on a global character. The main stakeholders—innovators, entrepreneurs and investors—now have an unprecedented degree of mobility in pursuing economic opportunities wherever they arise. As such, frictionless movement of goods, workers, services, and capital is becoming the "new normal".

This new economic and social reality has created multiple regulatory challenges for policymakers as they struggle to come to terms with the rapid pace of these social and economic changes. Moreover, these challenges impact across multiple fields of both public and private law. Nevertheless, existing approaches within legal science often struggle to deal with innovation and its effects.

Paralleling this shift in the economy, we can, therefore, see a similar process of disruption occurring within contemporary academia, as traditional approaches and disciplinary boundaries—both within and between disciplines—are being re-configured. Conventional notions of legal science are becoming increasingly obsolete or, at least, there is a need to develop alternative perspectives on the various regulatory challenges that are currently being created by the new innovation-driven global economy.

The aim of this series is to provide a forum for the publication of cutting-edge research in the fields of innovation and the law from a Japanese and Asian perspective. The series will cut across the traditional sub-disciplines of legal studies but will be tied together by a focus on contemporary developments in an innovation-driven economy and will deepen our understanding of the various regulatory responses to these economic and social changes.

The series editor and editorial board carefully assess each book proposal and sample chapters in terms of their relevance to law, business, and innovative technological change. Each proposal is evaluated on the basis of its academic value and distinctive contribution to the fast-moving debate in these fields.

All books and chapters in the Perspectives in Law, Business and Innovation book series are indexed in Scopus.

More information about this series at http://www.springer.com/series/15440

Steven Van Uytsel
Editor

The Digital Economy and Competition Law in Asia

Springer

Editor
Steven Van Uytsel
Graduate School of Law
Kyushu University
Fukuoka, Japan

ISSN 2520-1875 ISSN 2520-1883 (electronic)
Perspectives in Law, Business and Innovation
ISBN 978-981-16-0323-5 ISBN 978-981-16-0324-2 (eBook)
https://doi.org/10.1007/978-981-16-0324-2

This Springer imprint is published by the registered company Springer Nature Singapore Pte Ltd.
The registered company address is: 152 Beach Road, #21-01/04 Gateway East, Singapore 189721, Singapore

Preface

This edited collection brings together leading scholars based in Asia to detail how their respective jurisdictions respond to the competition law problems evolving out of the deployment of the digital economy, which can be broadly defined as the economy operating based on the interconnectivity between people and businesses. This approach is warranted, because the digital economy, though a global phenomenon, plays out in local economic, political, and regulatory contexts.

This volume is based on ideas explored at two symposia: (1) Multidisciplinary Perspectives on Algorithms: Regulation, Governance, Markets, and (2) Algorithms, Collusion and Competition Law. These symposia were held at Kyushu University, Fukuoka, Japan on 21–22 and 23 November 2019, respectively. Both symposia were instrumental for the development of the ideas presented in this book.

Steven Van Uytsel would like to thank Kyushu University and the Society for the Promotion of Science (JSPS) for their generous financial support. Kyushu University has been providing financial support for the organization of the above symposia through its *Progress 100: Research Hub for the Humanities, Social Sciences, and Interdisciplinary Knowledge (RINK) Grant.* This grant has been obtained for the research of *Multi-Disciplinary Perspectives on New Technology & the Law*. The financial support of JSPS, obtained within the category of Grant-in-Aid for Scientific Research (C), was for research on *Artificial Intelligence, Price Setting Strategies and Antitrust Law: Towards a Regulatory Framework.* This project carries the project number 18K01300.

The editor also owes a word of gratitude to Mrs. Y. Matsumura, whose help was instrumental for organizing the symposia and editing the footnotes. The editor is also grateful to Mrs. Intachan Chirachawee, who also assisted in the editing of the footnotes.

Fukuoka, Japan
January 2021

Steven Van Uytsel

Contents

Editor and Contributors

About the Editor

Steven Van Uytsel is Professor in the Faculty of Law at Kyushu University (Japan). He received his legal education at the University of Antwerp, including an exchange at Uppsala University. He completed his LL.M. & LL.D. at Kyushu University and his Master of Arts (Japanese Studies) at the Mercator Hogeschool (now Mercator Campus of Ghent Hogeschool). Steven specializes in competition law, for which he has received several grants from the Japanese Society for the Promotion of Science, such as the Grants-in-Aid for Young Scientists (B), No. 23730058, "Competition Law, Public Enforcement Authorities and Private Parties—Towards a More Effective Interrelationship" (April 2011–March 2014) and the Grants-in-Aid for Scientific Research (C), No. 15K03152, "Anti-Cartel Enforcement: Towards a Holistic Understanding of Leniency Policies" (April 2015–March 2018).

Steven was lead editor of the Research Handbook on Asian Competition Law (Edward Elgar, 2020). He also acted as editor of Regulating FinTech in Asia: Global Context, Local Perspectives (Springer, 2020), Networked Governance, Transnational Business and the Law (Springer, 2014) and Collective Actions: Enhancing Access to Justice and Reconciling Multilayer Interests (Cambridge, 2012).

More recently, Steven has expanded his research to include artificial intelligence. For his research on artificial intelligence, he has obtained several grants such as JSPS Grant-in-Aid for Scientific Research (C) (April 2018–March 2021) for doing research on Artificial Intelligence, Price Setting Strategies and Antitrust Law: Towards a Regulatory Framework (No. 18K01300) and Kyushu University's Progress 100—RINK Grant for researching Regulating Algorithms: Multi-Disciplinary Perspectives on New Technology & the Law (2018–2020). This book is an offspring of these two grants.

Contributors

Peerapat Chokesuwattanaskul Faculty of Law, Chulalongkorn University, Bangkok, Thailand

Nikita Koradia Institute of Law, Nirma University, Ahmedabad, India

Kiran Manokaran Kasthuri & Sundar Associates, Chennai, India

Angayar Kanni Ramaiah Faculty of Law, University Teknologi MARA (UiTM), Pulau Pinang, Malaysia

Mohammad Reza Faculty of Law, Universitas al Azhar Indonesia, Jakarta, DKI Jakarta, Indonesia

Zara Saeed Shanghai Electric Group, Karachi, Pakistan

Ningrum Natasya Sirait Faculty of Law, Universitas Sumatera Utara, Medan, Sumatera Utara, Indonesia

Aria Suyudi Faculty of Law, STIH Indonesia Jentera, Jakarta, DKI Jakarta, Indonesia

Toshiaki Takigawa Kansai University, Osaka, Japan

Yoshiteru Uemura Faculty of Economics, Hannan University, Osaka, Japan

Steven Van Uytsel Graduate School of Law, Kyushu University, Fukuoka, Japan

The Digital Economy and Asian Competition Law: An Introduction

Steven Van Uytsel

Abstract Digital economy is a concept that has been around for nearly three decades. During this period, the concept has developed to include three dimensions. The core dimension of the digital economy surrounds information and communication technology. The narrow dimension of the digital economy embraces digital platforms and the businesses that are built on these platforms. The broad dimension of the digital economy deals with the digitization of the economy, of which artificial intelligence, sensors, cloud-based databases are the core. Several Asian countries, such as India, Indonesia, Japan, and Thailand, are moving towards the broad dimension of the digital economy. Despite this evolution, competition law literature is only recently embracing the concept of digital economy. The preference in the literature was to either refer to specific technological evolutions, use high technology, or bring up the concept of New Economy. It is only recently that digital economy is more and more used by the community of competition law scholars. Much of this literature deals with platforms, data and privacy, thus the narrow dimension of the digital economy. This book will follow this trend. However, the last part of this book will already relate to the broad dimension by discussing the use of artificial intelligence in price setting strategies.

Keywords Digital economy · Digital sector · Digitalized economy · New economy · Internet · Artificial intelligence · Society 5.0 · Data · Privacy · Market definition · Asia · Competition law · Superior bargaining position · Unfair trade practice · Ride hailing · Go-Jek · Hub and spoke · Predictable agent · Digital eye · Cartel facilitator

A report sponsored by Google, Temasek, and Bain & Company found that the Internet Economy in South-Asia had reached USD $100 billion in 2019.[1] The same report

[1] Google et al. (2019, p. 13).

S. Van Uytsel (✉)
Graduate School of Law, Kyushu University, Fukuoka, Japan
e-mail: uytsel@law.kyushu-u.ac.jp

S. Van Uytsel (ed.), *The Digital Economy and Competition Law in Asia*,
Perspectives in Law, Business and Innovation,
https://doi.org/10.1007/978-981-16-0324-2_1

predicts that, by 2025, this number will triple to $300 billion.[2] Within the South-East Asian region, Indonesia and Vietnam are setting the pace, with a growth rate of more than 40% a year.[3] Similar figures can be found for countries outside the South-East Asian region. It is predicted that the $200 billion digital economy in India could expand to up to $1 trillion by 2025.[4] According to the China Academy of Information and Communications Technology, China's digital economy has already surpassed the $1 trillion mark to reach a $5.07 trillion in 2019.[5] Japan, in 2017, had its digital economy valued at $110 billion. By 2030, the Japanese digital economy would quadruple to $506 billion.[6] But, are these reports addressing the same issue? Google, Temasek, and Bain & Company refer to the Internet Economy, while the other authors commonly use digital economy in their respective articles.

It is certain that "economic changes were associated mainly with emergence of the Internet."[7] However, the Internet was a phenomenon of the 1990s. Technology has evolved, and, especially since the 2010s, we see that a "succession of new information and communication technologies (ICTs) has diffused and underpinned economic change. This includes the embedding of connected sensors into more and more objects (the Internet of things); new end-user devices (mobile phones, smartphones, tablets, netbooks, laptops, 3D printers); new digital models (cloud computing, digital platforms, digital services); growing intensity of data usage through the spread of Big Data, data analytics and algorithmic decision-making; and new automation and robotics technologies."[8] Could this evolution towards new technology shed any light on how we should understand the differences among the terminology in the above-mentioned reporting?

To answer this question, further insight is required on how the term digital economy has originated and developed. It is the purpose of this introductory note to the book to briefly summarize this evolution and put forward a definition of the digital economy that is widely accepted in policy documents. This will be done in Sect. 1. With a more profound understanding of the term digital economy, Sect. 2 will elaborate that various Asian countries, like India, Indonesia, Japan and Thailand, have developed or are developing plans to embrace the concept of digital economy in its widest sense. This is not necessarily so for competition law literature. Section 3 briefly reviews competition law literature to show that there was either just a reference to the technological problem, the general term of high technology, or the New Economy. Digital economy is only a recently used concept in the competition law literature to deal with platform related problems. With contributions linked to platforms in Asia, this book contributes to the literature on the digital economy and competition law. Section 4 provides a more detailed overview of the book.

---

[2]Google et al. (2019, p. 14).

[3]Google et al. (2019, p. 18).

[4]MeitY (2019, p. 6).

[5]Huaxia (2020).

[6]Bhatnagar (2020).

[7]Bukht and Heeks (2017, p. 2).

[8]Bukht and Heeks (2017, p. 2) and Podszun (2015, p. 102).

1 The Digital Economy

Digital economy was a concept first coined by Don Tapscott.[9] When Tapscott published his book, *The Digital Economy: Promise and Peril in the Age of Networked Intelligence*, in 1996, the commercial use of the Internet in the United States had only celebrated its first anniversary.[10] Despite the early stage of development of this technology, Tapscott already envisioned that the digital economy would be about the networking of humans through technology and in so doing, allow for a "combin[ing of] intelligence, knowledge, and creativity for breakthroughs in the creation of wealth and social development."[11] Tapscott's description of the digital economy was thus more a vision than a definition. With a focus on interactivity, Tapscott's vision went well beyond stacking information on websites.[12]

Subsequent studies on the digital economy made an attempt to materialize Tapscott's vision. One example in the literature was to emphasize the content of the economy. Neal Lane defined the digital economy in terms of e-commerce,[13] while Erik Brynjolfsson and Brian Kahin included all sectors of the economy that could be digitized.[14] Another example in the literature was to add the technology necessary to develop the digital economy. In this respect, Lynn Margherio et al. looked at what is needed for a digital economy.[15] Besides e-commerce,[16] the digital delivery of goods and services,[17] and retail sale of tangible goods,[18] they also stressed the need for a well-developed Internet.[19] These understandings of the digital economy were elaborated in various documents. Some valued more the e-commerce aspect, while others emphasized more the technology. Rob Kling and Roberta Lamb specified the commercial aspect by stating that the digital economy "includes goods and services whose development, production, sale, or provision is critically dependent upon digital technologies."[20] The Economist Intelligence Unit assessed the digital economy in function of the quality of the information and communication technology (ICT) infrastructure.[21]

---

[9]Tapscott (2016).

[10]Naughton (2016, p. 12) (the article describes that between 1967 and 1995, what we now know as the Internet was an experiment. At first, it was with a military focus. Gradually, a civilian dimension was added. However, the commercial use of the Internet only started from 1995).

[11]Tapscott (2016, p. xiv).

[12]Podszun (2015, p. 2012).

[13]Lane (1999).

[14]Brynjolfsson and Kahin (2000).

[15]Margherio et al. (1999).

[16]Margherio et al. (1999, pp. 12–23).

[17]Margherio et al. (1999, pp. 24–34).

[18]Margherio et al. (1999, pp. 35–40).

[19]Margherio et al. (1999, pp. 8–11).

[20]Kling and Lamb (2000, p. 297).

[21]Economist Intelligence Unit (2010).

Since 2016, an evolution is noticeable that scholars, government offices, international organizations and practitioners started to merge the different components of the digital economy. To understand the digital economy, the technological component cannot be separated from activities that are enabled by these technologies.[22]

In the light of the tendency to combine the different elements into one definition of the digital economy, Rumana Bukht and Richard Heeks embrace a model in which each step building upon ICT infrastructure.[23] At the core of the digital economy, Bukht and Heeks position the Information Technology (IT) and ICT sector.[24] The core is being named the digital sector and includes, among others, the telecommunication sector or the software industry.[25] The first to develop on the digital sector was the narrow understanding of the digital economy, which Bukht and Heeks just term the digital economy.[26] The narrow scope of the digital economy contains, among others, digital services (e.g. social network services) and the platform economy.[27] One step beyond is considered as the broad scope of the digital economy, which Bukht and Heeks call the digitalized economy.[28] The broad scope includes, for example, the algorithmic economy.[29] In between the narrow and broad scope, Bukht and Heeks position the gig economy and the sharing economy.[30] Figure 1 is how Bukht and Heeks represent their definition of the digital economy.

Bukht and Heeks' understanding of the digital economy has been adopted by several international organizations.[31] It is further in line with the observation made by the Economic Research Office of the Japanese Ministry of Internal Affairs and Communications.[32] The digital economy started out with the ICT industry. Gradually, the concept of the digital economy added more content with the development of new

---

[22]See, e.g., Dahlman et al. (2016, p. 11) ("The digital economy is the amalgamation of several general purpose technologies (GPTs) and the range of economic and social activities carried out by people over the Internet and related technologies. It encompasses the physical infrastructure that digital technologies are based on (broadband lines, routers), the devices that are used for access (computers, smartphones), the applications they power (Google, Salesforce) and the functionality they provide (IoT, data analytics, cloud computing)"); House of Commons (2016, p. 4) (the digital economy refers to both the digital access of goods and services, and the use of digital technology to help businesses); Knickrehm et al. (2016, p. 2) ("The digital economy is the share of total economic output derived from a number of broad "digital" inputs. These digital inputs include digital skills, digital equipment (hardware, software and communications equipment) and the intermediate digital goods and services used in production. Such broad measures reflect the foundations of the digital economy").

[23]Bukht and Heeks (2017). Compare with a summary of Tapscott's understanding, Podszun (2015, pp. 103–104).

[24]Bukht and Heeks (2017, p. 11).

[25]Bukht and Heeks (2017, p. 11).

[26]Bukht and Heeks (2017, p. 12).

[27]Bukht and Heeks (2017, pp. 12–13).

[28]Bukht and Heeks (2017, p. 12).

[29]Bukht and Heeks (2017, pp. 12–13).

[30]Bukht and Heeks (2017, p. 13).

[31]See, e.g., UNCTAD (2017, p. 4).

[32]Economic Research Office (2019, p. 16).

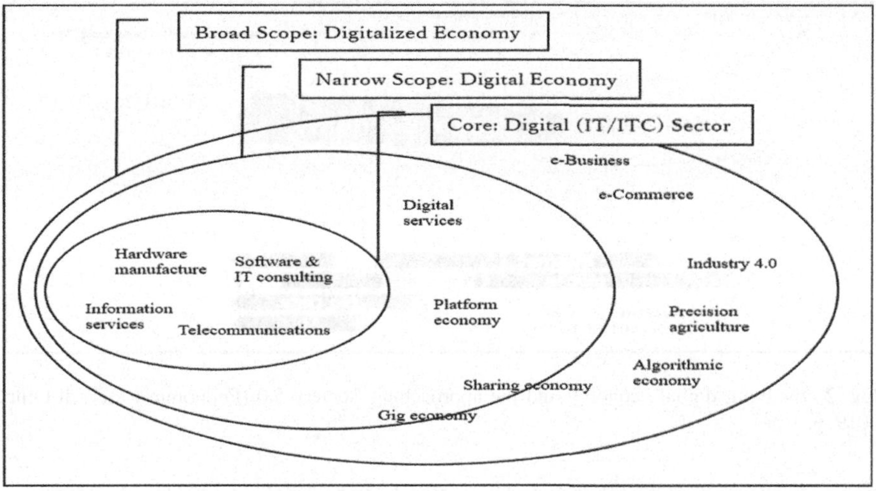

Fig. 1 Bukht and Heeks conceptualization of the digital economy (Bukht and Heeks 2017, p. 13)

technology. The introduction of the Internet in the retail sector created e-commerce. More recently, the development of mobile media technology has created new forms of economy, such as the sharing economy and the gig economy. There is a recognition that the further development of technology, more in specific the Internet of Things, the 5G telephony network, and Artificial Intelligence (AI), demands new classification.

2 Asia's Desire to Reach a Full-Fletched Digital Economy

Aware of the significant contribution the digital economy could have to their economic success, several Asian states have developed strategic plans for the future growth of all aspects of the digital economy. Japan is deploying *Society 5.0* since 2019.[33] Similar to Japan, India has launched *Digital India: Power to Empower* (Digital India) in 2015.[34] Thailand has developed the Thailand *Digital Economy and Society Development Plan* in 2017.[35] Indonesia has a more fragmented policy. The focus on e-commerce, called *Indonesia's e-Commerce Road Map* (Road Map),[36]

[33] Available at: https://www8.cao.go.jp/cstp/english/society5_0/index.html. Accessed 15 December 2020.

[34] Available at: https://digitalindia.gov.in/. Accessed 15 December 2020.

[35] Available at: https://www.onde.go.th/assets/portals//files/Digital_Thailand_pocket_book_EN.pdf. Accessed 15 December 2020.

[36] A translation of the policy, available at: https://www.amcham.or.id/images/Roadmap.pdf. Accessed 15 December 2020.

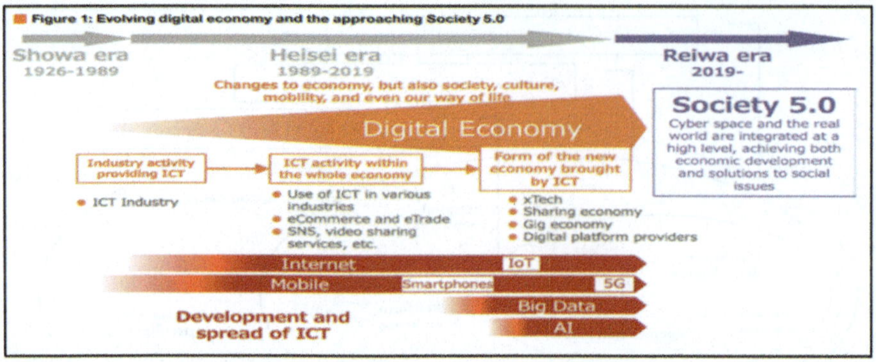

Fig. 2 Evolving digital economy and the approaching Society 5.0 (Economic Research Office 2019, p. 16)

is developing parallel with the *2020 Go Digital Vision*,[37] which aimed at incorporating e-commerce in various sectors of the economy such as agriculture, fisheries, small and medium sized enterprises, etc.[38]

Japan's idea with Society 5.0 is to integrate cyberspace with the real world. In other words, the technology developed in the fourth industrial revolution, such as Internet of Things, Big Data, AI, sharing economy, etc., should be incorporated into every industry and aspect of our lives.[39] The aim of this exercise would be to create new services making people's lives more comfortable and sustainable. Whereas Bukht and Heeks consider this the digitalized economy, the Economic Research Office of the Japanese Ministry of Internal Affairs and Communications uses the term Society 5.0.[40] In reality, both stand for the same thing: digitization of everything.[41] The digitization of everything could be described as the technology combining of sensors, cloud-based databases, and sophisticated algorithms and AI. The combination of all these technologies allow for collecting, aggregating and analyzing information and then, based on the analysis, offer personalized services to the end-users via networked software. The digital economy as understood by the Economic Research Office of the Japanese Ministry of Internal Affairs and Communications is presented in Fig. 2.

Five areas have been chosen by Japan for the initial focus of the development of Society 5.0: healthcare, mobility, supply chain, infrastructure, and fintech.[42] Cloud services, sensors, AI and other new technologies should enable the growth of more

---

[37] Edamadaka and Seiki (2019).

[38] Available at: https://partners.wsj.com/bkpm/indonesia-open-for-business/indonesia-set-to-become-a-digital-economic-powerhouse/. Accessed 15 December 2020.

[39] Available at: https://www8.cao.go.jp/cstp/english/society5_0/index.html. Accessed 15 December 2020.

[40] Economic Research Office (2019, p. 16).

[41] Brynjolfsson and McAfee (2013).

[42] Available at: https://www.japan.go.jp/abenomics/_userdata/abenomics/pdf/society_5.0.pdf. Accessed 15 December 2020. See also Fukuyama (2018, p. 48).

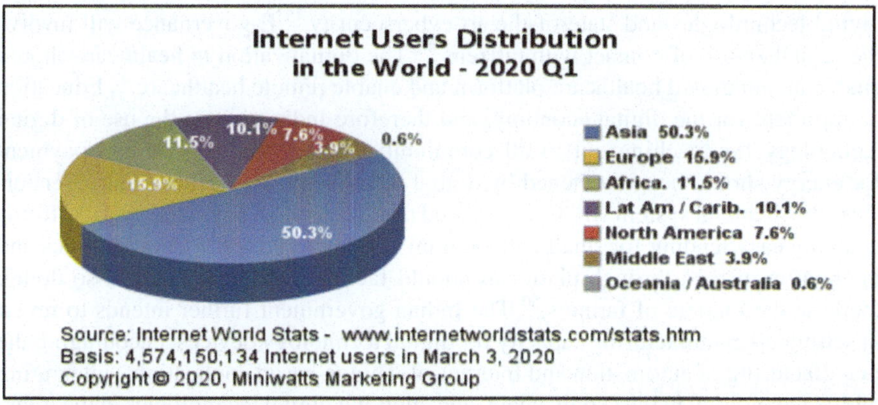

Fig. 3 Internet users distribution in the world—2020. Available at: https://www.internetworldstats.com/stats.htm. Accessed 15 December 2020

centrally controlled healthcare, in which action can be taken when some of the patient's parameters are distorted. Mobility will be taken over by autonomous vehicles of different kinds, relying on sensors, AI, Big Data and other new technologies, to provide smooth transport solutions for people in all kinds of circumstances. Equally, this kind of technology will enable the rethinking of the supply chain between firms. Robots, AI and sensors will be monitoring infrastructure and allow dispatching service teams from a more centrally located point. The financial sector will be transformed in order to operate a cashless society in which financial transactions can be done safely and conveniently.

India shares the same ambition with Japan. However, with only an Internet penetration of 40 percent, the goal to achieve is higher.[43] The ambition is incorporated in the government-led project Digital India. Within this project, India's Trillion Dollar Digital Opportunity (Digital Opportunity) was launched in 2019. The Digital Opportunity had to identify national goals and digital themes that could scale up the value of India's digital economy. The national goals, or key areas in which India wants to accelerate its progress, relate to: IT infrastructure, e-governance, healthcare, quality education, energy for all, next generation financial services, farmer income, production and supply chain, and jobs and skills for all.[44] The focus on IT infrastructure does not only cover access to the Internet, but also the creation and production of

[43]The Digital economy is booming in Asia. The basis for this success is the widespread Internet use in Asia. Fig. 3 depicts the percentage of Internet users in Asia compared to the world. More than half of the world Internet users live in Asia. Highlighting the Internet penetration in some of the Asian countries, the following observations can be made. In Japan, 93.8% of the population has access to the Internet. Thailand has an Internet penetration of 87.3%. Indonesia's population is for 60.2% connected to the Internet. Available at: https://www.statista.com/statistics/281668/internet-penetration-in-southeast-asian-countries/. Accessed 15 December 2020.

[44]MeitY (2019).

digital technologies and state-of-the art cybersecurity.[45] E-governance will involve the digitalization of contact with citizens.[46] The digitalization in healthcare should enable an integrated healthcare platform and enable remote healthcare.[47] Education is important for the digital economy, and therefore India stresses the use of digital technology for reaching out to all communities.[48] The delivery of and payment for energy should be smoothened by digital technology. To facilitate entrepreneurship, the financial system will be digitalized trough cashless payments and platforms enabling easy lending for small and medium sized enterprises.[49] Data analytics and integration of data through platforms should facilitate efficiency and in so doing, increase the income of farmers.[50] The Indian government further intends to invest in setting up manufacturing capacity for digital technology devices, encouraging the manufacturing of automation and Internet-of-Things-based applications, integrating digital technology in the supply chain, and applying digital technologies in the transportation sector.[51] In terms of jobs and skills, the Indian government bets on the one hand on offering skill building and on the other hand the integration of digital technology in the workplace to enable the connection of employers with work seekers and working from home or remote locations.[52]

The Digital Economy and Society Development Plan is Thailand's embracement of the digital economy. Also this plan is ambitious, as it will include the digital economy in all its aspects. Besides building high-capacity digital infrastructure,[53] Thailand aims at ensuring that digital technology is being integrated in the economy and that the society is able to operate and participate in such a digital economy.[54] This will require the development of a skilled workforce and trust and confidence in the use of the digital technology.[55] Besides, the government envisions its own transformation into a digital government.[56] In practice, this means that the government will first focus on the deployment of country-wide broadband Internet access,[57] followed by the creation of homegrown e-commerce,[58] the integration of smart technology in

---

45 MeitY (2019, pp. 127–152).

46 MeitY (2019, pp. 153–178).

47 MeitY (2019, pp. 179–192).

48 MeitY (2019, pp. 193–206).

49 MeitY (2019, pp. 217–224).

50 MeitY (2019, pp. 225–244).

51 MeitY (2019, pp. 245–266).

52 MeitY (2019, pp. 267–279).

53 ONDE (2018, p. 18).

54 ONDE (2018, p. 19).

55 ONDE (2018, pp. 20, 22).

56 ONDE (2018, p. 21).

57 ONDE (2018, p. 24).

58 ONDE (2018, p. 25). Thailand has close to no prominent homegrown players in the digital economy. The Thai digital economy is being served by international players. Alibaba owned Lazada and Singapore based Shoppee are the main e-commerce platforms, while Korean based Line is rolling out Line Shopping. An acquisition of the Hong Kong-based Chilindo by one of

agriculture and safety,[59] and the roll-out of an e-Payment system.[60] The government will also invest in the development of a digital personal health record system,[61] and in digital literacy, including the use of digital technology for education and lifelong learning.[62] The e-government will first emphasize paperless communication with citizens and building a platform to communicate with and obtain documents from the government.[63]

Indonesia's government is less ambitious. Even though Indonesia recognizes the premise that ICT technology is important for the development of the digital economy and that education is a valuable asset in a digital economy, the main focus of the government's policy is e-commerce.[64] The Indonesian government has rolled out the E-commerce Roadmap 2017–2019. This Roadmap included seven action programs: "facilitation of funding, tax incentives, customer protection, skills development [sic] logistics systems, acceleration of communication infrastructure, and cybersecurity."[65] Within the action programs for e-commerce, emphasis is put on startups. Grants will be created for e-commerce startups. Startup investor identification is another priority of the government. Investors in startups should enjoy tax benefits. Besides, regulatory schemes will be developed to protect e-commerce consumers. Stimulation packages will be offered for awareness raising of the existence of e-commerce and for digital technology skill training. To facilitate the shift towards e-commerce, the government will support the development of logistics, both in terms of setting up data transfer systems and of warehousing and courier systems.[66]

---

the leading Thai private companies, the Charoen Pokphand Group, gave Thailand a domestic player of importance. Available at: https://www.jpmorgan.com/europe/merchant-services/insights/reports/thailand; https://english.nna.jp/articles/9605; https://insideretail.asia/2020/08/09/thailands-cp-group-to-buy-hong-kong-e-commerce-platform-chilindo/. Accessed 15 December 2020.

[59] ONDE (2018, p. 19).

[60] Available at: https://www.itu.int/en/ITU-D/Regional-Presence/AsiaPacific/Documents/Events/2016/Apr-Digital2016/S2_Present_Pansak_Siriruchatapong.pdf. Accessed 15 December 2020.

[61] ONDE (2018, p. 20).

[62] ONDE (2018, p. 27).

[63] ONDE (2018, p. 26).

[64] This focus on e-commerce could be explained by the fact that Indonesia had already a well-developed homegrown e-commerce sector. Indonesia's main e-commerce platforms are Tokopedia or Bukulapak, who are competing in Indonesia with Asian grown Lazada (China) and Shopee Indonesia (Singapore). Indonesia is also the home of Go-Jek, a ride-hailing platform, and Traveloka, a travel service platform. Go-Jek has expanded well beyond ride-hailing and is now also active in the fintech sector, this besides a firm like Ovo. See Edamadaka and Seiki (2019, pp. 20–21).

[65] World Bank (2019, p. 103).

[66] Edamadaka and Seiki (2019, p. 22).

3 Digital Economy, a Recently Emerging Term in Competition Law Literature

3.1 *Microsoft, High Technology Markets or New Economy*

Digital economy is only a recently used term in the competition law literature, despite the term being around for nearly three decades. During this time, the term digital economy has developed into a rich concept. The digital economy has embraced three different dimensions. The core dimension centers around the ICT industry and its position in the economy, while the narrow dimension focuses on new business models brought by ICT and the broad dimension on change in society via the digitization of everything. Competition law has been dealing with problems in each of these dimensions. However, the literature has sided on the use of different terms to identify these dimensions.

If we start from the core dimension, which centers around ICT and IT, then the cases against Microsoft and Intel, a software developing company and a semiconductor company respectively, could be categorized as early examples of competition law enforcement situated within one of the dimensions of the digital economy.[67] Both cases centered around the foreclosure of competitors. Questions were raised as to the stance competition law should take towards these kinds of cases. However, these questions did not relate to effectiveness of the toolbox of the competition law. Instead, the questions related to the eternal conundrum of what goal(s) should be pursued by competition law. An answer to this conundrum is affected by various elements, such as politics, economics, or enforcement realities.[68] Depending on how the pendulum swings between these different elements, or even between different stances within these elements, the outcome of the competition law case will be different. The different outcomes were often the cause of discussion, if not in political or enforcement circles, then in the literature.

Even though the Microsoft and Intel cases could be situated within the boundaries of one of the dimensions of the digital economy, the concept was never used. At best, the problem of Microsoft or Intel was situated within the concept of the New Economy.[69] However, New Economy was not the only concept used. Competition law literature at the early 2000s also used concepts as high technology industries,[70] high-tech sector,[71] or technology markets.[72] Some other literature only refers to

---

[67] On Microsoft, see, e.g., Rubini (2010) and Gavil and First (2014). On Intel, see, e.g., Bernard (2010).

[68] Monti (2012, pp. 22–55) and Van Rompuy (2012, pp. 16–24).

[69] See, e.g., Graham and Smith (2004), Gordon (2002) and Sullivan (2001).

[70] See, e.g., Gal and Waller (2012) and Martin (2001).

[71] See, e.g., Baker (2001).

[72] See, e.g., Coates (2011).

innovation[73] or the Internet.[74] Kevin Coates indicates that all these concepts can be used interchangeably.[75] New Economy seems to be the most prevalent among them.

Few of the competition law scholars have attempted to define the New Economy. Cosmo Graham, for example, holds that the New Economy could be "restricted to the use of computer software and hardware and its application through digitalisation to the communications industry, especially the use of the Internet to business transactions."[76] Differently, Alison Jones and Brenda Sufrin provide a list of what the New Economy could encompass. The New Economy, they hold, "includes the telecommunications (electronic communications), media, and information technology sectors and high technology industries such as Internet based businesses (e.g. B2B marketplace), computer software, biotechnology and aerospace."[77] But more important than a definition, these scholars agree that it is better to provide the characteristics of the New Economy. To frame it in the words of Jones and Sufrin, the New Economy is characterized by "very rapid technological change, the creation and exploitation of intellectual property rights, the need for complementary products to work together, and a high degree of technical complexity."[78] Graham adds to this list the presence of some kind of a network and high fixed but low marginal costs.[79]

The New Economy-related literature acknowledged the usefulness of traditional competition rules and tools. The various competition rules in relation to pricing would still be relevant, if pricing issues were to occur. It has been held that the application of competition law in the New Economy will be less towards pricing, but the Intel cases have shown that, if high tech companies do not refrain from engaging in price setting strategies aiming to exclude competitors from the market, the enforcement agencies can act appropriately with provisions dealing with predatory pricing and rebates.[80] In relation to tempering innovation, something that is more likely in high tech markets than price related anti-competitive conduct, the Microsoft and Intel cases have shown that the competition laws are able, through concepts like tying or unfair competition, to deal with products designed to advantage other products of the firm marketing both products.[81]

With the rise of technology, the issues of standardization and interoperability became even more important than during the Microsoft cases. Standardization allows for economies of scale.[82] Interoperability will facilitate positive network externalities.[83] Despite these positive effects, standardization and interoperability have also

---

[73] See, e.g., Schmidt (2009) and Käseberg (2012).

[74] See, e.g., Surblytė (2015).

[75] Cf. Coates (2011, pp. 51–55).

[76] Graham (2004, p. 2).

[77] Jones and Sufrin (2011, p. 57).

[78] Jones and Sufrin (2011, p. 57).

[79] Graham (2004, p. 3).

[80] Coates (2011, pp. 57–89) and Schmidt (2009, pp. 77–105).

[81] See, e.g., Rubini (2010) and Gavil and First (2014).

[82] Jones and Sufrin (2014, p. 760) and Coates (2011, p. 183).

[83] Coates (2011, p. 184).

the potential of anti-competitive effects. The potential of competitors gathering "in a room together to discuss the future shape of the industry, and the products and services that might appear"[84] could trigger the "risks of collusion and cartelization, and of foreclosure of those not present in the room or as yet not present on the market."[85] Furthermore, "[w]hen intellectual property rights are included in standards, additional concerns appear, such as the concern that the IP owner might hold up adoption or dissemination of the standard through refusing to license, or offering to license on less favorable terms than it would have applied before the standard was adopted, or licensing on a discriminatory basis, favoring – for example- its own operations over those of third parties."[86] Collusion, as long as it can be proven, does not pose a problem for competition law.[87] Equally, interoperability can be tackled with traditional competition law rules. If it were not for unilateral refusal (or withdrawal) to supply,[88] the more permissive stance of copyright law on reverse engineering were offering solutions to guarantee interoperability.[89] Looking backwards, standardization seemed to have been a more controversial issue for competition law. With the risk of a patent ambush or patent hold-up, the New Economy competition law had to clarify the extent of licensing on (fair), reasonable and non-discriminatory terms ((F)RAND) more than ever before.[90]

Another important evolution, at least in various parts of the world, was the transition of a state-run media and telecommunication market to a liberalized one.[91] Competition law proved to be important to force access to media and telecommunication product and service markets that were being protected by the former monopolists.[92] In this respect, the essential facilities doctrine was first raised in relation to information,[93] which in later literature further developed in relation to Big Data.[94] The liberalization of the market increased the number of players in the market. However, as the business strategy changed towards multi-media characterized by an integration of different areas of the IT and ICT sector, competition law had to canalize the desire of telecommunications and media firms to merge or form strategic alliances.[95] With the development of multi-media, new issues arose as well. Competition law literature started also to discuss how it should be dealing with

---

[84]Coates (2011, p. 184).

[85]Coates (2011, p. 184). See also Jones and Sufrin (2014, p. 699).

[86]Coates (2011, p. 184).

[87]See, e.g., Kaplow (2013) and Harding and Joshua (2003).

[88]Coates (2011, pp. 212–239).

[89]Coates (2011, p. 235).

[90]See, e.g., Hayashi (2016), Jones and Sufrin (2014, p. 563) and Käseberg (2012, pp. 240–247).

[91]See, e.g., Nikolinakos (2006).

[92]Nikolinakos (2006, pp. 59–90). On access in general, see Moss (2005).

[93]Joined Cases C-241/91 P and C-242/91 P, *Radio Telefis Eiremann and Independent Television Publications Limited vs. Commission* [1995] ECR I-743.

[94]See, e.g., Graef (2016, pp. 123–279).

[95]See, e.g., Nikolinakos (2006, pp. 131–175).

the protection of data collected by multi-media entities[96] and various other online firms,[97] network effects,[98] multisided markets,[99] the development of sector-specific regulations,[100] or the creation of new pricing strategies.[101] All of these issues, being more controversial to the conceptualization of competition law than any of the intervention in early stages of the digital economy, started to further expand in the New Economy competition law literature. Not all literature dealing with these controversial issues, though, is using the concept of New Economy. Yet, some literature is already introducing the concept of digital economy to discuss these controversial issues.

Data collection by New Economy firms triggered the issue of privacy,[102] as some jurisdictions took a stricter view on data protection.[103] Such a stricter view, if it leads to legislation, could also impact innovation. The regulatory impact on innovation is not in all jurisdictions subject to competition law. Hence, one could see the emergence of a separate debate on the desirability to regulate data protection and, if it is considered desirable, to what extent.[104] However, if data protection is becoming an issue, then firms could start competing on privacy.[105] As such, this brings more product differentiation. It is possible that such a privacy-caring firm is being taken over by an incumbent in order to eliminate the offering of the new product. Competition law should thus offer an insight into whether it is going to take a specific stance towards this killing acquisitions.[106] Another way that competition law could relate to privacy competition is when an incumbent refuses access to its services because the other firm does subscribe to privacy. This question relates to whether data portability should be advocated for. Data portability is the possibility to move data from one provider to another and thus places the owner of the data in control.[107] Data portability could encourage competition or, if entrance is possible, enable easier access to the market.[108] Still another way in which competition law could be important concerns the competitive advantage that is created by gathering

[96] See, e.g., Nikolinakos (2006, pp. 333–355).

[97] Patterson (2017).

[98] See, e.g., Kwoka (2005, p. 17), Peritz (2005, p. 28), Etro (2007, pp. 57, 60–61) and Stucke and Grunes (2016, pp. 162–216).

[99] See, e.g., Frank (2015, pp. 81–100) and Etro (2007, pp. 61–64).

[100] See e.g., Nikolinakos (2006), Graham (2004, p. 10), Nihoul (2004, pp. 91–123) and Murray and Scott (2004, pp. 126–156).

[101] See, e.g., Wismer (2015, pp. 41–52).

[102] See, e.g., Competition Law Enforcement on Exploitative Abuse by Digital Platforms: Japanese Approach in a Global Context [this volume]; Gorecka (2020), Kemp (2019), Ng (2018) and Daly (2016).

[103] Wasastjerna (2020) and Patterson (2017, pp. 163–181).

[104] Coates (2011, pp. 364–365).

[105] Gal and Oshrit (2020) and Stucke and Grunes (2016).

[106] See, e.g., Griffith (2017). On the concept of killing acquisitions, see Cunningham et al. (2016).

[107] An early elaboration on the control over online information flows, see Daly (2016).

[108] Coates (2011, p. 405).

huge amounts of information.[109] The possession of a competitive advantage is not necessarily anti-competitive. To be anticompetitive, it is still required to show that the information gathering is done with the aim of excluding competitors from the market. Several enforcement agencies are currently investigating whether such a conduct is present.[110]

In order to protect privacy, more and more jurisdictions are creating a regulation separate from the competition law rules. Even though the privacy regulation is not the only (sector) specific regulation,[111] it is one that is triggering a debate on the goals of competition law. The existence of the European General Data Protection Regulation (GDPR) and its application in German courts has led to the observation that the New Economy is pushing the debate on the goals of competition law. It is claimed that competition law could be used to correct non-market failures such as the failure to protect privacy and personal data.[112] This embracement of several goals could create a polycentric competition law.

Early competition law intervention in markets with network effects is another controversial issue raised in the New Economy literature.[113] Network effects "lead to a tendency for markets to 'tip' to a single dominant vendor or technology. In the markets that tip, competition is *for* the market, not *in* the market, and the market is likely to end up highly concentrated."[114] Competition will therefore be vigorous at an early stage, but fade away once the race towards the monopoly has been won.[115] The

---

[109]Gal and Oshrit (2020).

[110]Even though not a formal enforcement investigation, the United States (US) Congress held a hearing with the tech executives of Facebook, Google, Amazon and Apple on their market power in 2020. The US Department of Justice charged Alphabet Inc., the company behind Google, for being a "monopoly gatekeeper for the Internet." Available at: https://www.theguardian.com/technology/2020/oct/20/google-antitrust-charges-threat-big-tech. Accessed 15 December 2020. Meanwhile, the Federal Trade Commission has focused its attention on Amazon and Facebook, of which the latter is formally sued. Available at: https://www.ftc.gov/news-events/press-releases/2020/12/ftc-sues-facebook-illegal-monopolization. Accessed 15 December 2020. The European Union has challenged Google and is now investigating Amazon. On Google, see https://ec.europa.eu/commission/presscorner/detail/en/IP_19_1770. Accessed 15 December 2020 and on Amazon, see https://ec.europa.eu/commission/presscorner/detail/en/ip_20_2077. Accessed 15 December 2020. More recently, China has announced similar actions towards its own homegrown platforms, Alibaba and Tencent. Available at: https://www.reuters.com/article/us-china-antitrust-idUSKBN28O0CQ. Accessed 15 December 2020. Tim Wu, in his book the curse of bigness, is already speculating on the occurrence of this kind of investigations. See Wu (2018, pp. 132–133).

[111]For other examples, see e.g., Nikolinakos (2006), Graham (2004, p. 10), Nihoul (2004, pp. 91–123) and Murray and Scott (2004, pp. 126–156).

[112]Lianos (2018).

[113]Network effects entail that new economy products or services increase in value the more people use the product or the service.

[114]Lind and Muysert (2002, p. 5).

[115]Wu (2018, pp. 117–126). One of the conclusions that Wu connects to the outcome of bigness, which is the result of failure to control excessive corporate power, is the rise of inequality, nationalism, populism, etc. A failing competition law could be the underlying reason. On this issue, The Nexus between Competition and Personal Data Protection Laws: Thailand's Perspective [this volume]. Competition law will, however, not always be the panacea for inequality caused in the

scholarly opinions are divided on this issue, though.[116] Not all scholars support the analysis leading to the conclusion that early intervention is necessary. Firms in the New Economy may be dominant or operate in a concentrated market, their dominance could be fragile and temporary.[117] The New Economy is also characterized by high pace of innovation, which can cause the market to "change radically quite quickly."[118]

In terms of pricing strategies, online platforms started to roll out price parity clauses or most favored nation clauses. Their effect on the price triggered various investigations, requiring the enforcement agencies to draw lines of what is acceptable under their respective competition laws.[119]

3.2 *The Shift Towards Digital Economy*

The rise of these controversial issues seem to have triggered an evolution in competition law literature from the use of the concept of the New Economy to the use of the concept of the Digital economy.[120] This literature addresses competition law issues related to the rise of platforms as a new business model,[121] the technological breakthroughs in artificial intelligence, connectivity, and the growing importance of Big Data. All of these, as we have described above, represent aspects of the broad dimension of the digital economy, also referred to as the digitized economy.

The digital economy, driven by platforms,[122] requires, so informs Pinar Akman, "a rethinking and reconfiguration of some core concepts of competition law in terms of whether and if so, how they should apply to particular practices of technology companies in these non-traditional market contexts? The way these businesses and competition operate on these markets (winner takes it all, competition for market, oligopoly competition, etc.) challenges the traditional understandings of market definition, market power, distinctions between unilateral conduct and agreement conduct, vertical and horizontal restrictions of competition, and so on."[123]

Indeed, delineating a market is being complicated by factors that do not fit within a traditionally applied SSNIP test.[124] These factors are, among others, the two- or

competitive process, see Ride Hailing Apps Enter in Competition with Ojek: Indonesia's Response to the Impact of Disruptive Innovation (this volume).

[116]See, e.g., Graham (2004) and Monti (2004, pp. 17–18, 24).

[117]Graham (2004, p. 4).

[118]Graham (2004, p. 4).

[119]See, e.g., Wismer (2015, pp. 41–52) and González-Díaz and Bennet (2015, pp. 26–42).

[120]See, e.g., Buthelezi and Hodge (2019); Ezrachi and Modral (2019); Teece (2012–2013).

[121]On the history of the platform economy, see Steinberg (2019).

[122]Platforms are "Internet sites where users and potential purchasers of services and products are matched and interact with advertisers, business users, service providers or suppliers." See Lundqvist (2020, p. 2).

[123]Akman (2019, p. 589).

[124]On the traditional approach of the SSNIP test, see, e.g., Van den Bergh (2017, pp. 142–150) and Jones and Sufrin (2014, pp. 69–73).

multi-sidedness of platforms, the absence of pricing for provided products or services, the potential for combining heterogeneous products or services on one side of the platform, and the possibility for the user to be active on more than one platform (multi-homing).[125] A way to avoid this complexity, though, may be to work with less demanding competition law concepts, such as unfair trade practices.[126]

Similarly, the delineation of market power used to depend on market share.[127] However, the difficulty with platforms is whether the market share on both sides needs to be taken into consideration, whether market share should be replaced by subscriber share, whether market power of a platform should be viewed in perspective to other platforms, or by just being a system leader. To answer these questions, scholars started to look into network effects and tipping.[128] Also the platform's position in acquiring data became an element for consideration.[129]

With the use of algorithms for price setting,[130] the blurring of the distinction between unilateral conduct and agreements on the one hand and vertical and horizontal agreements on the other hand can be exemplified. Pricing algorithms have opened questions for revisiting the issue of tacit collusion, thus moving price fixing rules closer to unilateral conduct.[131] Equally, pricing algorithms, in a hub-and-spoke setting, make it possible to sustain horizontal price fixing through the participation of an actor positioned vertically vis-a-vis the implementers of the price fixing.[132]

4 The Digital Economy in Asia and Competition Law

Digital economy is a concept gradually being embraced by the community of competition law scholars. The focus of the research being brought within the digital economy is on platforms and the businesses developed for these platforms. These platforms, often further denominated with the word digital, can be thought of as "the sum total of a place for exchanges of information, goods, or services to occur between producers and consumers as well as the community that interacts with said

---

[125] O'Connor (2016). See also Hauck (2015, pp. 58–60).

[126] On this topics, see Regulating Competition between Digital Platforms: The Japan Fair Trade Commission's Preference for Unfair Trade Practices [this volume]. For the United States, see Hauck (2015, pp. 53–61).

[127] Jones and Sufrin (2014, pp. 336–344).

[128] Peritz (2005, p. 28).

[129] Lundqvist (2020, pp. 13–14).

[130] On this topic, see, e.g., Van Cleynenbreugel (2020), Van Uytsel (2018), Gal (2019), Blockx (2017), Ezrachi and Stucke (2016) and Mehra (2015).

[131] See, e.g., Kupčík (2020), OECD (2017, p. 27) and Ezrachi and Stucke (2016, pp. 56–70). For an Asian context, Algorithmic Collusion and Indian Competition Act: Suggestions to Tackle Inadequacies and Naivety [this volume].

[132] See, e.g., OECD (2017, pp. 24–32) and Ezrachi and Stucke (2016, pp. 46–55). For an Asian context, Algorithmic Hub and Spoke Cartels: A Japanese Perspective [this volume].

platform."[133] These platforms are triggering different questions for competition law in Asia. Three themes are being addressed in this book. First, the book addresses how competition law could regulate unilateral conduct. More in specific, this part will address how competition law can be used to address exploitative unilateral behavior of the platform and how competition law could intervene against unilateral conduct of firms that have not established a dominant position. Second, the book will highlight the limits of competition law in the digital economy, either by showing that an ineffective competition law is a burden to the digital economy or by identifying the boundaries for addressing social harm done by the innovation of the digital economy. Third, the book will review whether some of the Asian countries are able to address the digitization of pricing strategies.

Part I—Platforms, Unilateral Conduct and Competition Law—discusses exploitative and exclusionary conduct by platforms in Japan. The first contribution deals with the Japanese approach of exploitative conduct of platforms toward their suppliers and consumers, while the second contribution highlights the Japanese approach of tackling exclusionary conduct by platforms.

Toshiaki Takigawa highlights, with exploitative abuse, a topic that is less covered in the competition law literature on platforms. The cause lies in the fact that not all jurisdictions accept that their competition laws apply to exploitative abuse, which concerns the practice of imposing disadvantageous contractual terms on suppliers. Takigawa informs that the Japanese Antimonopoly Act (AMA) is regulating the exploitative abuse via the abuse of a superior bargaining position, which is a further interpretation of the Article 19 AMA provision on unfair trade practices. The use of an abuse of a superior bargaining position could lead to excesses. Takigawa tackles two of these in his paper. On the one hand, he shows that, without limitations on how to interpret unreasonableness of contract terms, almost any contract may be explained as a consequence of an abuse of a superior bargaining position. On the other hand, he argues that, without appropriate legislation on the protection of the privacy of consumers, a too restricted interpretation of an abuse of superior bargaining position may weaken the position of the consumer. To prevent the former, Takigawa refers to a report of the Japanese Fair Trade Commission (JFTC) that advocates for some procedural fairness approaches in how to achieve a more objective judgement of what contract provisions could be considered unreasonable. To allow the latter, Takigawa identifies the government-wide drive to tackle the power of platforms as the reason why the JFTC has taken an active approach to protect consumers. The protection is, as Takigawa illustrates, not unlimited. Consumers will only be able to rely on the provision of the abuse of superior bargaining position if they are locked-in into the platform's network. In other words, they should be prevented from multi-homing.

Steven Van Uytsel and *Yoshiteru Uemura* continue the observations made by Takigawa by arguing that the unfair trade practices in general are the means of the JFTC to deal with anti-competitive conduct of digital platforms. The choice of the JFTC for unfair trade practices positions the Japanese approach in the middle of an academic debate that calls for, at first sight, opposite requirements. On the one hand, there is a

[133] Available at: https://www.bmc.com/blogs/digital-platforms/. Accessed 15 December 2020.

call for early market intervention to prevent a single platform from growing excessively big. On the other hand, there is an argument against government intervention because incumbent platforms are innovators and, if not careful in the intervention, these platforms can be challenged on their existence. Unfair trade practices, so argue Van Uytsel and Uemura, allow for both early and meticulous intervention. Early intervention can be realized because market power is not an important criterion, if at all one, in the conceptualization of an unfair trade practice offence. Meticulous intervention can be guaranteed because unfair trade practices focus on the conduct of an online platform. Unfair trade practices do, in other words, not aim to tackle the 'bigness' of the online platforms and so trigger a change in the competitive structure of the market.

Part II—The Limits of Competition Law in the Digital Economy—contains two contributions. The first contribution exemplifies the limits of competition law if this law only remains an empty façade. The second essay portrays the substantive limits of competition law to support market participants challenged by digital innovation.

Peerapat Chokesuwattanaskul posits that the digital economy is driven by data. Data is intrinsically linked with privacy. Privacy, so claims Chokesuwattanaskul, presupposes that all personal data should remain personal. Personal data can only be withdrawn from privacy through consent or a legitimate reason. This legitimate reason represents a trade-off between private and public interests. To guarantee a proper trade-off, Chokesuwattanaskul posists that this requires a competitive market, a redistribution system, and a government acting in the best interests of the public. However, Thailand presents a different story. Even though competition law exists, the government has never been able to make the enforcement effective. Close links between the business and political elites have prevented the establishment of a redistribution system in which wealth inequality is addressed. Moreover, Chokesuwattanaskul indicates that the government policies are often populist without aiming for structural change in function of the public good. Without changes, whereby competition law becomes effective and includes the idea of privacy protection, a proper balancing between private and public interests will not be assured in the near future.[134]

Ningrum Natasya Sirait, Mohammad Reza, Angayar Kanni Ramaiah and Aria Suyudi describe how the digital economy is disrupting the organization of public transport in Indonesia. The disruption is particularly grief for *Ojek*, which are motorcycle owners that have informally organized themselves to offer transport to the public. With the development of ride hailing apps, the Indonesian consumer was offered a convenient instrument to call for transport. The immense shift of the consumers towards the ride hailing apps caused social unrest among the *Ojek*, who, due to their tech-illiteracy, saw demand for their service decrease. Social unrest led to regulatory intervention. The intervention was drastic: ride hailing apps and *Ojek* were explicitly placed outside the law. Whereas the ride hailing app firms were able to challenge such a regulatory intervention in the Supreme Court, *Ojek* were not. The

[134]On the topic of inequality caused by unfettered growth of companies, partly because of failing competition policy, Wu (2018).

question then raised is whether the competition enforcement authority of Indonesia, the Commission for the Supervision of Business Competition, could somehow play a role in softening the social challenges of technological disruption. Sirait, Reza, Ramaiah and Suyudi see two possible scenarios. First, the KPPU can advise the government on the compatibility of new legislation with the competition policy. The KPPU has used this power, but mainly focused on creating equal access to the market for setting up a formal business. The informal sector has not been considered. Second, if there is an infringement of the competition law, the KPPU can take an enforcement action. KPPU has not been able to find an infringement. However, it is held that, if low price setting by the ride hailing apps can be addressed, the informal sector would benefit. Hence, the general conclusion is that competition law's role in addressing social inequality caused by innovation is limited.

Part III—Algorithms, Coordinated Price Setting, and Competition Law—details how algorithms are increasingly used in the price setting strategies of companies. The more these algorithms develop, the likelier it will become that they will be involved in coordinated price setting. With a contribution on India and Japan, this book offers an insight to what extent both jurisdictions are ready to deal with such a phenomenon.

Nikita Koradia, Kiran Manokaran, and Zara Saeed expound on the readiness of the Indian Competition Act 2002 for the various consequences of using algorithms in price setting strategies and how the Indian Competition Bill 2020 will change the situation. The main focus of Koradia, Manokaran, and Saeed's contribution is on a scenario in which the algorithms will be used as a facilitator positioned vertically in relation to the conspiring cartel members, the so-called hub and spoke scenario. Koradia, Manokaran, and Saeed meticulously argue, with reference to important jurisprudence, that the Competition Commission of India (CCI) has neglected to explain Article 3 of the Indian Competition Act 2002 in a way to also include hub and spoke types of cartels. One of the problems identified is the requirement that the participants to the agreement need to be active in an identical or similar trade. To overcome this problem, the legislator is considering to change the Competition Act 2002 and take out the requirement of identical or similar trade. Yet, this change will not be sufficient to weaponize the CCI with an instrument to also tackle new forms of algorithmic collusion that may prove to be problematic. In this respect, Koradia, Manokaran, and Saeed address the predictable agent scenario, which implies that the pricing decision of the algorithm is predictable after having seen the market conditions, and the digital eye scenario, which entails a situation in which algorithms are able learn how to fix prices. Therefore, Koradia, Manokaran, and Saeed formulates recommendations for the CCI to alleviate, as much as possible, the negative price consequences of algorithms.

Steven Van Uytsel investigates whether the Japanese AMA is able to deal with cartels that have been facilitated by algorithms. The focus is on the hub and spoke model of cartels. These types of cartels, in which a party in a vertical relationship towards the competitors is involved, has long been a conundrum for the JFTC. This conundrum started with the question of how to deal with bureaucrats who were enabling bid rigging in public procurement projects. A solution to the conundrum was the enactment of a separate legislation to facilitate legal action against cartel

facilitating bureaucrats. Van Uytsel analyzes various scenarios in which an algorithm can be used and comes to the conclusion that it may be difficult for the JFTC to successfully pursue legal actions against all such cartels. One way out, Van Uytsel argues, is the reliance on unfair trade practices. However, this will not enable the JFTC to impose an administrative fine on the price fixing firms using algorithms.

To conclude this overview, I would like to repeat the words of Graham and state that I "cannot pretend that the essays in this volume cover all aspects of the relationship between competition, regulation"[135] and the digital economy. I "hope that by bringing them together in this format, the collection raises some valuable questions and stimulates discussion on what will continue to be an important policy problem for the 21st century."[136]

Acknowledgements This chapter has received support of the project Artificial Intelligence, Price Setting Strategies and Antitrust Law: Towards a Regulatory Framework, a Grants-in-Aid for Scientific Research (C) with No. 18K01300.

References

Akman P (2019) Editorial: an agenda for competition law and policy in the digital economy. J Eur Competition Law Pract 10(10):589–590

Baker JB (2001) Can antitrust keep up? Competition policy in high-tech markets. https://www.brookings.edu/articles/can-antitrust-keep-up-competition-policy-in-high-tech-markets/. Accessed 15 Dec 2020

Bernard K (2010) The *Intel* cases—legal convergence or leaps of faith? CPI Antitrust J (2):1–12

Bhatnagar P (2020) Japan's digital trade benefits to quadruple to US$506 billion by 2030. https://www.hinrichfoundation.com/research/wp/digital/japan/. Accessed 15 Dec 2020

Blockx J (2017) Antitrust in Digital Markets in the EU: policing Price Bots. Radbound Economic Law Conference. https://papers.ssrn.com/sol3/papers.cfm?abstract_id=2987705. Accessed 15 Dec 2020

Brynjolfsson E, Kahin B (eds) (2000) Understanding the digital economy: data, tools, and research. MIT Press, Cambridge, MA

Brynjolfsson E, McAfee A (2013) In the second machine age: work, progress, and prosperity in a time of brilliant technologies. Norton & Company, New York

Bukht R, Heeks R (2017) Defining, conceptualizing, and measuring the digital economy. Development Informatics working paper series No. 68. https://papers.ssrn.com/sol3/papers.cfm?abstract_id=3431732. Accessed 15 Dec 2020

Buthelezi T, Hodge J (2019) Competition policy in the digital economy: a developing country perspective. Competition L. Int 15:201

Cunningham C, Ederer F, Ma S (2016) Killer acquisitions. https://www.cass.city.ac.uk/__data/assets/pdf_file/0020/434324/12.-Ma_Killer-Acquisitionsv2.pdf. Accessed 15 Dec 2020

Coates K (2011) Competition law and regulation of technology markets. Oxford University Press, Oxford

[135] Graham (2004, p. 15).

[136] Graham (2004, p. 15).

Dahlman C et al (2016) Harnessing the digital economy for developing countries. https://www.oecd-ilibrary.org/development/harnessing-the-digital-economy-for-developing-countries_4adffb24-en. Accessed 15 Dec 2020

Daly A (2016) Private power, online information flows and EU law: mind the gap. Bloomsbury, Oxford

Economic Research Office (2019) Overview of the 2019 white paper on information and communications in Japan. https://www.ituaj.jp/wp-content/uploads/2019/10/nb31-4_web-3_Report_2019WhitePaper.pdf. Accessed 15 Dec 2020

Economist Intelligence Unit (2010) Digital economy rankings 2010: beyond e-readiness. https://graphics.eiu.com/upload/EIU_Digital_economy_rankings_2010_FINAL_WEB.pdf. Accessed 15 Dec 2020

Edamadaka P, Seiki I (2019) Digitalization in Indonesia. BayCurrent Consult, 20–24. https://www.baycurrent.co.jp/en/our-insights/pdf/Digitalization%20in%20Indonesia.pdf. Accessed 15 Dec 2020

Etro F (2007) Competition policy for the new economy. In Katsoulacos Y (ed) Abuse of dominance. Athens University Press, Athens, pp 46–83

Ezrachi A, Modral J (2019) Rising to the challenge—competition law and the digital economy. Competition L. Int 15:117–125

Ezrachi A, Stucke ME (2016) Virtual competition: the promise and perils of the algorithm-driven economy. Harvard University Press, Cambridge

Frank JS (2015) Competition concerns in multi-sided markets in mobile communications. In: Surblytė G (ed) Competition on the Internet. Springer, Heidelberg, pp 81–100

Fukuyama M (2018) Society 5.0: aiming for a new human-centered society. Jpn Spotlight 27:47–50

Gal MS (2019) Algorithms as illegal agreements. Berkeley Technol Law J 34:67–118

Gal M, Oshrit A (2020) The competitive effects of the GDPR. J Competition Law Econ 16(3):349–391

Gal MS, Waller SW (2012) Antitrust in high-technology industries: a symposium introduction. J Competition Law Econ 8(3):449–457

Gavil AI, First H (2014) The Microsoft antitrust cases: competition policy for the twenty-first century. The MIT Press, Cambridge, MA

González-Díaz FE, Bennet M (2015) The law and economics of most-favoured nation clauses. CLPD 1(3):26–42

Google et al (2019) e-Conomy SEA 2019—Swipe up and to the right: Southeast Asia's $100 billion Internet economy. https://www.blog.google/documents/47/SEA_Internet_Economy_Report_2019.pdf. Accessed 15 Dec 2020

Gorecka A (2020) A confusing relationship between privacy and competition law—a way forward for EU competition law and algorithms pricing. Indian J Artif Intell Law 1(1):7–29

Gordon RL (2002) Antitrust abuse in the new economy: the Microsoft case. Edward Elgar, Cheltenham

Graef I (2016) EU competition law, data protection and online platforms: data as essential facility. Wolters Kluwer, Alphen aan den Rijn

Graham C, Smith F (eds) (2004) Competition, regulation and the new economy. Hart Publishing, Oxford

Graham C (2004) Introduction. In: Graham C, Smith F (eds) Competition, regulation and the new economy. Hart Publishing, Oxford, pp 1–12

Griffith E (2017) Will Facebook kill all future Facebooks? Business. https://www.wired.com/story/facebooks-aggressive-moves-on-startups-threaten-innovation/. Accessed 15 Dec 2020

Harding C, Joshua J (2003) Regulating cartels in Europe: a study of legal control of corporate delinquency. Oxford University Press, Oxford

Huaxia (2020) China's digital economy reaches $5 trillion in 2019. http://www.xinhuanet.com/english/2020-07/03/c_139186711.htm#:~:text=SHANGHAI%2C%20July%203%20(Xinhua),China%20Academy%20of%20Information%20and. Accessed 15 Dec 2020

Hauck R (2015) FTC v. Google: the enforcement of antitrust in online markets. In: Surblytė G (ed) Competition on the Internet. Springer, Heidelberg, pp 53–61
Hayashi S (2016) FRAND commitment and competition law limitations—for the enforcement of patent rights in Japan. Journal of Japanese Law 21(42):202–239
House of Commons (2016) The digital economy. https://publications.parliament.uk/pa/cm201617/cmselect/cmbis/87/87.pdf. Accessed 15 Dec 2020
Jones A, Sufrin B (2011) EU competition law: text, cases and materials, 4th edn. Oxford University Press, Oxford
Jones A, Sufrin B (2014) EU competition law: text, cases, and materials. Oxford University Press, Oxford
Kaplow L (2013) Competition policy and price fixing. Princeton University Press, Princeton
Käseberg Th (2012) Intellectual property, antitrust and cumulative innovation in the EU and the US. Hart Publishing, Oxford
Kemp K (2019) Concealed data practices and competition law: why privacy matters. European Competition Journal 16(2–3):628–672
Kling R, Lamb R (2000) IT and organizational change in digital economies: a sociotechnical approach. In: Brynjolfsson E, Kahin B (eds) Understanding the digital economy. MIT Press, Cambridge, MA, pp 295–324
Knickrehm M et al (2016) Digital disruption: the growth multiplier—optimizing digital investments to realize higher productivity and growth. https://www.accenture.com/_acnmedia/pdf-14/accenture-strategy-digital-disruption-growth-multiplier-brazil.pdf. Accessed 15 Dec 2020
Kupčík J (2020) European tacit collusion theory and its application to price theory. Eur Competition Law Rev 41:533–545
Kwoka JE (2005) Networks and natural monopolies. In: Moss DL (ed) Network access, regulation and antitrust. Routledge, Abingdon, pp 17–27
Lane N (1999) Advancing the digital economy into the 21st century. Inf Syst Front 1:317–320
Lianos I (2018) Polycentric competition law: current legal problems. SSRN: https://ssrn.com/abstract=3257296. Accessed 15 Dec 2020
Lind RL, Muysert P (2002) Innovation and competition policy: challenges for the new millennium. CRA Competition Policy Discussion Papers 4. http://ecp.crai.com/publications/CRA_DP4.pdf. Accessed 15 Dec 2020
Lundqvist B (2020) Regulating competition in the digital economy. In Lundqvist B, Gal MS (eds) Competition law of the digital economy. Edward Elgar, Cheltenham, pp 2–29
Margherio L et al (1999) The emerging digital economy. https://www.heartland.org/_template-assets/documents/publications/24388.pdf. Accessed 15 Dec 2020
Martin S (2001) Competition policy for high technology industries. J Ind Competition Trade 1:441–465
Mehra S K (2015) Antitrust and the Robo-Seller: competition in the time of algorithms. Temple University Legal Studies Research Paper Series No. 2015-15 https://papers.ssrn.com/sol3/papers.cfm?abstract_id=2576341. Accessed 15 Dec 2020
Ministry of Electronics & Information Technology—Government of India (MeitY) (2019) India's trillion-dollar digital opportunity. https://www.meity.gov.in/writereaddata/files/india_trillion-dollar_digital_opportunity.pdf. Accessed 15 Dec 2020
Monti G (2004) Article 82 EC and the new economy markets. In: Graham C, Smith F (eds) Competition, regulation and the new economy. Hart Publishing, Oxford, pp 17–54
Monti G (2012) EC competition law. Cambridge University Press, Cambridge
Moss DL (ed) (2005) Network access, regulation and antitrust. Routledge, Abingdon
Murray A, Scott C (2004) Controlling the new media: hybrid responses to new forms of power. In: Graham C, Smith F (eds) Competition, regulation and the new economy. Hart Publishing, Oxford, pp 126–156
Naughton J (2016) The evolution of the Internet: from military experiment to General Purpose Technology. J Cyber Policy 1(1):5–28

Ng W (2018) Privacy, data protection, and competition law in China: some preliminary considerations. Presentation at the 12 December 2018 Asian Competition Forum

Nihoul PLG (2004) Authorities, competition and electronic communication: towards institutional competition in the information society. In: Graham C, Smith F (eds) Competition, regulation and the new economy. Hart Publishing, Oxford, pp 91–123

Nikolinakos (2006) EU competition law and regulation in the converging telecommunications, media and IT. Kluwer Law International, The Hague

O'Connor D (2016) Understanding online platform competition: common misunderstandings. In Ortiz A (ed) Internet competition and regulation of online platforms. Competition Policy International. https://www.competitionpolicyinternational.com/wp-content/uploads/2016/05/INTERNET-COMPETITION-LIBRO.pdf. Accessed 15 Dec 2020

OECD (2017) Algorithms and collusion—background note by the secretariat. DAF/Comp (2017). https://one.oecd.org/document/DAF/COMP(2017)4/en/pdf. Accessed 15 Dec 2020

ONDE (2018) Thailand digital economy and society development plan. https://www.onde.go.th/assets/portals//files/Digital_Thailand_pocket_book_EN.pdf. Accessed 15 Dec 2020

Patterson MR (2017) Antitrust law in the new economy. Harvard University Press, Cambridge, MA

Peritz RJR (2005) Tipping. In: Moss DL (ed) Network access, regulation and antitrust. Routledge, Abingdon, pp 28–34

Pieter Van Cleynenbreugel (2020) Article 101 TFEU's Association of Undertakings Notion and Its Surprising Potential to Help Distinguish Acceptable from Unacceptable Algorithmic Collusion. The Antitrust Bulletin 65(3):423–444

Podszun R (2015) The more technological approach: competition law in the digital economy. In: Surblytė G (ed) Competition on the Internet. Springer, Heidelberg, pp 101–108

Rubini L (ed) (2010) Microsoft on trial: legal and economic analysis of a transatlantic antitrust case. Edward Elgar, Cheltenham

Schmidt H (2009) Competition law, innovation and antitrust: an analysis of tying and technological integration. Edward Elgar, Cheltenham

Steinberg M (2019) How Japan transformed the consumer internet. University of Minnesota Press, Minneapolis

Stucke ME, Grunes AP (2016) Big data and competition policy. Oxford University Press, Oxford

Sullivan LA (2001) Is competition policy possible in high tech markets: an inquiry into antitrust, intellectual property, and broadband regulation as applied to the new economy? Case W Res L Rev 52:41–90

Surblytė G (ed) (2015) Competition on the Internet. Springer, Heidelberg

Tapscott D (2016) The digital economy: promise and peril in the age of networked intelligence. McGraw-Hill, New York

Teece DJ (2012–2013) Next-generation competition: new concepts for understanding how innovation shapes competition and policy in the digital economy. JL Econ Pol'y 9:97

UNCTAD (2017) Information economy report 2017: digitalization, trade and development. https://unctad.org/system/files/official-document/ier2017_en.pdf. Accessed 15 Dec 2020

Van den Bergh R (2017) Comparative competition law and economics. Edward Elgar, Cheltenham

Van Rompuy B (2012) Economic efficiency: non-efficiency considerations under Article 101 TFEU. Wolters Kluwer, Alphen aan de Rijn

Van Uytsel S (2018) Artificial intelligence and collusion: a literature overview. In: Corrales M, Fenwick M, Forgó N (eds) Robotics, AI and the future of law. Springer, Singapore, pp 155–182

Wasastjerna M (2020) Competition, data and privacy in the digital economy: towards a privacy dimension in competition law. Wolters Kluwer, Alphen aan den Rijn

Wismer S (2015) A note on price-parity clauses in platform markets. In: Surblytė G (ed) Competition on the Internet. Springer, Heidelberg, pp 41–52

World Bank (2019) The digital economy in Southeast Asia: strengthening the foundations for future growth. http://documents1.worldbank.org/curated/en/328941558708267736/pdf/The-Digital-Economy-in-Southeast-Asia-Strengthening-the-Foundations-for-Future-Growth.pdf. Accessed 15 Dec 2020

Wu T (2018) The curse of bigness: antitrust in the gilded age. Columbia Global Reports, New York

Part I
Platforms, Unilateral Conduct and Competition Law

Competition Law Enforcement for Exploitative Abuse by Digital Platforms: The Japanese Approach in a Global Context

Toshiaki Takigawa

Abstract The enforcement of competition law's exploitative-abuse clause on digital platforms by competition agencies is aimed at abuse in two-sided markets intermediated by digital platforms: first, platform abuse of their trading-counterparts (suppliers); second, abuse of consumers (users). Abuse of suppliers needs to be identified mostly on procedural fairness; as long as contractual terms are negotiated transparently between platforms and their trading-counterparts, competition agencies are urged to refrain from intervening in substance of trading terms. Digital platforms which abuse consumers, exclusively concerns consumer data. In countries equipped with strong data protection rules, there exists no rationale for competition agencies to assume the role of data-protection agency. Yet, in those countries, where data protection rules and data protection agencies are lacking or weak, competition agencies might assume the role of data protection agency, as an interim measure.

Keywords Exploitative abuse · Digital platforms · Superior bargaining position · Unfair trading practices · Consumer data · GAFA · Antimonopoly law

1 Introduction

Powerful digital platforms, represented by GAFA (Google, Apple, Facebook, and Amazon) have come to play an increasingly larger role in citizens' lives, ushering in public demands to rein in platform conduct. Digital platforms affect the welfare of not only consumers (platform customers) but also their trading counterparts (suppliers to platforms). This is because platforms intermediate between the two-sided markets: first, the market for consumers; second, the one for product/service suppliers.

Several platforms, due to network effects coupled with scale merits, have achieved dominant positions (namely, market power) in the two-sided markets, inviting accusation that they exclude competitors through leveraging their market power. This accusation squarely points to a key aspect of competition law—addressing

T. Takigawa (✉)
Kansai University, Osaka, Japan

S. Van Uytsel (ed.), *The Digital Economy and Competition Law in Asia*, Perspectives in Law, Business and Innovation,
https://doi.org/10.1007/978-981-16-0324-2_2

anti-competitive exclusion, through enforcement of monopolization or abuse-of-dominance clauses. Yet, this aspect of competition law has already been well discussed, bearing fruits in actual competition cases, particularly in the EU, targeted at super platforms, represented by Google.

This chapter considers another target of competition law, so far not well covered—abuse in exploitative conduct, which, in the case of digital platforms, concerns contractual terms deemed disadvantageous against platform suppliers as well as against consumers.

Nevertheless, we have to first recognize that the use of competition law to tackle exploitative conduct has been met with opposition. Most prominently, the US courts and antitrust agencies have consistently rejected utilizing antitrust laws for intervening in exploitative conduct by dominant companies. This rejection is based on the argument that lawfully acquired market power should be left free to be exploited, as long as the exploitation does not amount to anticompetitive exclusion; otherwise enterprises would be deprived of motivation to grow.[1]

Not restricted to the US, influential opinions have also been expressed in the EU against use of competition law to tackle exploitative conduct. First, reputable economists commissioned by the European Commission expressed: "To the extent that non-dominant platforms, in their regulatory role, can be expected to be disciplined by competition, no further reaching general rules would be needed."[2] Second, in the UK, government-commissioned policy authors expressed opinions against exploitative-abuse regulation: 'the pro-competition approach is to agree rules upfront, providing clarity to businesses in the market about the rules of the game.' 'The approach [the policy paper] recommends is instead to use pro-competition policy tools to provide every chance for competition to succeed in digital markets.'[3]

These views against enforcement on exploitative-abuse hold strong theoretical cohesion, emanating from the consumer-welfare basis of competition law. Still, outside the US, use of competition law to tackle exploitation has become prevalent, across the EU, Japan, Korea, and China, all addressing exploitative conduct by dominant companies, or those with relative market power. Moreover, although restricted to the grocery (agricultural goods and foods) sector, the use of competition law to check bargaining power of powerful grocery chains over suppliers has been implemented or contemplated in Australia and the UK.

This situation indicates that we cannot, now, simply denounce the enforcement on exploitative abuse by competition agencies; instead, we have to contemplate how to delineate boundaries of exploitative conduct, against which competition agencies may take actions: in case of digital platforms, regarding contractual terms imposed

---

[1]See, for instance, Shapiro (2019, p. 79) (the goal of antitrust policy is to protect and promote competition. Antitrust is not designed or equipped to deal with many of the major social and political problems associated with the tech titans, including threats to consumer privacy and data. Addressing these major problems requires sector-specific regulation).

[2]Crémer et al. (2019, p. 69).

[3]Furman et al. (2019, p. 56).

by digital platforms on suppliers, as well as on consumers. This chapter focuses on this point.

Exploitative conduct by dominant firms has mostly concerned conduct toward trading-counterparts, most typically, suppliers to powerful grocery chains. This is because exploitation has been linked to monopsony power (or buying power) of big retailers.

Nevertheless, recently, platform exploitation of consumer data has surfaced as the new target of competition law, as manifested by the German Bundeskartellamt in its enforcement on Facebook,[4] as well as the recent announcement by the Japanese competition agency—JFTC—on application of superior-bargaining-position clause (of the Japanese Antimonopoly Act—AMA) to digital platforms, for their dealing with consumers.[5] This aspect of exploitative-conduct regulation for protecting consumers, in comparison with that for protecting suppliers, presents a novel issue, regarding its overlapping with consumer protection rules. This chapter discusses this issue as well.

Section 2 deals with digital platforms' exploitative abuse on their suppliers, namely abuse in the platform to business (P to B) transaction. Section 3 deals with digital platforms' exploitative abuse on consumers (P to C), with emphasis on distinction between competition law and consumer protection measures. The Conclusion, in Sect. 4, summarizes the policy implications.

2 How to Address Platforms' Exploitative Abuse of Their Suppliers

Big grocery chains have long been accused of abusing their bargaining power over their suppliers, through imposing on them unfair contractual terms, as most recently proclaimed by the European Commission in its 2019 Unfair Trading Practices Directive.[6] The bargaining power of big grocery chains over their suppliers has been attributed to the locked-in status of the suppliers. Australia showcases this apprehension on unbalanced bargaining power.[7] Such apprehension is shared by several European countries, including the UK, prompting the European Commission to set up the Unfair Trading Practice Directive, in order to avoid fragmented regulations across the EU.

---

[4] Bundeskartellamt (2019).

[5] JFTC (2019a).

[6] European Commission, Directive 2019/633 on Unfair Trading Practices in Business-to-Business Relationships in the Agricultural and Food Supply Chain (25 April 2019) (2019 Unfair Trading Practices Directive).

[7] Fels and Lees (2018).

2.1 *Reining in Buying Power of Powerful Platforms*

The same concern, in Japan, has been treated as abuse of 'superior bargaining position' (abbreviated as SBP) by big purchasers against their suppliers. The Japanese situation shows that there exists little reason to limit this issue to grocery chains,[8] since the Japanese competition agency (JFTC) has extended the condemnation to a wide range of industries, including convenience stores,[9] and even banks.[10] Indeed, theoretically, every industry where large companies have bargaining power over their trading counterparts may be targeted by regulation against abuse of power.

It was only a matter of time, then, before digital platforms have come to be accused of abusing their bargaining power over their suppliers, who suffer from an inferior bargaining position against powerful platforms, due to the difficulty of these suppliers in finding sales-outlets of equivalent size outside the major platforms. On this basis, the JFTC in 2019 commenced to tackle digital platform abuse of their suppliers.[11]

2.2 *Should Competition Agencies Become Regulators of Exploitative Conduct?*

Powerful enterprises which deal with small-and-medium enterprises (SMEs), have been condemned as exploitative when they impose disadvantageous or unfair contractual-terms on SMEs. Thus, regulation on exploitative conduct has become equivalent with regulation on unfair trading practices (UTPs). Nevertheless, UTPs need not be regulated by competition agencies; they may more aptly be regulated by public agencies assigned to protect SMEs.

Indeed, the European Commission's 2019 Unfair Trading Practices Directive does not stipulate that the Directive be enforced by competition agencies, but leaves it to member states to designate relevant agencies. Still, as long as exploitative abuse continues to be regulated by competition law (which is the case in many countries outside the US), competition agencies receive strong pressure to rein in UTPs.

The reason is institutional: competition agencies are equipped with powerful enforcement tools backed by power to impose sanctions; by contrast, agencies to protect SMEs generally have weaker enforcement tools. Then, once it is admitted

---

[8]The EU 2019 Unfair Trading Practices Directive limits its target to the grocery sector, reasoning that "Within the agricultural and food supply chain, significant imbalances in bargaining power between suppliers and buyers of agricultural and food products are a common occurrence. Those imbalances in bargaining power are likely to lead to unfair trading practices when larger and more powerful trading partners seek to impose certain practices or contractual arrangements which are to their advantage in relation to a sales transaction."—2019 Unfair Trading Practices Directive, para 1.

[9]JFTC Remedy Order against Seven-Eleven Japan Co., Ltd (22 June 2009). Shinketsushu 56(2):6.

[10]JFTC Remedy Order against Mitsui-Sumitomo Bank (12 December 2005). Shinketsushu 52:436.

[11]JFTC (2019b).

that competition agencies should tackle UTPs, it becomes difficult to limit the targeted areas, since competition law covers all industries, and populism-oriented pressure is exerted on competition agencies toward protecting SMEs.

It is in this context that the European Commission set up the 2019 Unfair Trading Practices Directive as a directive specific to the grocery (or agricultural product) sector. The Commission limited the area of UTP regulation to the grocery sector, in order to not spread the regulation of UTPs across industries, even though EU competition law is equipped with the clause on exploitative abuse—Article 102 TFEU (Treaty on the Functioning of the European Union). Still, member states are free to choose agencies assigned to enforce the UTP Directive, and many states would choose to put the enforcement task to each state's competition agency.

2.3 Digital Platforms' Bargaining Power Over Their Suppliers

Competition agency enforcement of exploitative abuse has been endorsed as one aspect of regulation on dominant enterprises. The focus on dominance is derived from competition law's objective of protecting competition; without this focus, competition law would become a general tool to intervene in any kind of business practices, deemed unfair, transforming competition agencies to super agencies in charge of a whole range of business conduct.

Yet, dominance (namely, market power) held by powerful enterprises is often hard to prove, leading to under-enforcement by competition agencies. This problem has been solved by the drafter of the Japanese AMA, through delineating enterprises targeted by the law's exploitative-abuse clause as those with 'superior bargaining position (SBP)', which may be short of market power. SBP is essentially equivalent to 'relative market power', which was adopted by German competition law (para. 20 ARC).[12] The Japanese SBP and German 'relative market power' commonly address dependency of small-and-medium suppliers on large purchasers.

Dependency of suppliers on large purchasers is caused by investments sunk by the suppliers for meeting specific needs of the purchasers, causing the suppliers to be 'locked-in' to the purchasers. Nevertheless, locked-in situations may be handled within the framework of market power, as famously shown by *Kodak v. Image Technical Services* decided by the US Supreme Court, which held that purchasers of Kodak copy-machines (which has only a miniscule market share) were "locked-in" to the Kodak machines.[13] Even so, locked-in status which leads to market power may be found only in a limited number of cases, as shown by 'post-Kodak' decisions in the US.[14]

---

[12] Act against Restraint of Competition (ARC), §20 (1), (2): see Wagner-von Papp (2018).

[13] Eastman Kodak Co. v. Image Technical Services, Inc. 504 U.S. 451, 476 (1992).

[14] For instance, Queen City Pizza, Inc. v. Domino's Pizza, Inc. 124 F. 3d 430, 440 (3d Cir.1997).

The adoption of SBP (alternatively, "relative market power"), then, functions to mitigate the burden that competition agencies have in proving market power held by big purchasers.[15] Yet, the other side of the coin is that the SBP clause brings a risk of overregulation, since those suppliers encountering only a small degree of discomfort in shifting their sales-outlets may still succeed in convincing competition agencies that they have suffered from SBP abuse by big purchasers.

As a rebuttal to this argument of overregulation, JFTC, in its recent Report Regarding Trade Practices on Digital Platform, explains why digital platforms are specifically prone to acquire SBP: those digital platforms that have accumulated big data bring about switching costs for the platforms' suppliers, due to their being locked-into the platforms, thus enabling those platforms to hold SBPs over their suppliers.[16] More specifically, those suppliers that rely largely on a unique platform cannot switch to other platforms due to a large number of customers that the platform retains, obliging the suppliers to deal with the platform even under disadvantageous contractual-terms.[17]

This logic definitely applies to several of the most powerful platforms, such as Google, Facebook, and Amazon; however, this logic should not be automatically applied to all platforms, since a considerable number of platforms do not hold power to lock-in suppliers.

Risk of overregulation is aggravated, regardless of the logic of the JFTC's trade-practices Report, since all digital platforms may easily become a target of SBP-abuse regulation. This is because JFTC has consistently identified SBPs whenever JFTC has identified unfair contractual terms, through reasoning that the fact that a supplier was obliged to accept disadvantageous terms proves SBP status of the purchaser.[18] Yet, this is a tautology, which effaces the role of SBP as the concept for delimiting a range of companies targeted by the abuse-regulation clause. Consequently, JFTC, equipped with the SBP clause, may now be regarded as having transformed itself from competition agency to general overseer of unfair trade practices.[19]

SBP, or 'relative market power' (in the European parlance), therefore, cannot delimit the targets of its regulation. This point was well grasped by the drafters of the EU 2019 Directive; as a remedy, therefore, the Directive adopted a numerical threshold: "[the Directive] should apply to the business conduct of larger operators toward operators who have less bargaining power. A suitable approximation for relative market power is the annual turnover of the different operators."[20] By contrast, JFTC's new standard shown in the trade-practices Report, has not adopted

---

[15] See Takigawa (2018) (JFTC's stance of distinguishing "superior bargaining position" from market power has resulted in identifying SBPs whenever SMEs encountered slight degrees of hardship in switching their dealings from the alleged abusers… to other retailers).

[16] JFTC (2019b, p. 7).

[17] JFTC (2019b, p. 22).

[18] JFTC (JFTC 2010, II-1) (SBP means that the trading party is unable to avoid accepting such a request that is disadvantageous to the party). This idea has been repeated in several SBP cases, most recently, JFTC Toys "R" Us Hearing decision (4 June 2015). Shinketsushu 62:119.

[19] See Takigawa (2018).

[20] 2019 Unfair Trading Practices Directive, para 11.

any numerical threshold. Actually, the JFTC could not adopt one, given that the new standard is only a subset of JFTC's general Guidelines on SBP abuse,[21] which has not set up any numerical threshold for identifying SBP.

2.4 *Criteria for Identifying Abusive Exploitation*

Given the tautological nature of the criteria for identifying SBP, the crucial point in the SBP regulation rests on criteria for identifying abusiveness in trading-terms, contracted between big buyers and their suppliers.

2.4.1 Need to Go Beyond the Unreasonableness Criterion

This criterion has been set up by the JFTC in its original SBP Guidelines. But, the criterion ends up delineating abusive terms as those which cause 'unreasonable' damage to the suppliers.[22]

Unreasonableness, in the same way as fairness, is a subjective concept, failing to delimit boundaries of regulation. A subjective criterion ends up backing citizens' intuitive support for small-and-medium suppliers, when the suppliers complain about trading terms contracted with big purchasers.

Yet, viewing from the side of big purchasers, they often have legitimate reasons for adopting such contractual terms. For instance, the JFTC's trade practices' Report[23] cites a complaint by suppliers to digital platforms, against platforms which calculate charges (to be collected by the platforms) based on summation of a product's price and transportation fee: Those suppliers have felt it unfair to pay a charge for transportation fees, because the fee is for the transaction between platforms and transportation companies, with no involvement of the suppliers.[24] In defense of this complaint, a platform explained that setting up a charge based solely on a product's price would induce suppliers to set their products' prices at an exceedingly low level, while setting transportation fees at an exceedingly high level, thus artificially lowering transaction charges.[25]

[21] JFTC (2010).

[22] Takigawa (2018); also see Wakui and Cheng (2015, p. 7) (a retailer's abusive practice can cause an unreasonable or unexpected disadvantage to the supplier in various ways. Thus, the factors that need to be taken into account in the evaluation will vary by the type of practice).

[23] JFTC (2019b).

[24] JFTC (2019b, p. 31).

[25] JFTC (2019b, p. 31).

2.4.2 JFTC's 2019 Report on Digital Platforms' Trading Practices

Realizing that the general criterion on SBP abuse—'unreasonable burden on suppliers'—is too ambiguous, the JFTC in its Report on digital platform trading practices[26] set up more concrete criteria, focusing on procedural fairness in revisions of contracts between platforms and suppliers. For the revision procedures to be judged as fair, platforms need to, first, notify in writing to their suppliers on the content of revisions; second, in case those suppliers express their opinions on the revision, platforms need to take these into consideration, at the same time, placing ample time before implementing the revision.[27]

These criteria which focus on negotiating procedure are generally more sensible and reasonable than those targeting the substance of trading terms. Nevertheless, the JFTC Report does not state that procedural fairness trumps substance of trading-terms. Therefore, even after the new JFTC standard, vagueness of criteria on unfair trading-terms persists. It is, therefore, hoped that JFTC adopts a view that as far as trading-terms (including fees) have been fairly and transparently negotiated between platforms and their suppliers, JFTC usually refrains from intervening in the substance of trading-terms. In this regard, JFTC might emulate the EU 2019 Directive, which prioritizes negotiation-procedural fairness.[28]

2.4.3 The Rakuten Case: The Need for Balancing Welfare of Businesses Against Those of Consumers

Even after the 2019 trading practices Report, vagueness of criteria on unfair trading-terms persists. This fact was laid bare in the 2020 Rakuten case initiated by JFTC. Rakuten is the second largest (after Amazon) platform for electronic commerce (E-commerce) in Japan. JFTC sought an interim order (for suspension) to Tokyo regional court, against Rakuten's contract-revision toward suppliers, on which Rakuten obligated suppliers to adopt transport-fee included pricing (for transaction exceeding 3980 yen).

Several suppliers, discontent with the contract-revision, brought complaint to JFTC, which took it so seriously as to seek an interim measure (for suspension) from the regional court. It is natural that many suppliers are discontent with the contract-revision, whereby their range of freedom in choosing sales-methods are narrowed. However, the existence of discontent on the side of suppliers, by itself, should not be deemed enough for identifying abuse, since such standpoint makes it impossible for big retailers and platforms to revise contract-terms toward suppliers.

---

[26] JFTC (2019b).

[27] JFTC (2019b, pp. 30, 35).

[28] 2019 Unfair Trading Practices Directive, para 16 (it is appropriate to distinguish between practices that are provided for in clear and unambiguous terms in supply agreements ... between parties and practices that occur after the transaction has started ..., so that only unilateral and retrospective changes to those clear and unambiguous terms of the supply agreement are prohibited. However, certain trading practices are considered as unfair by their very nature ...).

Although JFTC presents the reason for identifying abuse by Rakuten, the reason lacks convincingness, because JFTC's press release[29] merely states that '[contract-revision initiated by Rakuten] results in hampering free and voluntary decision by a considerable number of suppliers, thus …seriously harming fair and free market order'. This statement shows that JFTC prioritizes 'free and voluntary decision' by suppliers. Yet, this prioritizing results in robbing digital platforms of capacity to design their business methods through imposing conditions on suppliers regarding methods of sales.

Prioritizing free decision of suppliers not only contradicts the business models of digital platforms but also contradicts the meaning of contracts, since contracts are engaged for restricting freedom of decision by the parties of contracts. The JFTC is required to go beyond the 'free decision' argument, toward explaining why JFTC considers that the contract revision (adoption of transport-fee included pricing) exerts 'unreasonable burden on suppliers'.

Here, 'unreasonableness' needs to be examined in the spirit of 'fair and free market order'—namely, the objective of the competition law. Given digital platforms engage in two-sided markets, involving not only suppliers but also consumers, competition law objective mandates competition agencies to weigh welfare of suppliers against that of consumers.

Consumers evidently welcome transportation-included pricing because of its transparency, given the lack of transparency and cumbersomeness of pricing in which a transportation fee is added to a product's price, as practiced by Amazon for its platform business of its electronic commerce (which is distinct from electronic commerce directly operated by Amazon). Given benefit to consumers, it is dubious to conclude 'unreasonable burden' on suppliers, induced by the contract revision.

The Rakuten case practically ended on March 2020, when Rakuten vaguely acceded to JFTC by announcing: 'Rakuten is going to implement the new contract (regarding transportation-fee included pricing) only with several suppliers who are ready; for other suppliers, Rakuten is going to take measures to meet the intention of those who wish to be exempted from the new contract'.[30] Rakuten's announcement was followed by JFTC announcing the reversal of its appeal for interim order.[31]

It is necessary to recall that JFTC, in its 2019 Report on digital platform trading practices, wisely focused on the appropriateness of negotiating procedure, not on substance of contract-revision. JFTC, then, is advised to stick to the spirit of its 2019 Report, by focusing on negotiation procedure of contract revision, rather than substance of the revision. It seems that Rakuten was too hasty in implementing the contract revision, without giving suppliers ample time to prepare for the contract revision. Then, if Rakuten ameliorates its negotiating procedure, JFTC is advised to consider it as enough, without proceeding to examine 'unreasonable burden to suppliers'.

---

[29] JFTC (2020).

[30] Rakuten (2020).

[31] JFTC (2020).

2.5 How to Delimit the Use of the Exploitative-Abuse Clause by Competition Agencies

Populist sentiment prompts governmental agencies to intervene in trading terms between big merchants and SMEs, for the sake of fairness. However, the resulting intervention would become so pervasive as to end up undermining free market order.[32]

In order to minimize this risk, the SBP-abuse clause (and similar clauses on relative market power, or dependency) should be used by competition agencies only as the last resort, when SMEs have no other means for resolving their conflicts with big merchants.

Moreover, competition agencies, including JFTC, need to minimize interventions, through focusing on trading-term revisions made after conclusion of a contract.[33] Furthermore, trading-term revisions need to be left free, as long as conditions for revisions have been contracted in writing between platforms and their suppliers.[34]

3 How to Address Platform Exploitative Abuse of Consumer Data

Exploitative abuse has mostly been addressed by competition agencies with regard to terms offered by large-scale buyers to their suppliers, for addressing exploitative abuse of monopsony power (buyers' bargaining power). But exploitative abuse may also be addressed with regard to terms offered to end-consumers (customers). As an example, the European Commission has once applied Article 102 of the TFEU to a producer's pricing on consumers.[35]

It is not surprising, therefore, that several competition agencies have commenced tackling exploitative abuse of digital platforms over consumers. The most conspicuous example is Bundeskartellamt's enforcement on Facebook's handling of consumer data.

As to Japan, the JFTC has long eschewed applying the AMA's exploitative-abuse clause–SBP clause–to terms offered to consumers; instead, applying exclusively to terms offered to trading-counterparts (mostly, suppliers to big retailers). This is because the JFTC has regarded the SBP clause as a tool to address the vertical relationship between powerful purchasers and small-and-medium suppliers.

---

[32]See Wagner-von Papp (2018, pp. 243–244) (if one would have to regulate comprehensively all aspects of the contractual relationship, ...is not desirable in a free market economy).

[33]See Wakui and Cheng (2015, p. 28) (in the cases where the JFTC did take formal measures, the offending entrepreneur had imposed on the supplier some economic burden that was not specified in the contract).

[34]This is a policy stated in the European Commission 2019 Unfair Trading Practices Directive.

[35]*United Brands Company vs. Commission of the European Communities*, Court of Justice of the European Union, Case 27/76 (1978).

However, times have changed: in step with the Government-wide drive[36] to rein in powerful platforms, the JFTC has announced its new policy of applying the SBP clause to platforms' terms toward consumers.[37] In parallel with Bundeskartellamt's enforcement on Facebook, JFTC's new initiative focuses on digital platform and their handling of consumer data.

Competition law's exploitative-abuse clause covers a whole range of abusive terms which businesses impose on consumers; yet, as for digital platforms, the terms on handling of consumer data stand out. This is due to platforms having a business model of giving consumers free services, in exchange for obtaining consumer data, from which the platforms elicit profits, prominently, through making their targeted advertising more personal and accurate.

3.1 Which to Choose: Competition Law or Consumer Protection Law for Addressing Abusive Terms on Consumers

The application of competition law to rectify platform abuse of consumers (as opposed to suppliers) invites criticism that exploitative abuse on consumers have already been addressed by consumer-protection rules: regarding consumer data, by GDPR in the EU, and rules inspired by GDPR in countries outside the EU.

The JFTC should be well aware of this criticism, because JFTC ceded its consumer protection function (engaged through the AMA-affiliated law on false advertising) to the newly inaugurated Consumer Affairs Agency in 2009. Indeed, this criticism was expressed in public comments to the JFTC's draft Guidelines on digital platforms, to which JFTC responded by stating that exploitative abuse of consumers enables the abuser to transfer the resulting profit to resources for combatting the abuser's rivals, leading to exclusionary effects, thus legitimizing application of the AMA.[38]

However, this logic is exactly the same as the one used by JFTC for legitimizing enforcement on exploitative abuse in its original SBP Guidelines. Then, just in the same way as the logic in the SBP Guidelines, the connection of exploitative abuse to exclusionary effect is too remote, with JFTC automatically identifying exclusionary effect whenever it identifies exploitative conduct.

Automatically connecting exploitative conduct to exclusionary effect results in legitimizing SBP-clause application to a whole range of abusive terms, imposed by businesses on consumers. This radically broadens JFTC's task, going well beyond competition issues, extending its task to a whole range of consumer protection issues.

---

[36]See JFTC (2019a), Annex 2 (JFTC views on respondents' comments' mentioning that the JFTC Guidelines was issued in the wake of the Governmental decision, on June 2019, stating that application of SBP clause under the AMA to digital platforms' dealing with consumers is to be set on or before summer of 2019).

[37]JFTC (2019a).

[38]JFTC (2019a), Annex 2, which cites footnote 4 of the draft Guidelines.

True, JFTC has set up its new Guidelines specifically aiming it at digital platforms. But, there exists no reason to limit the application to digital platforms[39]; instead, same Guidelines, logically, may be extended to a whole range of consumer protection issues.

Looking globally, it is not only JFTC that protects consumers through the application of competition law's exploitative-abuse clause; Bundeskartellamt, regarding its Facebook decision, presents another prominent example. By contrast, the Italian authority applied its consumer protection law, rather than competition law, for addressing the data privacy issue.[40] Different treatments across countries reflect different institutional settings across countries, regarding relative strength of a consumer protection regime over a competition one.

Among these countries, Japan and Germany share a common characteristic: both hold powerful competition agencies, which coexist with relatively weak consumer-protection agencies. Regarding personal-data protection, Japan does have its data protection agency—Personal Information Protection Commission—, but it is a young agency with relatively weak enforcement tools; whereas JFTC is a well-established agency with ample staff equipped with powerful enforcement tools, in particular, the power to impose substantial fines on culprits. This is in parallel with the situation in Germany; Bundeskartellamt is a powerful agency, coexisting with no specific agency for protecting personal data.[41]

As a backdrop of this phenomenon, abusive conduct of powerful digital-platforms has become a prominent political and social issue in several developed countries, leading to demands for governmental action from citizens. Then, in countries where powerful competition agencies coexist with weaker consumer protection agencies, the competition agencies are urged to act, and those agencies equipped with exploitative-abuse clauses cannot reject the call for action, since exploitative abuse covers a whole range of abuse on consumers.

In the case of Japan, JFTC has taken the lead, among governmental agencies, in addressing abuse by digital platforms, although, at the first stage, restricting its enforcement on exclusionary abuse, through the AMA's monopolization clause, together with unfair-trade-practices clauses oriented to exclusionary conduct. At the second stage, however, JFTC has commenced applying the AMA's exploitative-abuse clause—SBP clause—to digital-platform abuse of suppliers—hitherto observed domain of the SBP clause.

Then, more recently, as the third stage, reining in digital platforms has become a Government-wide mandate in Japan, within which the JFTC has naturally become an

---

[39]JFTC, itself, admits that abuse against consumers is addressed by SBP clause in areas other than digital platforms. JFTC (2019a), Annex 2.

[40]See Botta and Wiedemann (2019, p. 428) (the Italian case has been decided under consumer, rather than competition law).

[41]Botta and Wiedemann (2019, p. 440) (in Germany, unfair commercial practices that affect consumers can only be enforced in civil courts by qualified institutions, associations, and chambers of industry and commerce).

indispensable player, with the Government prompting JFTC to widen the coverage of the AMA's SBP clause to abuse on consumers.[42]

For JFTC, the natural reaction is to meet with the Governmental prompt (in correspondence with public demand), for utilizing the SBP clause to protect consumers from abuse by powerful platforms. Nevertheless, utilizing the SBP clause for protection of consumers accompanies risk of overreach by JFTC, at the sacrifice of its core task—enforcing on collusions, mergers, and exclusionary conduct. Therefore, JFTC, as well as other competition agencies facing similar situations, should be careful to limit exploitative-abuse regulation to those consumer-protection areas where competition agencies are obliged to enter, due to lack or weaker capacity of consumer protection agencies.

3.2 *Proving Platform Bargaining Power Over Consumers*

In the same way as with the case of abuse on suppliers, abuse on consumers may be addressed by the SBP clause (or relative-market-power clauses) of the competition law only when the abuser manifests bargaining power over consumers. Bargaining power requirement needs to be interpreted as a mitigating device for lessening burden on competition agencies for proving market power of the abusers.

Generally, a higher hurdle should be set to prove bargaining power of platforms over consumers, as opposed to over suppliers, since consumers have less reason to stick to a single platform, in face of several alternatives. Indeed, a German Higher Regional Court (the Düsseldorf Higher Regional Court), in the Facebook decision (regarding the interim measure) rejected Bundeskartellamt's finding of Facebook's relative market power over consumers,[43] although the Federal Court overturned the Düsseldorf Court, in favor of Bundeskartellamt.[44] Still, the Federal Court's decision concerns only appropriateness of the interim measures (namely, suspension); decision on substance is pending at the Düsseldorf Court. Given that the Düsseldorf Court has already offered (in its decision on interim measures) detailed analysis denouncing substance of Bundeskartellamt's reasoning, very concise decision (on interim measures) by the Federal Court is weak for overruling the Düsseldorf Court.

As to JFTC, in its December 2019 Guidelines on digital platforms, it has put up two reasons for recognizing consumers' dependence on a few super platforms.

---

[42]See JFTC (2019a), Annex 2.

[43]Facebook/Bundeskartellamt, The Decision of the Higher Regional Court of Düsseldorf (Oberlandesgericht Düsseldorf) in interim proceedings, 26 August 2019, Case VI-Kart 1/19 (V). Available at: https://www.d-kart.de/wp-content/uploads/2019/08/OLG-D%C3%BCsseldorf-Facebook-2019-English.pdf. Accessed 15 December 2020. The Düsseldorf Court, not restricting its decision to the interim measure issue, wholly rejects the Bundeskartellamt's reasoning: First, behaviors by Facebook (which are prohibited by Bundeskartellamt) do not have the effect of restricting competition, thus do not constitute violation of the German competition law; Second, consumers have not suffered damage from giving Facebook additional personal-information.

[44]Bundesgerichtshof (The Federal Court) (2020).

First, consumers suffer from disadvantageous trading terms against businesses, due to information asymmetry, leading to discrepancies in bargaining power.[45] Nevertheless, this statement is true for whole situation of businesses vis-a-vis consumers, leading to the implication that the SBP clause would be applied widely to businesses, not restricted to digital platforms.

Second, JFTC posits that SBP is identified when "consumers are obliged to accept the disadvantageous treatment from digital platforms for the sake of continuing to utilize the services offered by the platforms."[46] This explanation appears to limit SBP identification to cases of 'locked in' status of consumers. But, the explanation is too loose to set any limitation on finding SBP, since 'locked in' status is identified whenever consumers feel that they suffer from disadvantageous trading terms, at the same time, continuing to use the service of the platform. This explanation by JFTC ends up identifying the SBP status of the business, whenever the business's trading terms are found unfair (or unreasonable, or alternatively, disadvantageous to consumers). This tautological reasoning is the same as that given by JFTC in its Guidelines on the SBP clause.[47]

Then, as with the general SBP Guidelines, this new policy statement on digital platforms has put no limits on identification of SBP regarding digital platforms; whenever JFTC identifies unreasonably disadvantageous terms on consumers, JFTC automatically recognizes SBP with the platforms.

Yet, it is necessary to limit the scope of SBP-abuse regulation applied to digital platforms, in order to give smaller platforms areas of safe harbors, thus mitigating risk of overreach by JFTC. For this purpose, JFTC might set up market-share thresholds, or, at least, quantitative volume thresholds, in step with the European Commission's adoption of numeric thresholds in its Guidelines on abuse in agricultural products sector.[48]

3.3 *Identification of Exploitative-Abuse in Platform Handling of User Data*

Due to platforms having a business mode which provides free services to consumers in exchange for obtaining their data, exploitative-abuse of consumers almost exclusively concerns platform and their handling of user data. Still, the description of exploitation is ambiguous, since, in the case of the AMA's SBP clause, exploitation is identified in trading terms which are 'substantially disadvantageous'[49] to customers. The JFTC, therefore, needs to explain about criteria, based on which 'substantially disadvantageous' nature of terms on the handling of consumer data is determined.

[45] JFTC (2019a, p. 3).

[46] JFTC (2019a, p. 4).

[47] JFTC (2010).

[48] 2019 Unfair Trading Practices Directive.

[49] JFTC (2010, II-1).

3.3.1 Bundeskartellamt's Facebook Case

In the Facebook case, Bundeskartellamt has put up as the reason for finding Facebook's handling of user data as exploitative, the fact that it is "in violation of the European data protection rules."[50] By putting up the data protection rules, namely GDPR, Bundeskartellamt has avoided the criticism oriented to vagueness of criteria for identifying exploitative abuse.

However, the GDPR, has its regulatory agencies, having no need to be enforced by competition agencies. Still, Germany, among EU member countries, may have special institutional reasons for the competition agency taking the role of a data-protection agency.

3.3.2 JFTC's 2019 Guidelines on Digital Platforms

By contrast to the EU, Japan has not yet strengthened its data protection rule—the Act on the Protection of Personal Information[51]—to the level equivalent with GDPR.

It is against this backdrop that the Japanese Government urged JFTC to tackle data protection issues through the exploitative-abuse clause—the AMA's SBP clause. One may interpret that the Japanese Government is not yet ready to enact GDPR-equivalent data protection rules; instead, as an interim measure, it is calling on JFTC to fill the void.

Then, in order to amend the vague definition of exploitative abuse—trading terms which inflict "substantial disadvantage" to the abusers' trading counterparts[52]—, JFTC is required to explain the criteria by which data-related terms offered by platforms would be identified as inflicting 'substantial disadvantage' to consumers.

Indeed, in its 2019 Guidelines on digital platforms, JFTC listed a limited number of terms (or modalities) on data use (set up by platforms) as abusive, although the Guidelines leave room for JFTC to identify abusive terms outside the listed terms. These listed terms are as follows[53]:

1. Purchase or use of personal data, without informing consumers of the purchase/usage objective.
2. Purchase or use of personal data, which surpass the degree necessary for the use objective, at the same time without gaining user consent.
3. Purchase or use of personal data, without taking necessary measures for securing safety.

[50] Bundeskartellamt (2019).

[51] Act No. 57 of May 30, 2003 (APPI), translation available at: http://www.japaneselawtranslation.go.jp/law/detail/?id=2781&vm=&re. Accessed 15 December 2020. The Act was amended (June 2020) to give greater protections to individuals: such as requiring companies to obtain consent from individuals for transfers of non-identifiable personal data to a third party. Available at: https://www.ppc.go.jp/en/news/archives/2020/20200618. Accessed 15 December 2020.

[52] JFTC (2010, II-1).

[53] JFTC (2019a, p. 7) (for data acquisition) and p. 9 (for data use).

4. Inducing client-consumers to offer to the platforms economic benefits or additional personal information, in addition to the personal information which consumers are offering to the platforms as a compensation for the free services given by the platforms.

These listed items all concern modalities of data purchase/use, and are sensible ones to be prohibited. These behaviors are mostly prohibited by the EU GDPR. Thus, JFTC's new Guidelines perform as virtual Guidelines on protection of personal data. The JFTC has thus assumed the role of personal data protection agency. This accompanies risk of overreach, to the sacrifice of the competition agency's core task of protecting competition. The current set up may be rationalized as an interim measure, until the personal-data protection rule[54] would be strengthened and be enforced by the Japanese data-protection agency–Personal Information Protection Commission.

4 Conclusion

Competition agency enforcement of the exploitative-abuse on digital platforms, is aimed at abuse in two-sided markets intermediated by digital platforms: first, platform abuse on their trading-counterparts (suppliers); second, abuse on consumers (users).

Platform abuse on suppliers is one variation of buying power (monopsony power) abuse. Buying power, from the consumer-oriented view of competition law, needs to be regulated through an exclusionary abuse clause, not through an exploitative abuse clause. Yet, outside the US, it has become prevalent for competition agencies to protect small-and-medium suppliers from big retailers, through application of exploitative abuse clauses. Therefore, now, it has become important to set limitation on application of the exploitative-abuse clause to digital platforms. For this objective, abuse needs to be identified mostly on procedural fairness; as long as contractual terms are negotiated transparently between platforms and their trading-counterparts, competition agencies are urged to refrain from intervening in the substance of trading terms. Indeed, JFTC's new Report on digital platforms focuses on procedural fairness.

As compared to protection of small-and-medium suppliers, protection of consumers (users of digital platforms), through application exploitative-abuse clauses, brings about the risk of competition agencies' taking on the role of consumer protection agency, at the sacrifice of competition agencies' core task of protecting competition. Indeed, regarding digital platforms, their abuse against consumers concerns exclusively consumer data. Therefore, in countries equipped with strong data protection rules (particularly EU member countries with GDPR) enforced by data protection agencies, there exists no rationale for competition agencies assuming the role of data-protection agency. Yet, in those countries, where data protection rules and data protection agencies are lacking or weak, competition agencies might

[54] Japanese personal-data protection rule—Act on the Protection of Personal Information—was amended in 2020; however, its degree of protection is still much inferior to that attained by GDPR.

assume the role of data protection agency, as an interim measure. Recently adopted Guidelines, by JFTC, on digital platforms may be rationalized in this context.

References

Botta M, Wiedemann K (2019) The interaction of EU competition, consumer, and data protection law in the digital economy: the regulatory dilemma in the Facebook odyssey. Antitrust Bull 64(3):428–446

Bundeskartellamt (2019) Bundeskartellamt prohibits Facebook from combining user data from different sources (Press release, 2 July)

Bundesgerichtshof (The Federal Court) (2020) Federal court of justice provisionally confirms the allegation of abuse of a dominant position by Facebook (Press release, 23 June). https://www.bundesgerichtshof.de/SharedDocs/Pressemitteilungen/DE/2020/2020080.html?nn=10690868. Accessed 15 Dec 2020

Crémer J, de Montjoye Y, Schweitzer H (2019) Competition policy for the digital era. Publications Office of the European Union, Luxembourg

Fels A, Lees M (2018) Unconscionable conduct in the context of competition law with special reference to retailer/supplier relationship within Australia. In: Di Porto F, Podszun R (eds) Abusive practices in competition law. Edward Elgar, Gloucestershire, pp 343–374

Furman J, Coyle D, Fletcher A, McAuley D, Marsden P (2019) Unlocking digital competition report of the digital competition expert panel. https://assets.publishing.service.gov.uk/government/uploads/system/uploads/attachment_data/file/785547/unlocking_digital_competition_furman_review_web.pdf. Accessed 15 Dec 2020

JFTC (2010) Guidelines concerning abuse of superior bargaining position under the anti-monopoly act. https://www.jftc.go.jp/en/legislation_gls/imonopoly_guidelines_files/101130GL.pdf. Accessed 15 Dec 2020

JFTC (2019a) Guidelines on abuse of superior bargaining position over consumers who provide personal information to digital platforms. https://www.jftc.go.jp/en/pressreleases/yearly-2019/December/191217DPconsumerGL.pdf. Accessed 20 Dec 2020

JFTC (2019b) Press release (31 October): report regarding trade practices of digital platforms (business-to-business transactions by online retail platform and app store). https://www.jftc.go.jp/en/pressreleases/yearly-2019/October/191031.html. Accessed 15 Dec 2020

JFTC (2020) Press Release (28 February): the JFTC has filed a petition for an urgent injunction against Rakuten, Inc. https://www.jftc.go.jp/en/pressreleases/yearly-2020/February/200228.html. Accessed 15 Dec 2020

Rakuten (2020) Press release (10 March): Kousei torihiki iinkai ni yoru kinkyuu teishi meirei no saru-tate no torisage ni tsuite [Notice regarding petition for urgent injuction by the Japan Fair Trade Commission]. https://corp.rakuten.co.jp/news/press/2020/0310_01.html. Accessed 15 Dec 2020

Shapiro C (2019) Protecting competition in the American economy: merger control, tech titans, labor markets. J Econ Perspect 33(3):69–93

Takigawa T (2018) Restraining bargaining power through competition law: superior bargaining position regulation in Japan as compared with the EU. In: Di Porto F, Podszun R (eds) Abusive practices in competition law. Edward Elgar, Gloucestershire, pp 265–282

Wakui M, Cheng TK (2015) Regulating abuse of superior bargaining position under the Japanese competition law: an anomaly or a necessity? J Antitrust Enforcement 3(2):302–333

Wagner-von Papp F (2018) Unilateral conduct by non-dominant firms: a comparative reappraisal. In: Di Porto F, Podszun R (eds) Abusive practices in competition law. Edward Elgar, Gloucestershire, pp 225–264

Regulating Competition Between Digital Platforms: The Japan Fair Trade Commission's Preference for Unfair Trade Practices

Steven Van Uytsel and Yoshiteru Uemura

Abstract The Japan Fair Trade Commission (JFTC) has shown an increasing interest in the digital economy. Since the JFTC's Chairman, Kazuyuki Sugimoto, spoke about this topic in the New Year's address in 2016, the JFTC publicized several studies on the digital economy. One important issue raised in some of the reports was the central role unfair trade practices could play to force the players in the platform economy to abide with the principles of the Japanese Act on Prohibition of Private Monopolization and Maintenance of Fair Trade (AMA). This conclusion runs parallel to the enforcement actions of the JFTC. In the only cease-and-desist order of the JFTC, a platform was ordered to comply with the AMA through an unfair trade practice. Various decisions to close an investigation on a suspected violation of the AMA, such as against Amazon, Airbnb, or Rakuten, also document the importance of the unfair trade practices as a tool to bring these firms in compliance with the AMA. The evolution to revert to unfair trade practices could be seen as positive. We argue that unfair trade practices allow the JFTC to balance two opposite views in the literature on the platform economy. On the one hand, there is a call for early market intervention to prevent a single platform from growing excessively. On the other hand, there is an argument against intervention because incumbent platforms are innovators and, if not careful, can be challenged on their existence. Unfair trade practices allow for both early intervention and meticulous intervention. Early intervention can be realized because market power is not an important criterion, if at all one, in the conceptualization of an unfair trade practice offence. Meticulous intervention can be guaranteed because unfair trade practices focus on the conduct of an online platform. Unfair trade practices do, in other words, not aim to tackle the 'bigness' of the online platforms and so trigger a change in the competitive structure of the market.

S. Van Uytsel (✉)
Graduate School of Law, Kyushu Universit, Fukuoka, Japan
e-mail: uytsel@law.kyushu-u.ac.jp

Y. Uemura
Faculty of Economics, Hannan University, Osaka, Japan

S. Van Uytsel (ed.), *The Digital Economy and Competition Law in Asia*,
Perspectives in Law, Business and Innovation,
https://doi.org/10.1007/978-981-16-0324-2_3

Keyword Digital economy · Online platforms · Platform economy · Unfair trade practices · Japanese Antimonopoly Act · Japan Fair Trade Commission · Amazon · Airbnb · Rakuten · Minna no Pet

1 Introduction

The Japan Fair Trade Commission (JFTC) has recently been very active in researching how it should position itself towards developments in the digital economy, of which the platform economy is part. The first start was given by Chairman Kazuyuki Sugimoto in his New Year's message of 2016.[1] In this message, Sugimoto recognized that the digital economy, and in specific the platform economy, has changed business models, requiring the JFTC to carefully consider the extent to which its *Act on Prohibition of Private Monopolization and Maintenance of Fair Trade*[2] (Antimonopoly Act or AMA) should be applied.

After having participated as an observer in the *Cross-sectional System Study Group for the Fourth Industrial Revolution* of the Ministry of Economy, Trade, and Industry (METI),[3] the JFTC released several reports relevant to the digital and platform economy. In June 2017, a first study on the relationship between data and competition policy was released.[4] From 2018, the focus shifted to digital platforms. Together with METI and the Ministry of Internal Affairs and Communications, the JFTC issued a notice summarizing the fundamental principles necessary to allow digital platforms to grow.[5] Being general in nature and transgressing competition law issues, the JFTC continued its research on digital platforms and made considerable progress in 2019. In a short period of three months, the JFTC publicized its vision on the application the abuse of superior bargaining position to transactions between digital platform operators and consumers,[6] collected public comments on its suggested revision to the guidelines applicable to the review of business combinations (mergers) in order to accommodate platforms,[7] and issued its report in relation to trade practices on digital platforms.[8]

As the most comprehensive, the *Report Regarding Trade Practices on Digital Platforms* is one of the more interesting instruments to further analyze.[9] At the

[1] Sugimoto (2016).

[2] Law No. 54 of 1974, shiteki dokusen no kinshi oyobi kousei torihiki no kakuho ni kan suru houritsu [Law Concerning the Prohibition of Private Monopolies and the Assurance of Fair Trade] (hereinafter AMA).

[3] Ministry of Economy, Trade and Industry (2016).

[4] Japan Fair Trade Commission (2017a).

[5] Ministry of Economy, Trade and Industry, Japan Fair Trade Commission, and Ministry of Internal Affairs and Communications (2018).

[6] Japan Fair Trade Commission (2019b).

[7] Japan Fair Trade Commission (2019c).

[8] Japan Fair Trade Commission (2019a).

[9] Japan Fair Trade Commission (2019a).

end of this document, the JFTC survey concludes with possible solutions to the anticompetitive conduct that could occur in the digital market.[10] Of interest in the fight against anti-competitive behavior in the Japanese digital market are: abuse of superior bargaining position, interference with a competitor's transactions, and trading on restrictive terms.[11] Each of these three suggestions are further qualifications of what in the AMA is termed 'unfair trade practice'.[12]

The reliance on unfair trade practices implicates that the application of another provision in the AMA is excluded. This provision is the one on monopolization. For outside observers, preferring unfair trade practices above monopolization may be awkward, especially because the JFTC seems to identify the digital market as oligopolistic, thus with the presence of a few dominant players. This chapter will argue, after identifying the use of unfair trade practices in the platform economy cases in Japan, that unfair trade practices have an advantage. These provisions allow for intervening in markets before dominance has been achieved. For markets in which dominance already exists, it allows for swift action.

The Chapter is structured as follows. In Sect. 2, the Chapter discusses how the AMA regulates anti-competitive conduct. This introduction is given to show that the AMA has provisions that overlap in scope. Despite the overlap in scope, one provision is easier in its enforcement than the other. Section 3 elaborates on enforcement examples. By concluding that the JFTC prefers to use unfair trade practices in relation to anticompetitive conduct of online platforms, Sect. 4 seeks to deliver a rationale for this choice. The conceptualization of the unfair trade practices allows for both early and meticulous intervention in the market. Section 5 concludes.

2 Regulating Anticompetitive Conduct Under the Antimonopoly Law

Competition law came to Japan under the pressure of the United States in the aftermath of the Second World War.[13] In an attempt to democratize the Japanese economy, the Allied Powers, in which the United States had the main influence,[14] obliged the Japanese government to elaborate and adopt a competition law.[15] When the first drafts were not in line with the US understanding of what the content of competition law should be,[16] the Supreme Commander of the Allied Powers requested an American lawyer to draft a law.[17] Even though the Japanese government could scrutinize the

---

[10] Japan Fair Trade Commission (2019a).

[11] Japan Fair Trade Commission (2019a, pp. 22–95).

[12] Wakui (2018, pp. 135 and 178–206).

[13] See, generally, Haley (2001) and First (2000).

[14] Augustine.

[15] Wakui (2008, pp. 7–12).

[16] Wakui (2008).

[17] Wakui (2008).

drafts and suggest changes,[18] the AMA was generally considered to be an amalgam of the different laws regulating competition in the United States.[19]

2.1 An Historical Perspective on Anticompetitive Conduct in Japan

The drafting of the AMA started well with the appointment of Posey T. Kime,[20] a bureaucrat working at the Antitrust Division within the Department of Justice. Kime had to provide a draft competition law for Japan. For this job, he almost mechanically transferred the conceptualization of forbidden conduct under the United States' antitrust laws to his draft for the Japanese competition law. One article would deal with the conduct prohibited in the Sherman Act, another article would deal with the conduct regulated in the Federal Trade Commission Act and still another article would deal with the Clayton Act. If the conduct encoded in the Clayton Act is disregarded, Kime suggested that the Japanese competition law should regulate unreasonable restraints of trade and private monopolization on the one hand and unfair methods of competition on the other. Unlike in the United States, price fixing agreements were still the subject of another article in Japan. Just like in the United States, unreasonable restraints of trade and monopolization would be subject to criminal sanctions, while unfair methods of competition would not be.[21]

Positioning unreasonable restraints of trade and unfair trade practices next to each other caused confusion. In order to overcome their confusion, the Japanese negotiators formulated their understanding of unfair trade practices in a document

[18]See, e.g., Matsushita (1997, pp. 151–156) and First (2000, pp. 67–70).

[19]Competition law in the United States was not regulated by just one statute. Three different statutes have been enacted over time: The Sherman Act (1890), the Federal Trade Commission Act (1914), and the Clayton Act (1914). The Sherman Act prohibited unreasonable restraints of trade (Sect. 1) and monopolization (Sect. 2). Enforcement powers were given to the Department of Justice, in which an Antitrust Division was established. The Federal Trade Commission Act banned unfair methods of competition. The enforcement power over these unfair methods was given to the Federal Trade Commission. The Clayton Act addressed practices that were not regulated in the Sherman Act, such as mergers and acquisitions and interlocking directors. This Act further allowed private parties to sue for triple damages for harm caused by violations of the Sherman Act or the Clayton Act. Regarding the amalgam, Schaede (2000, p. 75), Murakami (2003, p. 41), and Seita and Tamura (1994, p. 122). Compare Kameoka (2014), p. 12 (putting an emphasis on some of the original and unique features of the AMA); Wakui (2008, p. 13) (focusing on the more severe provisions of the AMA compared to the United States' antitrust laws).

[20]Posey T. Kime had served two terms at the Indiana State Court of Appeals before he transferred to the Antitrust Division within the Department of Justice. In this capacity he was asked to lead the newly formed Antitrust Legislation Branch within the Supreme Command of Allied Powers. This branch was to implement the Edwards Report. Kime headed this branch for less than one year. Haley (2001, p. 30).

[21]There is only one draft available made by Kime. This draft introduced the prohibition on monopolization with criminal sanctions, prohibition of agreements in restraint of trade subject to criminal penalties and unfair methods of competition without criminal sanctions. Haley (2001, p. 31).

titled *Questions Pertaining to the Interpretation of Anti-Trust Laws*.[22] In relation to unfair trade practices, the negotiators developed two understandings. Harry First, writing on the original intent of the Japanese AMA, summarizes their position as follows

> …there are two categories of unfair methods of competition. The first covers practices which are designed to bring about a monopoly or a restraint of trade, but fail. These practices 'generally [tend] to lessen competition by resorting to weapons other than superior quality or cheaper price of services or commodities' (what we might today call exclusionary practices). The second category covers methods of competition that adversely affect "particular customers or competitors, apart from substantially lessening competition. Citing a Brookings Institute study, Government and Economic Life, the Questions Pertaining Memorandum states that this second category of unfair methods of competition relates to 'the intended maintenance of certain ethical standard[s] in the business world.'[23]

The Japanese negotiators saw the latter described understanding of unfair practices as a duplication of other laws existing in Japan and preferred therefore to limit unfair trade practices to former understanding.[24]

In addition, the Japanese negotiators sought clarification on conduct, such as price discrimination, tying and exclusive dealing, which could be categorized both as private monopolization and unfair methods of competition. The clarification was important since a different categorization would require another standard of proof. The Japanese negotiators noticed that private monopolization in the United States required an impact on competition, while an unfair method of competition does not.[25]

In last instance, the Japanese negotiators questioned whether it would be appropriate to apply criminal sanctions to restraints of trade and private monopolization and only apply cease and desist orders to unfair methods of competition. At the end, unfair methods of competition reflected behavior that could lead to private monopolization but was still short of fulfilling all criteria. An order to stop the behavior should be enough. Only when the order was not followed, further severe sanctions would be suitable.

Kime's successor, Lester N. Salwin, did not address the issues raised by the Japanese negotiators. Despite the remaining uncertainties, the structure of the forbidden conduct did not change.[26] The AMA, as was enacted on March 31, 1947, contained therefore a dual structure. Article 3 stipulated that private monopolization and unreasonable restraints of trade would be declared illegal. Article 19 held that no enterprise shall employ unfair methods of competition.[27]

When the Allied Occupation ended in 1953 and Japan regained its sovereignty, politicians and bureaucrats within the Ministry of Trade and Industry[28] (MITI)[29]

---

22 Haley (2001, p. 50).

23 Haley (2001, p. 51) (footnotes omitted).

24 Haley (2001).

25 Haley (2001).

26 Haley (2001).

27 For a further definition of unfair methods of competition, see Yamamura (1966, p. 199) and Haley (2001, p. 53) (giving the text of original Article 2 AMA, which detailed the content of Article 19 AMA:

seized the occasion to voice their critiques to the "occupation's legacy of competition law"[30] and advocate for an industrial policy geared towards sustaining the economic expansion of Japan. An early step was to reduce the personnel of the JFTC[31] awaiting a more drastic revision of the AMA itself. The Diet enacted the revisions of the AMA in 1953. The revision kept the distinction between Article 3 and Article of the 19 AMA, but substituted the term unfair methods of competition for unfair business practices. At the same time, the concept was redefined to include even broader practices.[32]

To be illegal under Article 19, though, the JFTC had to designate that particular business conduct as an unfair trade practice. In other words, the JFTC had to further specify the list of unfair trade practices as it was described in then Article 2 (7)

---

1. Unwarranted refusal to receive from or to supply to other entrepreneurs commodities, funds, and other economic benefits;
2. Supplying commodities, funds, and other economic benefits at unduly low prices;
3. Supplying of commodities, funds and other economic benefits at unduly discriminative prices.
4. Unreasonably inducing or coercing customers of a competitor to deal with oneself by offering benefits or threatening disadvantages;
5. Trading with another party on condition that said party shall, without good cause, refuse acceptance of supply of commodities, funds, and other economic benefits from a competitor of oneself; and
6. Supplying commodities, funds, and other economic benefits to another party on such conditions that shall unduly restrain transactions between said party and his suppliers of commodities, funds, and other economic benefits or customers or that shall unduly restrain relations between said party and his competitors, or on condition that the appointment of officers (hereinafter referring to director, unlimited partners who are executives, auditors, or persons similar thereto, manager or chief of the main branch office) of the company of said party shall be subject to prior approval on part of oneself.

In order to provide flexibility, the last subparagraph stipulated that the Japan Fair Trade Commission could expand the list of unfair methods of competition and that based on its rule making power derived from Article 71 and 72.

[28]Haley (2001, p. 53).

[29]The Ministry of International Trade and Industry (MITI) evolved out of the Ministry of Commerce and Trade in 1949. See Johnson (1982, p. 176). Compare Haley (2001, p. 53) (who indicates that the Ministry of Commerce and Trade was reestablished in 1952 as MITI). Other scholars indicate that MITI underwent tremendous changes in 1952, but indicate it was established in 1949, see, e.g., Scalapino (1977, p. 234).

[30]Haley (2001, p. 53).

[31]Haley (2001, p. 53).

[32]For a further definition of unfair trade practices, see Yamamura (1966, p. 199) and Haley (2001, p. 53) (providing the text as adopted in 1953:

1. Unduly discriminating against other entrepreneurs;
2. Dealing at unfair prices;
3. Unreasonably inducing or coercing customers of a competitor to deal with oneself;
4. Trading with another party on such conditions as will restrict unjustly the business activities of said party;
5. Dealing with another party by unwarranted use of one's bargaining position; and
6. Unjustly interfering with a transaction between an entrepreneur who competes in Japan with oneself or with the company of which oneself is a stockholder or an officer and his customer;

of the AMA. The JFTC issued the General Designation of Unfair Trade Practices (1953 General Designation) soon after the changes to the AMA were in force. The 1953 Designation included twelve broadly worded items, including, among others, "refusals to deal, price discrimination, predatory or unfair pricing practices, customer and supplies restrictions, tying arrangements, and abuses of dominant bargaining position."[33] The 1953 General Designation was revised in 1982 (1982 General Designation) to include a total of 16 designations that could be captured by the following broad categories: refusal to deal, discriminatory pricing or treatment, unfair pricing, unfair inducement and coercion (including tying), exclusive dealing, resale price maintenance, exclusive or restrictive dealing, resale price maintenance, abuse of dominant bargaining position and interference with a competitor's transaction.[34]

A last revision of the 1982 General Designation, together with Article 2(9) AMA,[35] occurred 2009 (2009 General Designation).[36] This revision reduced the

---

or, in case such entrepreneur is a company, unjustly inducing instigative or coercive means on stockholders against the interest of such a company or an officer of such a company to act.)

[33]Haley (2001, p. 53).

[34]Haley (2001, p. 53).

[35]Article 2 (9) AMA reads now as follows:

The term "unfair trade practices" as used in this Act means an act falling under any of the following items:

(i) Engaging, without justifiable grounds, in any of the following acts, in concert with a competitor:

 (a) Refusing to supply to a certain enterprise or restricting the quantity or substance of goods or services supplied to a certain enterprise
 (b) Causing another enterprise to refuse to supply a certain enterprise, or to restrict the quantity or substance of goods or services supplied to a certain enterprise

(ii) Unjustly and continually supplying goods or services at a price applied differentially between regions or between parties, thereby tending to cause difficulties to the business activities of other enterprises
(iii) Without justifiable grounds, continuously supplying goods or services at a price far below the cost incurred to supply them, thereby tending to cause difficulties to the business activities of other enterprises
(iv) Supplying goods to another party who purchases said goods from oneself while imposing, without justifiable grounds, one of the restrictive terms listed below:

 (a) Causing said party to maintain the selling price of the goods that one has determined, or otherwise restricting said party's free decision on the selling price of the goods
 (b) Having said party cause an enterprise that purchases the goods from said party maintain the selling price of the goods that one has determined, or otherwise causing said party to restrict said enterprise's free decision on the selling price of the goods

(v) Engaging in any act specified in one of the following by making use of one's superior bargaining position over the counterparty unjustly, in light of normal business practices:

 (a) Causing said counterparty in continuous transactions (including a party with whom one newly intends to engage in continuous transactions; the same applies in (b) below) to purchase goods or services other than those to which said transactions pertain

designations to 15.[37] Yet, the broad categorization mentioned in relation to the 1982 General Designation did not change.

2.2 *Using Unfair Trade Practices to Enforce the AMA Against Unilateral Conduct and Vertical Agreements*

As mentioned above, the Japanese AMA was modeled after US antitrust laws. The original AMA provided for *unreasonable restraint of trade* based on Sect. 1 of the US Sherman Act and *private monopolization* on Sect. 2 of the Act in addition to *merger control*. Considering that the JFTC was established as the sole competition authority in Japan, it was enough for the AMA to have only one provision prohibiting *unreasonable restraint of trade* and *private monopolization*.[38] However, the original AMA provided for another provision modeled after Sect. 5 of the US Federal Trade Commission Act,[39] which substantially includes all conduct violating Sects. 1 and 2 of the Sherman Act. In this way, the AMA has come to have a unique structure

---

(b) Causing said counterparty in continuous transactions to provide money, services or other economic benefits
(c) Refusing to receive goods in transactions with said counterparty, causing said counterparty to take back such goods after receiving them from said counterparty, delaying payment to said counterparty or reducing the amount of payment, or otherwise establishing or changing trade terms or executing transactions in a way disadvantageous to said counterparty

(vi) Any act falling under any of the following items, which tends to impede fair competition and which is designated by the Fair Trade Commission, other than the acts listed in the preceding items:

(a) Unjustly treating other enterprises in a discriminatory manner
(b) Engaging in transactions at an unjust price
(c) Unjustly inducing or coercing the customers of a competitor to deal with one
(d) Dealing with another party on such conditions as will unjustly restrict the business activities of said counterparty
(e) Dealing with the counterparty by making use of one's superior bargaining position unjustly
(f) Unjustly interfering with a transaction between an enterprise in competition with one in Japan or a corporation of which one is a shareholder or an officer and another transaction counterparty; or, if such enterprise is a corporation, unjustly inducing, instigating or coercing a shareholder or officer of such corporation to act against the corporation's interests.

[36] Kameoka (2014, p. 60) (footnote 10).

[37] Designation of Unfair Trade Practices (Fair Trade Commission Public Notice No. 15 of June 18, 1982 as revised in 2009). Available at: https://www.jftc.go.jp/en/legislation_gls/unfairtradepractices.html. Accessed 15 December 2020 (2009 General Designation).

[38] AMA, Article 3.

[39] AMA, Article 19.

under which violations of Sects. 1 & 2 of the Sherman Act and Sect. 5 of the FTC Act are regulated by only one competition agency, the JFTC.

As all basic infringements of competition laws are covered by Article 3 of the AMA, Article 19 of the AMA, which prohibits *unfair trade practices,* is not a necessary part of the AMA. This may be understood easily when compared with the structure of competition law of the European Union. It is obvious that Article 101 of the Treaty of the Functioning of the European Union (TFEU) corresponds to Sect. 1 of the Sherman Act and Article 102 TFEU to Sect. 2 of the Sherman Act in terms of what types of conduct are prohibited. Accordingly, in competition law, there exists no such article originating from Sect. 5 of the US Federal Trade Act because the European Commission acts as the sole agency responsible for the enforcement of EU competition law.

It can be said that both Articles 3 and 19 of the AMA would cover most of ex-post violations in the AMA and that they are therefore overlapping. Therefore, Murakami points out that the inclusion of Article 19 of the AMA was a clear mistake and has become an "original sin" in the enactment of the AMA.[40] Furthermore, he pointed out that Article 19 of the AMA has caused substantial confusion in the subsequent application of the AMA, bringing about unique regulatory and theoretical problems in the law.[41] Firstly, the JFTC declared, in a formal decision in early times after the enactment of the AMA, that the standard for the illegality of Article 19 of the AMA (likelihood of impeding fair competition or endangering fair competition) was much lower than that of Article 3 of the AMA, which required a substantial lessening of competition in the relevant market.[42] Since the JFTC took full responsibility over the enforcement of the AMA in 1953, the provision on unfair trade practices has become the most frequently used provision for addressing unilateral conduct. The private monopolization prong of Article 3 of the AMA has only been used six times between 1953 and 1992.[43]

This evolution is for sure a discontinuation of the history and the structure of the United States antitrust law in which unfair methods of competition only played a supplementary role.[44] This has generally become known as an expression of the 'incipiency doctrine' for unfair trade practices.[45] This doctrine entails that the unfair trade practices provision is justified because of the coverage of trade practices at "the early stage where harmful competitive effects start to be felt thereby preventing the possibility of developing into substantial competition restrictions."[46] Secondly, the unfair trade practices designated by the JFTC in 1953 have come to include new types of conduct such as abuse of superior bargaining position, which has less association with market competition. As a result, the prohibition of unfair trade practices was

40 Murakami (2003, p. 43).

41 Murakami (2003).

42 JFTC Decision of 28 March 1953, 4 Shinketsushu 119.

43 Iyori and Uesugi (1994, p. 100).

44 See, e.g., Arai and Harris (2014, p. 72).

45 First and Shiraishi (2013, p. 238).

46 First and Shiraishi (2013).

considered to be a kind of unfair competition law, which deals with day-to-day transactions and business activities of enterprises, far apart from competition laws in general.

Despite a renewed debate on the necessity of Article 19 of the AMA,[47] Article 19 of the AMA is the one chosen to deal with unilateral conduct in digital markets of Japan.

3 Unfair Trade Practices Regulating the Platform Economy

3.1 The JFTC's Enforcement Actions in the Platform Economy

3.1.1 DeNA Aiming at Exclusivity Over Game Providers

The JFTC interfered in the competitive relationship between DeNA Co., Ltd (DeNA) and Gree Inc. (Gree) on June 9, 2011.[48] Both DeNA and Gree were firms operating on the Internet.

DeNA started in 1999, when Tomoko Namba left her life as a partner at the consulting firm McKinsey & Co. and founded the firm. The core business of DeNA was for a long time online auction services. During its early years, we saw an expansion into e-commerce service and the establishment of mobile auction and shopping sites. In 2006, the company decided to launch Mobage Town. Mobage Town was established as a portal and social network for games. Another social network service, Shumee-to Club, was added in 2007 to DeNA's business activity.[49]

Gree was set up in December 2004 to incorporate a social networking service that Yoshikazu Tanaka had developed in his free time in 2003 while working at Rakuten.[50] The social networking service, provided under the name GREE,[51] offered a platform where people could connect based upon common interests.[52]

Both DeNA and Gree started to provide social games, i.e. games provided to users through mobile network services and which were equipped with a communication

---

[47] Lin and Hiroshi Ohashi (2014, p. 22). Takashi Negishi and Masayuki Funada are reporting that there is a renewed advocacy for requiring a similar adverse effect to that indicating a substantial restraint of trade. By requiring the same adverse effect on the market for exclusionary conduct under Article 3 and 19 AMA, the necessity of having a dual structure of substantive law provisions prohibiting such conduct can be more than ever questioned. See Negishi and Funada (2010).

[48] JFTC, Cease and Desist Order against DeNA Co., Ltd. (9 June 2011). Available at http://www.jftc.go.jp/houdou/pressrelease/h23/jun/110609honbun.files/110609betten.pdf (15 December 2020). A translation of the DeNA case by the authors, Van Uytsel and Uemura (2019, p. 259).

[49] DeNA (2017).

[50] Ernkvist (2017, p. 104).

[51] In Japanese, the name of the company and the platform are distinguished by the use of different alphabets. The company name is written in the Japanese katakana alphabet, while the platform's name is in the Roman alphabet and in capital letters.

[52] Available at: http://corp.gree.net/jp/en/corporate/vision/ (accessed 15 December 2020).

function among the users, through their respective mobile social networking services. Gree did so already since 2005, while DeNA only started this kind of activity in 2006. At first, both DeNA and Gree in-house developed social games. This business model changed in 2010. DeNA decided that a wide variety of genres of games was preferable and therefore opened its network in January 2010 for third-party social game developers. In June of the same year, Gree made the same shift in its business model and started to attract third-party social game developers to offer their games on GREE.[53]

Based upon the assessment made by the JFTC, DeNA had become the largest provider of social games by January 2010. This conclusion was drawn from the total revenue the firm obtained out of the social game industry. Gree was assessed to be the second largest.

To maintain its leadership, DeNA selected the most influential social game developers and approached them with the instruction only to provide social games through Mobage Town. If the identified social game developers continued to provide their games through GREE, DeNA would disconnect the links of these social game developers on the Mobage Town website. Further, DeNA also offered support for developing social game developers that chose to exclusively offer their games through Mobage Town. The majority of these influential social game developers complied with the request of DeNA. These developers either did not offer new games anymore or withdrew their newly developed games from GREE.[54]

In a rather short cease and desist order,[55] the JFTC issued a cease and desist order against DeNA after having done an on-the-spot investigation on December 8, 2010. The JFTC found that DeNA held the leading position within the market, while Gree was occupying the second position. This conclusion is only drawn by referring to the revenue both competitors make in relation to mobile social games. No reason was given on why the market should be limited to mobile social games. The judgment does not reveal any information on other competitors, whether domestic or foreign. Further, no information is given in relation to the ease of entering the market.[56] Even if there are no direct competitors, other enterprises may be able to shift their business model and challenge the position of the incumbent enterprises.[57] Having seen the specificities of the service offered by DeNA and Gree, one would also expect reference to multi-sided markets and related concepts of network effects and multi-homing.[58]

After establishing that the position within the mobile social game market, the JFTC investigated DeNA's conduct. The JFTC found that DeNA aimed at exclusively binding the most influential social game providers to its social networking service, Mobage Town. In doing so, the JFTC held that Gree would face difficulties

[53] Ernkvist and Qi (2014).

[54] JFTC, Cease and Desist Order against DeNA Co., Ltd. (9 June 2011).

[55] For the length of the cease and desist order, see Van Uytsel and Uemura (2019, p. 259).

[56] JFTC, Cease and Desist Order against DeNA Co., Ltd (9 June 2011).

[57] JFTC, Cease and Desist Order against DeNA Co., Ltd. (9 June 2011).

[58] JFTC, Cease and Desist Order against DeNA Co., Ltd (9 June 2011).

in competing with DeNA. At the end, DeNA contacted the most influential social game developers, of which the majority complied with DeNA's request not to offer games anymore to Gree.[59]

Despite DeNA having terminated the behavior of exclusive dealing at the time of the dawn raid, the JFTC decided that DeNA had unjustly interfered with the transactions between Gree and some of the social game developers. In deciding so, the JFTC held that DeNA infringed Article 19 of the AMA and this in combination with paragraph 14 of the 2009 General Designation, which stipulates that

> Unjustly interfering with a transaction between another enterprise who is in a domestic competitive relationship with oneself or with the corporation of which one is a stockholder or an officer, and its transacting party, by preventing the effecting of a contract, or by inducing the breach of a contract, or by any other means whatsoever.[60]

By classifying the infringement under paragraph 14 of the 2009 General Designation, and thus holding DeNA's behavior is a specific example of an unfair trade practice, the JFTC could only issue a cease-and-desist order based upon Article 20 of the AMA (DeNa case). This order included the request of officially adopting a resolution at the board of directors that DeNA has terminated the behavior of exclusively binding influential social game developers to Mobage Town and that it will never engage in this kind of behavior anymore. Further, DeNA has to disseminate this message to all its employees, the social game developers and Gree. In line with the above, DeNA was also obliged to work out a proper compliance regime.[61]

3.1.2 Amazon Japan Forcing Its Retailers to Prioritize Amazon Marketplace

Amazon Japan G.K. (Amazon Japan) was established on 1 May 2016, as a new entity emerging from the merger between Amazon Japan K.K. and Amazon Japan Logistics K.K. Amazon Japan operates on the one hand Amazon Marketplace, allowing third party sellers to sell and offer goods to the consumer, and sells on the other hand goods directly to consumers on Amazon.co.jp. As an e-commerce platform, Amazon Marketplace also uses Amazon.co.jp. to reach customers.[62]

The e-commerce platform, Amazon Marketplace, is only available for third party sellers after making a seller contract. Up to 30 April 2016, these third party sellers made a seller contract with Amazon Services International, Inc. (Amazon International). This changed on 1 May 2016. From that moment onwards, the contracts were made with Amazon Japan. All seller contracts made up to 30 April 2016 were transferred to Amazon Japan Logistics K.K. However, since this entity merged

---

[59] JFTC, Cease and Desist Order against DeNA Co., Ltd (9 June 2011).

[60] 2009 General Designation, Paragraph 14.

[61] JFTC, Cease and Desist Order against DeNA Co., Ltd (9 June 2011).

[62] Kasubuchi (2017), slide 5.

with Amazon Japan K.K. to Amazon Japan, the latter is now the party to all seller contracts.[63]

The seller contracts with Amazon International of Amazon Japan contain either price parity clauses[64] or selection parity clauses. With the price parity clause forbidding third party sellers from offering their products at better prices elsewhere or with the selection parity clauses forbidding the third party sellers to offer a better product selection elsewhere, the JFTC was of the opinion that competition is negatively affected.[65] There are three reasons.[66] First, the business activities of a seller are restricted. He has no freedom anymore in terms of pricing or product lineup. Second, the lowest prices and the biggest product lineup are guaranteed on the online shopping mall imposing these clauses without making any competitive effort. Third, any incentive to innovate the online market place or enter the online e-commerce market is destroyed. Innovation is not necessary because the clauses do not allow the third party sellers to reduce their prices if an innovative platform charges less fees. Entering a market is also difficult, because a new platform has no freedom to negotiate a better product lineup. These concerns are aggregated by the fact that Amazon Japan K.K. and later Amazon Japan, actively monitored the third party sellers' compliance with the various parity clauses.

The notice documenting the closing of the investigation on the suspected violation of the AMA is silent on how the JFTC would qualify the possible infringement. Isao Kasubuchi, the Director General of the JFTC's Trade Practices Department in 2017, reported during a meeting of the International Competition Network on unilateral conduct in Rome that paragraph 12 of the 2009 General Designation would be most suitable for dealing with the parity clauses.[67] Paragraph 12 of the 2009 General Designation deals with trading on restrictive terms and determines that "trading with another party on conditions which unjustly restrict any trade between the said party and its other transacting party or other business activities of the said party"[68] is forbidden.

Amazon Japan engaged in negotiations with the JFTC.[69] During these negotiations, Amazon Japan made the following proposals:

- Amazon Japan will delete the price parity clauses from concluded seller contracts, or will waive and will not exercise the rights of the price parity and selection parity clauses;
- It will not provide those parity clauses in seller contracts;
- Amazon JP will notify all sellers of these measures;

[63] Japan Fair Trade Commission (2017b).

[64] Amazon Marketplace Participation Agreement and Amazon Service Business Solution are two types of agreements containing price parity clauses.

[65] Japan Fair Trade Commission (2017b).

[66] Japan Fair Trade Commission (2017b), point 5.

[67] Kasubuchi (2017).

[68] 2009 General Designation, paragraph 12.

[69] Japan Fair Trade Commission (2017b), point 6.

- Amazon JP will annually report the implementation status to the JFTC in writing for 3 years.[70]

The JFTC accepted the suggested proposals and closed, without issuing a cease and desist order, the investigation on 1 June 2017.[71]

3.1.3 Minna no Pet Online Preferring to Be the Exclusive Intermediary Platform

Minna no Pet Online Co, Ltd. (MPO) is a company offering a digital platform aiming to match dog and cat breeders with possible customers. MPO, which saw its members increase, started a Premium Partner System (PPS) in November 2017. Breeders who were allowed to register on the PPS were not allowed anymore to use the services of competing websites. Moreover, the breeders had to withdraw advertisements from other pet intermediary sites. If breeders' advertisements were to be found on competing websites, MPO would exclude such breeders from its PPS. Exclusion from the PPS would result in the termination of several benefits. These benefits were, among others, rebates on commission fees due to MPO or preferential treatment in the MPO's search results.[72]

The JFTC conducted a dawn raid on MPO on the 27th of February 2018.[73] The JFTC was of the opinion that exclusively binding breeders to the MPO website restrains fair competition with competing platforms. The unfair restraint of competition was twofold. On the one hand, the conditions to be part of the PPS decrease the trading opportunities for the breeders. On the other hand, the reduction of information on competing platforms would divert possible consumers from these competing platforms to MPO.

The JFTC was of the opinion that such restraint could be qualified as trading on exclusive terms.[74] Trading on exclusive terms is defined in paragraph 11 of the 2009 General Designation as "[u]njustly trading with another party on condition that the said party shall not trade with a competitor, thereby tending to reduce trading opportunities for the said competitor."[75] Aware that the JFTC could take an action, MPO decided to cancel its PPS.[76] This made the investigation of the JFTC without cause. The JFTC therefore closed the investigation on the 23rd of May 2018.[77]

[70] Kasubuchi (2017), slide 9.

[71] Japan Fair Trade Commission (2017b), point 7.

[72] Fuchikawa (2020, p. 111).

[73] Japan Fair Trade Commission (2018a).

[74] Japan Fair Trade Commission (2018a), point 4.

[75] 2009 General Designation, Paragraph 11.

[76] Japan Fair Trade Commission (2018a), point 5.

[77] Japan Fair Trade Commission (2018a), point 6.

3.1.4 Airbnb Japan Denying the Right to Enlist Accommodations on Other Platforms

Airbnb Ireland UC, in Japan active as Airbnb Japan K.K. (Airbnb Japan), is a company offering arrangements for lodging. These arrangements are made through a platform that intermediates between providers of private housing for lodging, a so-called private lodging service, and potential users of this service. Rather than taking care of the private lodging services themselves, the providers or hosts can engage a co-hosting service. The co-hosting service will take care of the listing of the private lodging service on the platform, manage the reservation, clean the house, and respond to inquiries from the guests.[78]

Hosts or the co-hosting service could use a management tool to manage the private lodging service. Co-hosting service providers can even hook up their management tool to various private lodging service platforms by using an application programming interface. As this allows for integrating the reservation management, the exchange of messages with guests and setting prices across different private lodging services platforms, the management tool is widely used by co-hosting service providers.[79]

The JFTC decided to do a dawn raid on Airbnb Japan in the Autumn of 2017 because there was a concern about the contracts with some co-hosting services providers and management tool providers.[80] More in specific, the contracts stipulating that Airbnb's application programming interface would be used, restricted the possibility of listing the private lodging services on other platforms. This policy was revised to a restriction on listing private lodging services on other platforms to cases in which the co-hosting service providers and management tool providers did so through an application programming interface. This led to the fear that other platform operators could be excluded from the business of private lodging service platforms as the trading partners of Airbnb have restrictions placed on their businesses from freely seeking access to these platforms.

Fumio Sensui reports that the investigation of the suspected violation was both based on Article 3 in combination with Article 2(5) of the AMA and on paragraph 11 of the 2009 General Designation.[81] The former is the provision dealing with monopolization, while the latter is related to trading on exclusive terms.

Soon after the dawn raid, Airbnb approached the JFTC with a proposal not to enforce the clauses restricting its trading partners' business freedom. This proposal was perceived by the JFTC as sufficient to eliminate the suspected violation of the AMA. Therefore, the JFTC decided to close the investigation on 10 October 2018.[82]

---

[78] Japan Fair Trade Commission (2018b).

[79] Japan Fair Trade Commission (2018b), point 2.

[80] Japan Fair Trade Commission (2018b), point 4.

[81] Sensui (2018), slide 9.

[82] Japan Fair Trade Commission (2018b), point 6.

3.1.5 Travel Booking Websites Requesting to Be the Main Benchmark for Price Setting

Travel booking platforms, operated by, among others, Rakuten, Inc. (Rakuten) and Japanese subsidiaries of Booking.com and Expedia, were dawn raided by the JFTC on the 10th of April 2019. The JFTC suspected a violation of the AMA by the travel booking platforms in the form of parity clauses imposed on accommodation operators.[83] As has already been indicated in relation to the Amazon Japan case, the parity clauses, if present, could be regarded as violations of paragraph 12 of the 2009 General Designation.[84]

The JFTC has only published information in relation to Rakuten.[85] In its first commitment approval since the inception of the Commitment Procedure on the 30th of December 2018, the JFTC announced that Rakuten's contracts with accommodation operators had "set the conditions to require the operators to make the prices and the numbers of rooms which they place on the website [Rakuten Travel] equal to or better than those through other distribution channels with the minimum number of rooms requirement."[86]

In response to the JFTC's investigation, Rakuten decided to formulate a commitment plan in order to prevent the finding of a violation or the levying of a fine.[87] The commitment plan included the following.[88] First, Rakuten would cease the activity of including parity clauses in the contracts with the accommodation operators. Second, the board of directors would adopt a resolution approving the cessation of these kinds of clauses for the next three years. Third, Rakuten promised not to engage in suspected activities for the next three years. Fourth, Rakuten will inform the accommodation operators, its employees, and consumers of the change in policy. Fifth, Rakuten will develop a competition compliance manual and offer competition law compliance sessions to its personnel. Sixth, Rakuten will regularly update the JFTC on the above-mentioned commitments.

Agreeing with the commitment plan, the JFTC acknowledged that approval requirements were fulfilled and closed the investigation on the 25th of October 2019.[89]

---

83 Sakurada (2019).

84 See Sect. 3.1.2 above.

85 Japan Fair Trade Commission (2019d).

86 Japan Fair Trade Commission (2019d), point 2.

87 As long as the commitment procedure runs, there are only suspected violations of the law. Available at: https://www.jftc.go.jp/en/pressreleases/yearly-2018/June/180629_file/180629_3.pdf (accessed 15 December 2020).

88 Japan Fair Trade Commission (2019d), point 3.

89 Japan Fair Trade Commission (2019d), point 4.

3.1.6 Amazon Japan G.K.'s Forced Price Discounting and Other Financial Contributions

Amazon Japan has again come under investigation of the JFTC in 2018. The allegations were plenty. First, Amazon Japan kept the right to discount products and made third party sellers bear the costs of these discounts.[90] Second, Amazon Japan would not stipulate in advance how much of the profit would be given to the third party supplier in order to safeguard Amazon Japan's own target profit.[91] Third, under the Joint Marketing Agreement, third party sellers were requested to financially contribute to, often unspecified, marketing services.[92] Fourth, the third party sellers were asked to invest in Amazon Japan for unspecified system upgrades and improvements.[93] Fifth, Amazon Japan had the right, with some qualifications, to return inventory it judged as excess.[94]

The JFTC identified that all of these practices could qualify as an abuse of a superior bargaining position. This infringement resorts under Article 19 of the AMA, further explained by Article 2(9)(5) of the AMA, and is thus an unfair trade practice.

Just like in the Rakuten case mentioned above, the JFTC notified Amazon Japan about the allegations. Amazon Japan had to work out a plan with commitments to rectify the situation and submit such a plan to the JFTC for approval.[95] The commitment plan of Amazon Japan included that it would terminate any kind of behavior it was accused of and should not enter in similar behavior in the next three years. To facilitate this, Amazon Japan should create a competition law compliance manual and organize regular competition law compliance training sessions for its employees. Further, Amazon Japan took up the obligation to restore the damage by refunding the excess of money obtained through the alleged violations. This obligation had to be facilitated by a duty of Amazon Japan to notify the third party sellers of the results of the investigation.

With a duty to inform the JFTC of Amazon Japan's compliance with the commitment plan, the JFTC approved the commitment plan and closed the investigation on 10 September 2020. The JFTC also indicated that the damages to be paid by Amazon Japan would roughly reach 20 billion yen to be paid to around 1400 third party sellers.[96]

[90] Japan Fair Trade Commission (2020), point 2(1)
[91] Japan Fair Trade Commission (2020), point 2(2).
[92] Japan Fair Trade Commission (2020), point 2(3)
[93] Japan Fair Trade Commission (2020), point 2(4).
[94] Japan Fair Trade Commission (2020), point 2(5)
[95] Japan Fair Trade Commission (2020), point 3(1)-(8).
[96] Japan Fair Trade Commission (2020), point 4.

3.2 The Competitive Advantage of the Use of Unfair Trade Practices

The JFTC chose to regulate the platform economy based upon the following unfair trade practices: abuse of a dominant bargaining position, trading on exclusive terms, trading on restrictive terms and interference with a competitor's trade and business operations. All, except the first, of these unfair trade practices belong to the category of unfair trade practices which weakens free competition in the market.[97] Besides this category of unfair trade practices, there are unfair trade practices that are unfair as a means of competition[98] or they invade or infringe upon the basic right of participants to compete freely in the market.[99] An abuse of a dominant bargaining position is an example of the latter. The importance of distinguishing these three categories of unfair trade practices relates to the presence of some kind of competition-restrictive effect. The first-mentioned category requires the limitation of free competition in the market by some competition-restrictive effects in a relevant market, while the second and the third categories do not.

The requirement of competition-restrictive effects means that the difference between the interpretation of Article 3 of the AMA and Article 19 of the AMA has become smaller. The Tokyo High Court and the Supreme Court of Japan pointed out that defining the relevant market was required in the case of unfair trade practices dealing with limitation of free competition in the market.[100] Moreover, in a formal decision on the interpretation relating to the illegality of the competition-restrictive types of unfair trade practices, the JFTC held that the 'likelihood of impeding fair competition' does not necessarily require the occurrence of a concrete anticompetitive effect arising from the conduct at issue.[101] However, the JFTC mentioned that the 'likelihood of impeding competition' should not be interpreted as a vague possibility of anticompetitive effects, so emphasizing the importance of analyzing the quantitative and qualitative effects of the conduct in detail.[102]

There is still discussion to what extent an analysis of the anticompetitive effects needs to be made. The anticompetitive effects can be brought about by both restrictive or exclusionary practices. As has been mentioned above, unfair trade practices allow for tackling the anticompetitive effects at an early stage, at a moment when they commence. With a reference to the work of Fumio Sensui, Masako Wakui reports that the following guidelines have been worked out to identify this early stage anticompetitive effect:

---

[97]This includes 2009 General Designation, paragraphs 1, 2, 3, 4, 5, 6, 7, 11, and 12. In addition, 2009 General Designation, paragraphs 10 and 14 could have this role as well. Wakui (2008, p. 105).

[98]This includes 2009 General Designation, paragraphs 8, 9, and 15. In addition, paragraphs 10 and 14 of the 2009 General Designation could have this role as well. Wakui (2008, p. 105).

[99]This includes 2009 General Designation, paragraph 13. Wakui (2008, p. 105).

[100]Tokyo High Court judgment of 17 February 1984, 30 Shinketsushu 136; Supreme Court Judgment of 14 December 1989, 43 Minshu No. 12, 2078.

[101]JFTC Decision of 16 September 2008, 55 Shinketsushu 380.

[102]JFTC Decision of 16 September 2008, 55 Shinketsushu 380.

- "Establishment, maintenance or enhancement of an economic power that is less than what would be regarded as market power;
- Establishing, maintaining or enhancing market power to a minor degree;
- Facilitating the exercise of market power."[103]

This suggested framework of Sensui is not generally accepted in the Japanese competition law community. However, since there is no guiding case law, the alternative viewpoints could seem as random as Sensui's explanation. Wakui summarizes these viewpoints as follows. On the one hand, there are scholars arguing that there is no substantial difference between substantial lessening of competition relevant in the interpretation of Article 3 of the AMA and the lessening of free competition relevant in the interpretation of Article 19 of the AMA.[104] On the other hand, there are scholars who argue that a restriction or an elimination of free business is sufficient for determining a lessening of free competition.[105] Wakui herself advocates for interpreting the lessening of free competition as appreciably hampering. To reach this conclusion, a rigorous analysis of the relevant market would not be required.[106]

Practice of the JFTC seems to be close to Wakui's analysis. A rigorously defined relevant market is barely done. JFTC cease-and-desist orders seldom expand on how the relevant market is conceptualized. To use the words of Wakui, the "body of the text [of the cease-and-desist order] assumes that the JFTC adequately defined the relevant market."[107] This statement has been made in relation to the Nordion case, in which the market was assumed to be the Japanese market for Molybdenum-99. Cease-and-desist orders are still rare in the platform economy. However, considering the text of the DeNA case, there is no reason to belief the JFTC will deviate from this practice.[108] The other digital platform cases only dealt with suspected violations. In such kind of cases, the JFTC does not at all refer to a relevant market and the specific market share in any of their official documents.

In a market in which swift intervention is required, the absence of going through extensive market analysis is an advantage. The JFTC can focus on examining the alleged violations rather than wasting resources on positioning the investigated enterprise in a relevant market.

---

[103] Wakui (2018, p. 145).

[104] Wakui (2018, p. 145).

[105] Wakui (2018, pp. 145–146).

[106] Wakui (2018, p. 146). In relation to appreciable, reference can be made to the JFTC Guidelines Concerning Distribution Systems and Business Practices under the Antimonopoly Act (JFTC Distribution Guideline). This JFTC Distribution Guideline identifies that behavior on the market will be appreciable if it is done by an enterprise that is influential in the market. Such an influential position in the market is attained by a certain market share. For the application of the JFTC Distribution Guideline, the market share is set at 20% or above. Japan Fair Trade Commission (2017c), Point I.3(4).

[107] Wakui (2018, p. 189) footnote 127.

[108] Van Uytsel and Uemura (2019, p. 259) (Appendix) (barely any description of what the relevant market is).

4 The Flexibility of Unfair Trade Practices in Perspective

The JFTC has prioritized the use of unfair trade practices to enforce its AMA against anti-competitive vertical agreements and unilateral conduct. The unfair trade practice thus forbids both restraints of competition and exclusionary conduct. From an enforcement perspective, the unfair trade practices have the advantage of not requiring a rigorous market delineation. Market power, if relevant at all, is positioned at a very low level. The main focus of the unfair trade practices is on the conduct. The flexibility that flows from this conceptualization of the unfair trade practices allows either early intervention in the market or swift intervention without too much disturbing the market. The reason for both types of intervention is, as repeatedly mentioned, the relative unimportance of market power. Early intervention has been advocated as necessary by one part of the legal scholarship. Swift intervention without too much disturbing the market could be a response to the literature emphasizing not to hasten intervention.

4.1 Unfair Trade Practices Allowing Early Enforcement of the AMA

The literature on the platform economy has forwarded the idea that early intervention of competition law may be a necessary. The arguments behind this conclusion are built upon the characteristics of the platform economy.[109] Platform economy markets are generally characterized by high fixed costs (or sunk costs), but low marginal costs, economies of scale, and network effects and consumer lock-in.[110]

The high fixed costs relate to the investment the firms need to make for research and development or for setting up the network. Thus, the creation of the product or service or the setting up of the infrastructure to deliver the product or service will be capital intensive. The low marginal costs can be explained by the fact that it is inexpensive to produce additional units of the product or to add additional users to the service.[111] Due to the low marginal costs, the industries in the platform economy exhibit economies of scale. In other words, the returns for the firm will increase "as the scale economies grow."[112] Network effects entail that platform economy products or services increase in value the more people use the product or the service. By adding additional subscribers, the product or service becomes a

[109]Graham (2004, pp. 2–4).

[110]See, e.g., Graham (2004, pp. 2–4) and Ahlborn (2001, pp. 159–161).

[111]See, e.g., Graham (2004, p. 4). An example often cited in the literature is the one of Microsoft as a software developer. The initial investment to make products like Microsoft Office or Microsoft Word requires a huge investment in human resources. However, once the coding of the software is finalized, it can be reproduced at a cheap cost. Ahlborn (2001, p. 159) and Litan (2000, p. 430).

[112]Jonathan M. Jacobson (2001, p. 89).

more useful product for all its subscribers as the network of people that can potentially be contacted expands. In other words, the utility of the network enhances. The more popular a product or service becomes, the more attractive it will be for other product or service developers to create products or services usable in relation to that original product or service and so create indirect network effects.[113] Network effects could cause consumer lock-in. Once consumers have chosen for a product or service, very often based upon its popularity,[114] and have invested time to familiarize themselves with the product or service, the consumers tend to stay with that product or service. Consumers tend only to shift when obviously superior technology becomes available.[115]

Markets in which high fixed costs, economies of scale and network effects operate, tend to, it is said, lead towards monopolies. High fixed costs can be categorized as an entry barrier. The entry barrier is further fortified by the low marginal costs and the economies of scale. Network effects "lead to a tendency for markets to 'tip' to a single dominant vendor or technology. In the markets that tip, competition is *for* the market, not *in* the market, and the market is likely to end up highly concentrated."[116] Competition will therefore be vigorous at an early stage, but fade away once the race towards the monopoly has been won. Against this background, an argument has developed that enforcement authorities need to be more vigilant in relation to firms in the platform economy. Some even go as far as to defend the claim that competition law intervention prior to gaining dominance.[117]

Elsewhere, we have argued that the DeNA case could be conceptualized as an example of early market intervention in the mobile game industry. Four arguments have been put forward.[118] First, the market for social games on social networking services platforms was still in full expansion when the JFTC intervened. Even though DeNA and Gree were major players in the market, several other social networking services were introducing social games on their network. Second, user multi-homing among the platforms was possible. Third, the reliance on an exceptional unfair trade practice, namely paragraph 14 of the 2009 General Designation regulating the interference with a competitor's transaction, can only be explained because it is one of the few unfair trade practices not requiring any analysis of the market power. This unfair trade practice focuses on the methods adopted by DeNA and not the effects of these methods on competition.[119] Fourth, the other unfair trade practices that could have

[113]Russo and Stasi (2016, p. 3).

[114]Shapiro and Varian (1998, p. 179).

[115]Litan (2000, p. 430).

[116]Lind and Muysert (2002, p. 89).

[117]Jones and Sufrin (2011, p. 362) (and the footnotes cited in this respect).

[118]Van Uytsel and Uemura (2019).

[119]Despite the focus on methods, the JFTC officials still elaborate extensively on market characteristics. A summary of their argument goes as follows. At that time, DeNA held the largest share of the social game market in terms of revenue and was the most important business partner for many social game providers. This was possible because, about half a year earlier than Gree Inc., DeNA had implemented an open-door policy that allowed social game developers to provide their social games

applied to this case, such as paragraph 11 or 12 of the 2009 General Designation, would require some form of market analysis.

4.2 *Unfair Trade Practices Permitting Swift Action in Concentrated Markets*

Not all scholars support the analysis leading to the conclusion that early intervention is necessary. Firms in the platform economy may be dominant or operate in a concentrated market, their dominance could be fragile and temporary.[120] The platform economy is also characterized by its high pace of innovation, which can cause the market to "change radically quite quickly."[121] This argument, the proponents of the early intervention argument claim, has flaws. They do not deny that there are high rates of innovation in the platform economy, but they indicate that the innovation is driven by the incumbent firm and not by new firms. Daniel O'Connor, elaborating on the characteristics of the online platforms[122] in his article *Understanding Online Platform Competition: Common Misunderstandings*,[123] admits that much of the innovation comes from incumbent firms.[124] Nevertheless, there are enough examples, he indicates, of new entrepreneurial firms that have successfully challenged incumbent

through DeNA's mobile social networking service, named Mobage-Town, by disclosing information about its application programming interface. In addition, according to the facts found by the JFTC, the links on the game top page of the Mobage-Town website were key channels to attract registered users to the social games' websites provided by social game developers. Considering the influential top market share of DeNA, it was obvious that the website links on the Mobage-Town were vital for social game developers to secure more users. Under the circumstances, DeNA told the specified social game developers that DeNA would not list the website links of the games the developers provide through Mobage-Town if the developers also offered their social games through GREE, Gree Inc.'s gaming platform. At the same time, DeNA suggested that they would give game developers generous support regarding development and provision of their social games if the developers decided not to provide their new social games through GREE. In response to the request from DeNA, the majority of the specified social game developers did not provide new social games through GREE. Although there were some developers that had created new social games to provide through GREE, they gave up offering them through GREE to avoid the situation where the website links of their social games would be deleted from the more popular Mobage-Town website of DeNA. Added to this, when DeNA discovered that such specified social game developers were providing new social games through GREE, DeNA would actually counter the action and delete the website links of the social games provided by the developers on the Mobage-Town website. However, DeNA stopped such countermeasures when the game developers cancelled the provision of their games through GREE. Ohgo et al. (2011).

[120]Graham (2004, p. 4).

[121]Graham (2004, p. 4).

[122]These online platforms could be defined as "an online service that can function as an intermediary between two or more clearly defined groups." Examples include Amazon, eBay, Facebook, Google and Uber. O'Connor (2016).

[123]O'Connor (2016).

[124]O'Connor (2016, pp. 14–15) (holding that Amazon, once an e-retailer, is now competition with Google and Yahoo! In providing cloud services. With its extensive data and knowledge "from

dominant firms. O'Connor further opines that innovation has become easier and cheaper through the possibility of integrating services of different players.[125] Hence, market entry has become much easier, even for small players in the market. O'Connor formulates it as follows:

> Instead of the Internet drifting towards a world where Internet giants cement their market positions, each successful wave of Internet platform development has given would-be enterprises new tools. Now, Internet companies can build on top of an increasing array of other platforms providing global reach.[126]

Furthermore, O'Connor believes that intervention should not be too hasty because multi-homing allows for competition between the online platforms. Multi-homing prevents one of the negative externalities connected to network effects: customer lock-in.[127] As long as users are able to easily switch between platforms or even be active on different platforms at the same time, network effects will not create or fortify barriers to competition.[128]

O'Connor's holding that incumbent online platforms are innovating is well-exemplified by Amazon. The technological innovation of Amazon has been tremendous, and this not only on the Japanese market. Amazon introduced the Amazon *1-Click* to speed up the ordering process. *Recommendations* allow for the consumer to easily see what may be of interest based upon his previous purchases. With *Kindle*, Amazon has introduced one of the earliest user-friendly e-readers. *Amazon Marketplace* has opened the selling platform of Amazon to other business operators, referred to as third party operators. Another innovation is *Amazon Prime*, allowing customers to get access to additional services such as streaming movies online. These are just a few examples of how Amazon has kept innovating to stay relevant in a highly fast moving environment.

The constant stream of innovation is welcomed from a competition perspective. Early market intervention may hamper this process of innovation. Heavy intervention may stop this innovation. However, and this is the consequence of O'Connor's view, intervention should not be excluded. Intervention may be required when the negative externality of network effects is forming a barrier to competition. This would be the case if, due to some action, multi-homing is made impossible. O'Connor is not clear how the intervention should occur. It is for sure that the Japanese approach allows for swift action. The unfair trade practices allow the JFTC to investigate, and this almost with immediate focus, on the conduct of the online platform. Unfair trade

---

running the world's largest online store to offering an advertising platform," Amazon is also entering in competition with Google, Facebook and Yahoo!. Other examples of online platforms that are extending their businesses are Facebook challenging YouTube in video sharing or Google has entered market of mobile platforms and is so competing with Apple. This is not to say that all attempts to enter another market are successful. Google was unsuccessful to enter the social network service and Amazon failed in the mobile phone market).

[125] O'Connor (2016, pp. 15–16).

[126] O'Connor (2016, p. 15).

[127] O'Connor (2016, pp. 17–24).

[128] O'Connor (2016, p. 20).

practices do not require a focus on market power and the therewith related concept of relevant market.

4.3 The Absence of Real Sanctions, a Weakness

The swift and early intervention that the JFTC can undertake based upon the unfair trade practices has a weakness. The weakness relates to the administrative surcharge, which is an administrative penalty to take away the profits made due to an infringement. Since 2010, the JFTC is able to impose such a surcharge on the following unfair trade practices: refusal to trade, discriminatory pricing, predatory pricing, resale price restriction, and abuse of superior bargaining position.[129]

The power to levy a surcharge differs according to the type of unfair trade practice. In relation to a refusal to trade, discriminatory pricing, predatory pricing, and resale price restriction, the JFTC can only impose a surcharge if the enterprise has engaged in a similar infringement during the past 10 years. Such a condition does not exist for an infringement of the 'abuse their superior bargaining position' provision. For this type of infringement, the surcharge can be levied even if it is the first time that the enterprise commits an abuse of a superior bargaining position.[130]

It has to be noted that the surcharge is substantially lower than a surcharge that can be imposed on, for example, price fixing. The basic rule is that the percentages of the surcharge for price fixing is 10%, while it is only 3% for the following unfair trade practices: refusal to trade, discriminatory pricing, predatory pricing and resale price restriction.[131] Abuse of superior bargaining position is only subject to a surcharge of 1%.[132] The surcharge is calculated by "multiplying the sales amount of the relevant goods or services (in case of abuse of superior bargaining position pertaining to the receipt of supplied goods or services, the purchase amount of the relevant goods or services) during the period for the prohibited conduct (up to three years)"[133] with the above-mentioned surcharge rates. Moreover, since the cease-and-desist order is always preceded by a notification, it is seldom that an investigation of the JFTC reaches a final decision. Often, the enterprises voluntarily comply with the views put forward by the JFTC in the notification.[134]

The absence of a substantial financial sanction could incentivize enterprises to check out their options. Swift action by voluntarily complying with the requests of the JFTC could indeed also minimize the reputational damage.

---

[129] AMA, Article 20(2)-(6). For more analytical details, Kawai et al. (2018, p. 13).

[130] Wakui (2018, p. 140). It is also stipulated that only the unfair trade practices qualified in the AMA can be subject to a surcharge.

[131] Wakui (2018, p. 234).

[132] Wakui (2018, p. 234).

[133] Kawai et al. (2018, p. 12).

[134] Kawai et al. (2018, pp.14–15).

4.4 *Commitment Plans as a Formalization of Voluntary Compliance*

The DeNA case is one of the exceptional cases in which the JFTC has taken a formal decision against a digital platform. All the subsequent investigations against platforms have resulted in a discontinuation of the investigation. This decision was taken subsequent an indication of the alleged AMA infringer that she was to voluntarily comply with the viewpoints of the JFTC. This practice changed in the Rakuten case and the subsequent Amazon Japan case. These cases were terminated by an acceptance of a commitment plan.

The practice of commitment plans is relatively new to Japan and are a consequence of a legislative change following the conclusion of the Trans-Pacific Partnership Agreement.[135] This legislative change makes it possible for the JFTC and an enterprise to voluntarily resolve through consent a case in which the enterprise is suspected of violating the AMA.

In broad lines, the commitment procedure will apply to cases in fair and free competition is hampered. Explicitly excluded are price fixing cartels and bid rigging cartels. The JFTC is obliged to notify the enterprise of the suspected violations and link them with the relevant provision of the AMA. Within 60 days, the enterprise has to work out a plan to eliminate the suspected violation and submit an application to the JFTC. If the JFTC considers the plan to be sufficient to reach an elimination and expects the applicant to effectively implement the plan, the JFTC will approve the so-called commitment plan. In principle, the JFTC will not issue any order (cease-and-desist order whether or not combined with a surcharge order). The JFTC can resort to such orders if the enterprise does not apply for a commitment plan, the commitment plan is dismissed, or the commitment plan is revoked.[136]

By implementing this kind of procedure, the legislator has thus formalized a practice that already existed. However, with procedural rules in place, the JFTC'S practice has become more transparent.

5 Conclusion

The conceptualization of the AMA is complex. With on the one hand a provision dealing with agreements and unilateral conduct, and on the other hand a provision handling vertical agreements and unilateral conduct, the JFTC had to make a choice on how to set the enforcement practice. In relation to the digital economy, and more in specific the platform economy, the JFTC is obviously giving preference to unfair trade practices. This is exemplified in the cease-and-desist order of the DeNA case.

[135] Available at: https://www.jftc.go.jp/en/legislation_gls/antimonopoly_rules_files/policies_concerning_commitment_procedures.pdf (accessed 15 December 2020).

[136] A brief overview of the commitment procedure, available at: https://www.jftc.go.jp/en/pressreleases/yearly-2018/June/180629_file/180629_3.pdf (accessed 15 December 2020).

Later closures of investigations on suspected violations of the AMA, such as in the Amazon case, the Airbnb case, the Minna no Pet case, and the Rakuten case, also reveal the prevalence of unfair trade practices to tackle potential anti-competitive behavior by these online platforms.

The choice for unfair trade practices has its advantage. There is no unanimous line of argument in the literature on when and how to intervene in the platform economy. Some prefer early intervention, others conclude that, if any intervention is required, it should be limited. Unfair trade practices allow for both. Early intervention is possible due to the relative unimportance of market power. Meticulous intervention can be done by only focusing on the conduct under dispute without looking at the strength of the firms under investigation.

Acknowledgements This chapter has received support of the project Artificial Intelligence, Price Setting Strategies and Antitrust Law: Towards a Regulatory Framework, a Grants-in-Aid for Scientific Research (C) with No. 18K01300.

References

Ahlborn C (2001) Competition policy in the new economy: is European competition law up to the challenge. ECLR 22:156–167

Arai K, Harris HS (2014) Japan's antimonopoly act: Recent developments in private monopolization. J Antitrust Enforc 2:69–99

Augustine MR, A research guide to research on the allied occupation of Japan. http://www.columbia.edu/~hds2/BIB95/02occupation_augustine.htm. Accessed 15 December 2020

DeNA (2017) Milestones. http://dena.com/intl/company/milestones/. Accessed 15 December 2020

Ernkvist M (2017) The role of dual institutional and technological entrepreneurship in the formation of the Japanese social-game industry. In: Fung A (ed) Global game industries and cultural Policy. Palgrave Macmillan, London, pp 91–124

Ernkvist M, Qi Z (2014) The Japanese social gaming industry. http://creativeindustries.com.cuhk.edu.hk/wp-content/uploads/2014/12/Japanese-Game-Industry-Report-2013.pdf. Accessed 15 December 2020

First H (2000) Antitrust in Japan: the original intent. Pac Rim Law & Policy J 9:1–71

First H, Shiraishi T (2013) Japan: the competition law system and the country's norms. In: Fox EM, Trebilcock MJ (eds) The design of competition law institutions: global norms, local choices. Oxford University Press, Oxford, pp 235–265

Fuchikawa K (2020) Regulations of digital platform markets under the Japanese Antimonopoly Act: does the regulation of unfair trade practices solve the Gordian knot of digital markets. Antitrust Bull 65(1):102–119

Graham C (2004) Introduction. In: Graham C, Smith F (eds) Competition, regulation and the new economy. Hart Publishing, Oxford, pp 1–12

Haley J (2001) Antitrust in Germany and Japan: the first fifty years, 1947–1998. University of Washington Press, Seattle

Iyori H, Uesugi A (1994) The antimonopoly laws and policies of Japan. Federal Legal Publications, New York

Jacobson JM (2001) Do we need a "New Economy" exception for antitrust? Antitrust 61:89–91

Japan Fair Trade Commission (2017a) Report of study group on data and competition policy. https://www.jftc.go.jp/en/pressreleases/yearly-2017/June/170606_files/170606-4.pdf. Accessed 15 December 2020

Japan Fair Trade Commission (2017b) Closing the investigation on the suspected violation of the Antimonopoly Act by Amazon Japan G.K. https://www.jftc.go.jp/en/pressreleases/yearly-2017/June/170601.html. Accessed 15 December 2020
Japan Fair Trade Commission (2017c) Guidelines concerning distribution systems and business practices under the Antimonopoly Act. https://www.jftc.go.jp/en/legislation_gls/imonopoly_guidelines_files/DistributionSystemsAndBusinessPractices.pdf. Accessed 15 December 2020
Japan Fair Trade Commission (2018a) minna no petto onrain kabushiki geisha ni tai suru dokusen kinshi hou ihan higi jiken no shori ni tsuite [Closing the investigation on the suspected violation of the Antimonopoly Act by Minna no Pet Online K.K.]. https://www.jftc.go.jp/houdou/pressrelease/h30/may/180523_files/180523happyoubun.pdf. Accessed 15 December 2020
Japan Fair Trade Commission (2018b) Closing the investigation on the suspected violation of the Antimonopoly Act by Airbnb Ireland UC and Airbnb Japan KK. https://www.jftc.go.jp/en/pressreleases/yearly-2018/October/181010.html. Accessed 15 December 2020
Japan Fair Trade Commission (2019a) Report regrading trade practices on digital platforms—business-to-business transactions on online retail platform and app store. https://www.jftc.go.jp/en/pressreleases/yearly-2019/October/191031Report.pdf. Accessed 15 December 2020
Japan Fair Trade Commission (2019b) Guidelines concerning abuse of a superior bargaining position in transactions between digital platform operators and consumers that provide personal information, etc. https://www.jftc.go.jp/en/pressreleases/yearly-2019/December/191217DPconsumerGL.pdf. Accessed 15 December 2020
Japan Fair Trade Commission (2019c) Request for public comments on the revised "Guidelines to application of the Antimonopoly Act concerning review of business combination" (draft) and the revised "policies concerning procedures of preview of business combination. Available at: https://www.jftc.go.jp/en/pressreleases/yearly-2019/October/191004.html. Accessed 15 December 2020
Japan Fair Trade Commission (2019d) Approval of the commitment plan submitted by Rakuten, Inc. https://www.jftc.go.jp/en/pressreleases/yearly-2019/October/191025.html. Accessed 15 December 2020
Japan Fair Trade Commission (2020) Amazon Japan goudou kaisha kara shinsei ga atta kakuyaku keikaku no nintei ni tsuite [Approval of the commitment plan submitted by Amazon Japan GK]. https://www.jftc.go.jp/houdou/pressrelease/2020/sep/division3/200910_honbun.pdf. Accessed 15 December 2020
Johnson C (1982) MITI and the Japanese miracle: the growth of industrial policy: 1925–1975. Stanford University Press, Stanford
Jones A, Sufrin B (2011) EU competition law: text, cases and materials, 4th edn. Oxford University Press, Oxford
Kameoka E (2014) Competition law and policy in Japan and the EU. Edward Elgar, Cheltenham
Kasubuchi I (2017) Investigation of parity clauses in Japan. https://www.jftc.go.jp/en/int_relations/icn_files/UCWGWS.pdf. Accessed 15 December 2020
Kawai K, Fujii K, Tsunoda T (2018) Antimonopoly & unilateral conduct 2018: Japan. https://www.jurists.co.jp/sites/default/files/tractate_pdf/en/56280.pdf. Accessed 15 December 2020
Lin P, Hiroshi Ohashi H (2014) Treatments of monopolization in Japan and China. In: Blair RD, Sokol DD (eds) The Oxford handbook of international antitrust economics. Oxford University Press, Oxford, pp 188–232
Lind RC, Muysert P (2002) Innovation and competition policy: challenges for the new millennium. ECLR 24:87–92
Litan RE (2000) Antitrust and the new economy. U Pitt L Rev 62:429–436
Matsushita M (1997) The Antimonopoly law of Japan. In: Richardson JD, Graham EM (eds) Global competition policy. Institute for International Economics, Washington DC, pp 151–198
Ministry of Economy, Trade and Industry (2016) Report of the cross-sectional system study group for the fourth industrial revolution (2016). https://www.meti.go.jp/english/press/2016/pdf/0915_02c.pdf. Accessed 15 December 2020

Ministry of Economy, Trade and Industry, Japan Fair Trade Commission, and Ministry of Internal Affairs and Communications (2018) Fundamental principles for improvement of rules corresponding to the rise of digital platform businesses. https://www.jftc.go.jp/en/policy_enforcement/survey/index_files/190220.1.pdf. Accessed 15 December 2020
Murakami M (2003) nihon no dokusen kinshihou [The Japanese Antimonopoly Act]. Shouji Houmu, Tokyo
Negishi T, Funada M (2010) dokusen kinshihou gaisetsu [Overview of the Antimonopoly Law], 4th edn. Yukihaku Publishing, Tokyo
O'Connor D (2016) Understanding online platform competition: common misunderstandings. In Ortiz A (ed) Internet competition and regulation of online platforms. https://www.yumpu.com/en/document/read/55924325/edited-by-aitor-ortiz. Accessed 15 December 2020
Ohgo M, Konno A, Matsuda T (2011) kabushiki gaisha dii enu ee ni tai suru haijo sochi meirei nit suite [Cease and desist order against DeNA Co., Ltd.]. Kouseitorihiki [Fair trade] 733:91–96
Russo F, Stasi ML (2016) Defining the relevant market in the sharing economy. Internet Policy Rev: J Internet Regul 5:2–13
Sakurada Y (2019) Japan's booking-site clampdown exposes industry's arm-twisting. https://asia.nikkei.com/Business/Business-trends/Japan-s-booking-site-clampdown-exposes-industry-s-arm-twisting. Accessed 15 December 2020
Scalapino RA (1977) The foreign policy of modern Japan. University of California Press, Berkeley
Schaede U (2000) Cooperative capitalism: self-regulation, trade associations, and the antimonopoly law in Japan. Oxford University Press, Oxford
Seita AY, Tamura J (1994) Historical background of Japan's antimonopoly law. Univ Ill Law Rev 1:115–185
Sensui F (2018) Digital platform and competition law in Japan. https://www.jftc.go.jp/cprc/koukai/sympo/181207sympo01.pdf. Accessed 15 December 2020
Shapiro C, Varian H (1998) Information rules: a strategic guide to the network economy. Harvard Business Review Press, Boston
Sugimoto K (2016) 2016 new year message. http://www.jftc.go.jp/en/about_jftc/MessagefromChairma/150115.html. Accessed 15 December 2020
Van Uytsel S, Uemura Y (2019) Online platforms and the Japan Fair Trade Commission: the DeNA case as an example of early market intervention. In Lundqvist B with Gal MS (eds) Competition law for the digital economy. Edward Elgar, Cheltenham, pp 231–263
Wakui M (2008) Antimonopoly law: competition law and policy in Japan. Arima Publishing, Suffolk
Wakui M (2018) Antimonopoly law: competition law and policy in Japan. Independently Published
Yamamura K (1966) Economic policy in postwar Japan: growth versus economic democracy. J Asian Stud 25(4):713–728

Part II
The Limits of Competition Law in the Digital Economy

The Nexus Between Competition and Personal Data Protection Laws: Thailand's Perspective

Peerapat Chokesuwattanaskul

Abstract This chapter argues that the data-driven economy needs to figure out how to apply both competition and personal data protection laws. The implementation has to aim at preventing the situation where a group of people disproportionately gains at the expense of another group of people, whose data have been processed by the former. Without proper enforcement of competition and personal data protection laws, we argue that the feedback loop of having more data, better performance and greater talents will eventually worsen the problem of inequality. Thailand serves as a good case study of how the problem exists, while the implementation of both laws is still in retard. We propose that the line separating between personal and public interests has to be drawn and the effective enforcement of competition and personal data protection laws is at the heart of it.

Keywords Data-driven economy · Privacy · Competition law · Personal data · Data protection law · Private and public interest · GDPR · Personal Data Protection Act · Thailand

1 Introduction

This chapter discusses how personal data protection[1] and competition law will play a substantial role in the so-called data-driven world, where data are historically abundant and their utilization has been ubiquitous and extensive. The current dominance of data has omnipresent impacts on various aspects of the society spanning from business and economy to politics, which in turn has a significant impact on individuals. Data are generally the records of facts or what are believed to be facts and are neutral

[1] A caveat is that personal data protection can be seen as a subset of privacy when the subject of rights is data, therefore, in the context of this chapter, personal data protection and privacy may be used interchangeably.

P. Chokesuwattanaskul (✉)
Faculty of Law, Chulalongkorn University, 10330 Bangkok, Thailand
e-mail: Peerapat.ch@chula.ac.th

S. Van Uytsel (ed.), *The Digital Economy and Competition Law in Asia*,
Perspectives in Law, Business and Innovation,
https://doi.org/10.1007/978-981-16-0324-2_4

in terms of values and characteristics. Scientists have been observing and collecting natural data, including that of human nature for centuries. They have made enormous progress in a scientific discovery, which in turn benefits humanity as a whole.

However, when it comes to personal data, one must be more careful to consider how and when it should be used, especially when the scope is beyond scientific purposes. The world has never experienced a period when we can virtually track human behaviors at this level of granularity, and at the same time, possess the colossal computational power required to analyze and use these data. We call the economy where data have become an essential driving force of its members as *the data-driven economy*.

The fact that data are ubiquitous is generally neutral and rather optimistic when we consider the world as a single unit. However, when we look a little closer, the concern should be that this innovation should not be used by one group in exploiting the others. It is probably the whole reason we need to govern the data-driven world in such a way that the progress can be made for the benefit of the sum, yet still prevent the exploitation that could be done by the few. Therefore, we discuss how the largest users of data, firms, and the largest sources of data, individuals, should be interacting under legislation introduced by the government. It turns out, it is not that straightforward to govern this interaction especially in the situation where group like individuals are framed by the system to incur net loss, while another may curb the system to be the net profiteer. This so-called *dysfunctional equilibrium* cannot be sustained in the long run (Farrell 2012).

This chapter is structured as follows. Section 2 explains the principles underlying the rights over personal data should be characterized. Moreover, it also discusses the criteria under which personal data may be processed. In Sect. 3, we discuss further how privacy can be compromised and, more importantly, how some underlying presumptions differ across contexts. Such variation of context-specific factors affects how the interpretation and enforcement of data protection law should be altered accordingly. Section 4 explores what empirical evidence in a specific context, i.e., Thailand, has to say about the points mentioned above. In Sect. 5, we discuss a petition for the closer merger between personal data protection and competition laws. Before concluding in Sect. 7, we propose the needs of redrawing the line or threshold determining the optimal level of tradeoffs between two conflicting concepts such as privacy and utility or privacy and security. Section 7 concludes the chapter.

2 The Principle: Personal Data Should Remain Personal

The most important principle of privacy regarding personal data is that personal data can only be processed by the data subject, i.e., the one who is identified or identifiable by the data.[2] However, the principle is not absolute. There is some basis for exceptions.

---

[2]Solove (2008).

There are at least three ways by which someone else may process personal data. Firstly, the data subject explicitly or implicitly allows her data to be processed in a particular way. We have seen this principle translated into consent and contractual bases which are lawful bases in data protection laws, including the General Data Protection Regulation (GDPR).[3]

Secondly, data controller, i.e. the entity who has an authority to decide how the data will be processed, has a legitimate reason to collect personal data and process them in such a way that they also have their "contribution" to the utility of data. At the same time, a data controller has to make sure that during the process, data subjects' rights and freedoms are not disproportionally compromised.[4] The rationale has been translated into the legitimate interest basis in data protection laws.

Thirdly, in some scenarios, the personal data of someone may benefit the rest of the society. For example, when there is an outbreak of a contagious disease, having data on people's health conditions help mitigate the epidemic, which benefits the whole society. Therefore, in some situations, the government may have to take action and forgoes private rights for the sake of public interests, i.e. the mandatory internalization of externalities.

We will explore these "tradeoffs between private and public interests" further and try to understand when we should protect the privacy of individuals and when we should forgo it for the sake of the others and the society as a whole who may have better legitimacy.[5] The objective is to identify the factors determining these tradeoffs in order to analyze different countries' approaches to the topic of privacy, which arguably has a much wider implication than just the scope of privacy but the economic and political freedom of the society as a whole.

3 Giving up Privacy for a Greater Good

For simplicity, without losing generalizability, there are three main entities in our discussion: individuals or citizens, firms, and the public, each of which interacts with each other under certain rules of law. We assume that personal data are collected from individuals by firms and the public. We assume further that the public, a space in which both individuals and firms are co-existing, is overseen by the state. The fundamental function of the state is to coordinate among individuals and firms in order to achieve what serves the public best. The state employs the government as the means through which the state's power is organized. Therefore, there must be lines separating between the stakes of individuals and firms and also individuals and

[3]Houser and Voss (2018). The more-recent California Consumer Privacy Act (CCPA), which has just come into effect after the end of last year, does not require these legal bases in collecting data but still allow data subjects to opt out or delete their data anytime. I expect similar laws to be enacted really soon in other states within this year.

[4]Robinson et al. (2009).

[5]Cate (1994).

the public. Most of the time, the state has to judge when and where these lines can be drawn and, more importantly, crossed.

3.1 *The Tradeoff Between Private and Public Interests*

Even though the principle is that privacy must be protected, it is arguable that sometimes giving up a certain level of privacy is necessary for the benefits of the public, which in turn will also benefit each individual at an even greater degree.[6] For example, the government may use personal data of individuals to design more effective public policies, which eventually benefit the wider society such as the case where citizens give up personal health data for the government to mitigate pandemics. As long as no other unintended parties may process data for their interests, public interests seem to outweigh private interests.

Giving up private interests for public security is more justifiable when the degree of market failures is substantial. For example, the government may sometimes find it necessary to separate suspects or criminals from innocents. The separation ensures that people do not exercise their rights in such a way that adversely affects the others (i.e., the tragedy of commons), or to make sure that those who forego their private interests and contribute to the public eventually get rewards.[7] Due to these necessities, under the data protection law, data controllers and processors may process personal data on the bases of public tasks and legal obligation apart from asking for consent and relying on a contract.[8] As the government has to ensure that public goods like security are sufficiently provided and individuals internalize their externalities which may cause harm to others, the government should be able to process or assign someone to process personal data of individuals to achieve these purposes. In turn, the government has its authority to collect taxes from citizens in order to cover the expenses for these tasks. By doing these public tasks, there are a good set of principles and mechanisms in place to ensure that the government will exercise their power within the legitimate scope. For example, despite being exempted from some articles regarding lawful bases,[9] the government still has to ensure that data collected from individuals are safely kept and data processing is adequate, necessary and minima.[10] Not limited to privacy, most of the government actions that compromise basic human rights have to be done together with an impartial third party's approval, e.g., courts, and has to be proportional to the necessity of each task on a case-by-case basis.

---

[6]Rodwin (2010).

[7]Mena (2003).

[8]Šidlauskas (2019).

[9]For example, Article 4 of the Thailand's Personal Data Protection Act has exempted a few purposes of data processing from the provisions of the act, one of which is the government processes personal data for the purpose of security including fiscal and public securities. Similar exemptions exist in the Article 2 of the General Data Protection Regulation (GDPR) of the European Union.

[10]Mourby et al. (2018) and Langheinrich (2001).

The tradeoff between private and public interests may be more apparent in the relationship between a state and its citizens. However, the relationship among private entities in the market economy could be subject to the tradeoff between private and public interests as well. Firms, through some means, observe individuals' behaviors and attributes and process these data for their benefits. The processing ensures that firms understand individuals, mostly customers, better. By understanding individuals better, the transaction costs can be lowered. It is also easier for an individual to find the right firm who sells goods or services she/he is looking for. It is also easier to know the prices where other firms set and other individuals are willing to purchase. In other words, having individual data, firms can create a more informed market where everyone benefits.[11] As a consequence, the market will allow consumers to get access to better goods and services at the most reasonable prices as per the standard prediction of neoclassical economic theory. This is evident judging from the rise of the platform economy, which is broadly defined as the online structures that enable a wide range of human activities we have experienced worldwide in the past few years.[12]

Apart from that, in the labor market, these individuals also trade their labor with firms for wages. Given that these firms are able to perform better due to data possession, wages should increase as a consequence.[13] An increase in wages will not only benefit those who earn but also the whole economy due to an increase in the purchasing power. Moreover, as we will discuss later, as firms are able to process more and more data while being more competent in data analytics, they can earn higher margins and pay higher taxes. The government then with higher tax revenue will be able to provide better welfare to its citizens. Moreover, the government can spend this extra money to develop talents to feed the data-driven firm, in which human capital plays a crucial role.

We have seen so many contributions an individual can make by giving up her own data for the sake of "utility." We also have seen that the utility of data does not just benefit firms but also each individual at the end of the day.

The narrative provided above has some implicit yet strong presumptions, which will be discussed.

3.2 Presumption 1: Competition Is in Place

Competition in the data-driven world is two-fold. On the one hand, firms may compete in terms of data protection, knowing that consumers value personal data protection as

---

[11] Dolnicar (2002).

[12] Drahokoupil and Fabo (2016) and Kenney and Zysman (2016).

[13] An increase in wages is not necessary. It depends largely on the skilled required and, at the same time, may lead to some further capital-labor substitutions. However, it is reasonable to say that, on average, wages should increase. Even though some middle- and low-skilled labor will be substituted partly by high-skilled labors and partly by machines.

one of the quality aspects.[14] In other words, some have proposed that consumers have increasingly treated privacy as a non-priced characteristic of products or services, especially in countries where data protection law has been implemented and people are aware of this issue.[15] On the other hand, firms may compete using personal data as resources to gain competitive advantages.[16] On this regard, some have argued that data are non-rivalry in nature so it should not provide any competitive advantage to any firm.[17] Therefore, competition using data should set everyone on the same level playing field. However, it is also debatable that there are "multi-homing" users who regularly switch across firms and hence have left footprints, i.e. data, everywhere.[18]

Regardless of how and to what extent data may play their role in driving competition, it is hard to imagine how the narrative earlier will be true in the absence of competition. Frederick Hayek wrote in the Road to Serfdom that "[i]t is only because the control of the means of production is divided among many people acting independently that nobody has complete power over us, that we as individuals can decide what to do with ourselves."[19] Without a certain level of competition, data subjects will not really have much choice and the validity of a decision to give up personal interests for public interests becomes questionable.

In the data-driven economy, competition may suffer from quite a few factors. In the platform ecosystem where most data are generated nowadays, network effects have locked in most consumers in one or just a few firms. However, as we will discuss further, the possession of data alone will not take anyone far. What really creates the so-called "sustainable competitive advantage" are the resources that are valuable, rare, inimitable, and organized. Possessing data alone will not create any competitive advantage.[20] "Talent" is supposed to be the key ingredient in the process of turning data into insights and, eventually, profits for firms.[21] Nevertheless, the facts of having more data and more talents are not independent, but closely connected or even interdependent. It is hard to imagine any completion engineer who would accept to work on the oil rig that has no oil. Likewise, good data scientists go to those companies with data, with which they can work and experiment.

Moreover, in the context of the data-driven economy, a firm needs certain scale in order to optimally utilize data.[22] The firms who possess more data are in a better

---

[14]OECD (2020).

[15]Esayas (2019).

[16]Pitruzzella (2017), European Commission (2008), and European Data Protection Supervisor (2016).

[17]Acquisti et al. (2016).

[18]Choi (2010).

[19]Hayek (1945).

[20]Mata et al. (1995).

[21]Pepper and Gilbert (2015).

[22]It is true that we now have cloud services that smaller firms can also get access to a state of the art data infrastructure but again these cloud service providers are usually some of the biggest data processors in terms of volume of data as well. Therefore, we can consider this as the business model where they can capitalize their spare resources, by doing which they can reach a larger scale and enjoy more efficiency.

position to outperform firms who do not and tends to get larger by having more customers. As we discussed earlier, it is true that the possession of data alone is insufficient. More importantly, as they are more capable of financially and operationally attracting better talents and setup better infrastructure, they are more capable of squeezing out more information from the same amount of data they possess. This cycle is what some scholars called the 'feedback loop.'[23]

The data-driven economy would have not been possible without the introduction of the platform economy, where two groups of economic agents (e.g. seller and buyers) are matched and trade with each other. Connecting different groups of economic agents through intermediaries is referred to as multi-sided markets.[24] They usually have the so-called lock-in effect, where each group of users finds it difficult to switch to other services due to the value generated from having the other users within the same platform. It is hard or even almost impossible for new entrants to achieve the same level of competitiveness. At the same time, people have so little bargaining power against the big firms in terms of their data as a single unit of data values so little comparing to the whole set of data. A straightforward solution should be that consumers act collectively to bargain for their benefits against these larger firms. However, in the world where data subjects are mostly strangers to each other, it is hard to imagine how they may collectively form a collective body and bargain for their own rights. As a consequence, it turns out that big firms are more likely to become a monopoly in terms of data, i.e. dataopoly.[25]

After being able to enjoy the status of dataopoly, firms care less about individuals and individuals enjoy fewer benefits both in terms of consumption and return for labor inputs.[26] Competition in product and labor markets are arguably similar in nature. The key difference is just that sellers and buyers have relatively larger bargaining power in product and labor markets respectively. Without the fear of having someone stealing customers or workers away, firms find less incentive to do their best to meet the needs of individuals. Moreover, having less or no alternatives, individuals find it harder to compare characteristics of goods and services including prices and quality.

Besides, being a dominant player in one sector, firms try to penetrate into other industries to enjoy the economies of scope as well. We have seen this horizontal expansion ubiquitously. One clear example is how social network firms expand into delivery and financial sectors through both organic expansion and merger and acquisition.[27] What follows is that firms have more data both in terms of volume and variety, which exponentially enhances their ability to influence individuals.[28] An absence of sufficient competition in the goods and services market also influences how the labor market may behave. Holding the labor law constant, less competition suppresses the bargaining power of individuals in terms of wages as well. Therefore,

---

[23] Gal and Rubinfeld (2019) and Krzepicki et al. (2020).

[24] Evans (2003).

[25] Stucke and Grunes (2016).

[26] Ibid.

[27] Tepper (2018).

[28] Zuboff (2015).

having given up their data, there is too little to guarantee that the benefit will eventually redistribute to individuals as data subjects if healthy competition is not yet in place.

3.2.1 On the Data-Sharing Initiative

Lately, there has been a proposition that, by forcing firms to share their data, it should help promote data-related competition. The proponents of "data sharing" among those who collect data believe that data sharing may assure that data will be used by more parties and prevent dataopoly. Having more firms gain access to data usually means better products or services provided to customers because firms are now stepping on the level playing field, the situation where consumers usually benefit.[29]

Related to the data-sharing initiative is the essential facilities doctrine (EFD) by which, in many jurisdictions, a firm may request to get access to another firm's assets if access is necessary to provide another good or service.[30] In this sense, data can be seen as essential facilities as potential entrants may need specific data from the incumbents in order to enter the market.[31] However, the argument based on EFD is still at best theoretical and has not been tested in practice yet.

The data sharing initiative has at least three issues of concern. Firstly, not all firms are able to handle the same amount of data. It is costly to provide and maintain the infrastructure where reliable and efficient operations on data are guaranteed. One may argue that it is possible to make it in the form of a service provided by larger firms with reasonable fees paid by smaller firms. However, that is also another source of protectionism as long as the control of data fees is not properly established. Moreover, the data collected by one firm are usually not readily transferable to other firms. For example, some context-specific data such as users' behaviors on a travelling website are not readily utilizable by the news website. Secondly, in the data-driven economy, data have become the proprietary assets of firms and the source of its competitive advantage. By forcing a firm to share its competitive advantages with competitors, the government may be sending the wrong signal to the market and firms. This will eventually lead firms to have no incentive to develop the data-driven technologies in the first place. Data collection is not really accidental or by-products but a thoroughly designed process, into which blood, sweat and tears have gone. Thirdly, despite having data shared among firms, there is no guarantee that the data subjects will actually benefit from better goods or services or from cheaper prices. At the minimum there should be a guarantee that data subjects will not be influenced even more by these firms, both in terms of degree (better data lead to a better prediction) and breadth (not only more products and services but also socio-political decisions as well) of the influences. Last but not least, even though we might gain some additional

---

[29] Longo and Drazen (2016).

[30] OECD (2020).

[31] Diker and Ünver (2017).

surplus from the data-sharing policy, data themselves can serve as an additional tool to *facilitate* price-fixing and other anti-competition behaviors.[32]

A milder and upcoming proposition is the concept of data portability and interoperability. The data portability rights are explicitly stated in personal data protection laws including the GDPR. However, the same obstacles in data sharing also span the case of data portability. The concept may work in relatively more traditional industries such as mobile phone services where a consumer is able to ask a service provider to transfer her number and personal data to another service provider. However, in multi-sided markets, consumers find substantially less incentive to port data across as a unilateral move of user typically leads to less utility for most parties except the recipient.[33]

3.3 Presumption 2: A Redistribution System Is in Place

Individuals may indeed enjoy greater benefits from giving up their privacy, especially if the other end is the business whose products or services are used by themselves or is their own government, but the point is whether they get a "fair share" of their contribution or not. The share of fairness depends largely on the redistribution within and across societies.

In the worst case, it could be the case that individuals may just provide data and purchase goods and services they never need without any chance of having their wages or redistributive benefits from tax at all. Moreover, most developing countries also suffer from the polarization of labors.[34] In other words, laborers who enjoy higher wages from data-driven advancement are usually those who are relatively highly skilled or very low skilled while most developing countries' laborers are generally those who lose their jobs to technology (middle-skilled laborers). These middle-skilled laborers also suffer from the 'original sin' by being born in the countries where the educational system has not prepared them for the technological disruption. We discussed earlier that if competition and other institutions are not in place so that the system directly or indirectly pays back a portion of surplus acquired from the utilization of data either by firms or by the government to individuals whose data have been processed, individuals will not simply get back the fair share they deserve out of altruism.

We have seen how each individual finds it difficult to have any bargaining power against larger firms who collect her data. The scenario resembles a *take-it-or-leave-it* contract where terms are not usually read by consumers. As the argument goes, an individual both factually realizes and mentally believes that her data alone are

---

[32]Duffy and Feltovich (2002) and Sutter and Strassmair (2009).

[33]Gal and Aviv (2020) and Nicholas and Weinberg (2019).

[34]Gregg (1996).

meaningless at least to her. Not the least does she know how her data could be used and what the 'end product' can potentially be.[35]

3.3.1 The Alienation of Labor Force Revisited

The fact that data subjects are not fully aware of how their data may contribute to the profits of firms can be seen from the Marx's concept of 'alienation of labor force.' However, this time, the alienation is done at the most granular and profound way ever.

A low-wage worker in a factory in Vietnam is probably able to tell that the final product assembled on the other side of the world is a smartphone. A smartphone typically costs 3 times of the worker's monthly salary despite having spent just a few minutes to assemble one, yet many are surprisingly willing to be in debt to own one.

On the contrary, a user contributing data may perceive that she is 'experiencing' the social network or the Internet in general and does not even know that she is producing anything. At the same time, an ad shown in the side column seems to be what she really wants or what she just realizes that she may want it for the first time! It is through this process that data subjects in the data-driven economy resembles how proletariats were exploited by the bourgeoisie in Marx's thesis.

Even though the analogy allows us to consider the problem through the lens of Marxism, this study will not go so far as to claim that there will be any revolution or uprising of the same sort. However, there are two generalizable predictions which are more relevant to our scope of analysis: the ever-increasing degree of inequality and the fact that larger firms will hit the dead-end once the disparity has loomed too large. To put it in a bit of context, given that the main source of income of most social networks nowadays is through advertisement, people working on the ads will have to work harder to squeeze an extra dollar from the pocket of poorer consumers.

For this reason, looking through the same lens or not, some recent scholars and movements have started to consider data as the "off-springs" of laborers. Therefore, for laborers to have more bargaining power, some sorts of collective action might be needed. Posner and Weyl (2018) proposed that data can be seen as labor and advocate for the idea of "data labor unions" to represent the benefits of data subjects collectively.[36] Some businesses also realized this fact and came up with a new business idea of empowering a collection of users to monetize their data (e.g. Streamer) or form a data union (e.g. Swash).[37]

---

[35] Cui (2019).

[36] Posner and Weyl (2018).

[37] Chakravorti (2020).

3.3.2 Cross-Border Problems and the Digital Services Tax Initiative

A good amount of data-driven firms are now operating on the Internet providing free services and feeding themselves with commissions. They are usually registered and operate within just a few jurisdictions, most of which are larger economies by necessity and some tax havens by choice. The business model is called *zero-price economy*.[38] The problem is that there are a number of individuals whose data have been processed who live in other jurisdictions. Therefore, these individuals have no chance in getting any benefits from higher wages or more taxes collected from these firms. This reason explains why most data protection laws adopt the extraterritoriality principle[39] and enforce laws on firms who are situated outside of the country as well. In terms of taxes, there has been some movement in Europe where the Digital Services Tax (DST) has been charged by some countries such as Norway (at a surprisingly high rate of 25%), France and the United Kingdom to those firms processing the data of their citizens. Most recently, Malaysia has just introduced the tax while more countries in Asia are seriously considering the introduction.[40]

However, without these mechanisms, it is hard to identify how individuals will get their fair share of their contribution in terms of data apart from the benefits they may get from goods and services which in turn are subject to a sufficient level of competition as we discussed earlier.

3.4 Presumption 3: The Government Always Does What Is Best for Individuals and Each Individual Knows What Is Best for Herself

3.4.1 Individuals Are Easily Influenced to Pay Beyond Their Means

The data-driven economy significantly contributes to the cycle by stimulating the "trickle-down consumerism" situation, i.e. the situation where people with lower income or wealth try to imitate the consumption patterns of these whose income or wealth are beyond their means.[41]

---

[38]Newman (2015).

[39]Article 3 of GDPR defines the territorial scope of GDPR. The regulation applies to the processing of personal data in the context of the activities of an establishment of a controller or a processor in the Union, regardless of whether the processing takes place in the Union of not. Moreover, even those controllers or processors not established in the Union may be applied if the processing activities are related to the offering of goods and services to data subjects in the Union and to the monitoring of behavior of data subjects that takes place within the Union.

[40]Cui (2019).

[41]Stiglitz (2012).

In the old days, this trickle-down consumerism has happened all along, just to a lesser degree and scope.[42] In other words, through social constructs and settings, the rich would not really mingle with people far below their social status so the imitation did not occur between the classes that were too far apart. With the social construct where classes were structurally clear, the incentive for the cross-class imitation was also limited. Therefore, it was the period when people may be able to say that inequality was at the "healthy" level so that people had an incentive to work harder to climb up the ladder, which was arguably true as long as the inequality was not extreme or, more importantly, structural.

Back to the present day, when individualistic and liberal notions are promoted across different contexts, most people were taught to expect that all individuals are equal and anyone can be at the top of the pyramid. Together with modern technologies, globalization allows individuals to be informed of the consumption patterns of those who are relatively well-off, especially those whose wealth or income are far above the majority of the society, e.g., celebrities or the super-rich.

Given that individuals spend more and more time on the Internet, especially after the invention of social media, the breadth and depth of psychological impacts these technologies have on individuals are evidently increasing fast. Having been 'nudged' to spend beyond their means, it is not entirely surprising to witness the figure of household debts shooting up all over the world. To give an example, Thailand's household debt now accounts for 80% of the country's gross domestic product (GDP) (a historical level) and the figure is indifferent if not worse elsewhere.

This nature of trickle-down consumerism is coherent with the distinctive nature of "increasing returns to scale" of the two-sided market, where the more users the more average profit for firms. However, an increase in profits in this case is not from a decrease in unit costs due to the spread of fixed costs across more units of production as in the traditional economies of scale. Quite the contrary, an increase of average profit is derived from the network effects where consumer's willingness to pay is increasing in the number of consumers in the market.[43] Therefore, a dominant firm in the two-sided market is killing two birds in one shot as it gains the scale merely by having more users and, in turn, uses these users' data to generate further turnover by coming up with better recommendations and incentives to lock more users within the network.

3.4.2 Individuals also Pay for Unhappiness

Even the happiness derived from using these data-driven products and services, e.g. social networks, is still a subject of debate. The debate revolves around whether the products or services positively or negatively contribute to their well-being. One stream of research tries to estimate the value of being on the platform or social network by evaluating the willingness-to-get (WTG) value of the subjects, i.e. the

[42]Furman and Stiglitz (1998).

[43]Evans (2011).

researchers asked subjects how much they are willing to get in order to stop using Facebook for a day.[44] Most of these works found a positive value of being on the social network site.

On the contrary, another stream of research reversed the process by asking a group of subjects to deactivate Facebook for four weeks before the 2018 US midterm election and compare the subjective well-beings, political polarization, family and friends' social qualities, and persistent post-experiment use of Facebook pre- and post-deactivation. It turns out that deactivating Facebook has improved all areas of well-being being measured.[45] It might not be too far from truth to compare such behavior to other kinds of addiction where most individuals, once they get addicted, choose what is sub-optimal for themselves.[46]

This *irrational* trait of individuals directly challenges the concept of informational self-determination, which is at the heart of the modern data protection law, including GDPR of the EU and Personal Data Protection Act (PDPA) of Thailand. It is also called the *privacy paradox*, the situation in which individuals care about their privacy but do not act accordingly.[47] In other words, there is a discrepancy between stated and revealed preferences of users.[48] The key explanation of this paradox is the lack of ability. "Even if users put effort into making an informed choice, this is not (or barely) possible for them."[49]

Therefore, it might be hard to expect that people would value their personal data over the value of enjoying convenience from data-driven products and services. Having discussed a mismatch between actual and perceived values of individuals in this scenario, the establishment of transferable private ownership of personal data deems risky. Most individuals might be not fully aware of what is best for themselves when it comes to trading between addicted convenience and personal data.

3.4.3 The Government May Have No Incentive to Mitigate the Risks

Having known this adverse influence that firms and social constructs may have on individuals, the government should try to mitigate this systematic risk caused by over-consumerism discussed earlier. However, what worsens the situation is the fact that some governments might be reluctant to issue any policy that may impact the wealth of the wealthier due to the influence they have over the government. The government therefore needs to rely on the relatively short-term policies such as consumption stimuli which team up well with trickle-down consumerism, where people are ready to incur more debts just to consume beyond their means. It emphasizes an important

---

[44] Vock et al. (2013).

[45] Allcott et al. (2019).

[46] Chaloupka et al. (2000).

[47] Kerber (2016).

[48] OECD (2020).

[49] Botta and Wiedemann (2019).

point of our discussion below where public interests seem to gain more weight, which is particularly problematic in the society where inequality is evident.

To put things at the extremity, the magnitude of the problem is particularly strong in countries where inequality is persistent and large. This situation causes younger generations to be myopic as they have no hope to save up or invest for the long-run catchup. Unaffordable price of properties driven by the high purchasing power of the wealthier is one of the factors, which led the younger generation to find no hope in savings. As a consequence, we have started to see some push back from the pressure created by inequality in several places, including the recent uprising in Hong Kong.[50] The trajectory of the situation leaves little hope in closing the gap within each society and also across different countries.

The subsequent sections will discuss how the case of Thailand may fit into the framework we discussed earlier.

4 Digging Deeper into the Case of Thailand

On May 24, 2020, a couple of days before the PDPA was due to come into effect, the cabinet approved a royal decree seeking for the enforcement of the PDPA. The deference was justified as an attempt to relieve burdens on businesses amidst the period of the COVID-19 pandemic. "The compliance costs are too high for business operators," the government claimed. The decision, widely criticized, serves well as a mirror image of how the state prioritizes different parties within society. During the same period, the app 'Thai-Chana' introduced by the government to keep track of people's transportation since the announcement of the multi-stage easing of the lockdown starting in mid-May was also criticized for its poor data governance and how the government has expanded the scope of data collection beyond the scope of pandemic ramification.

Meanwhile, over 74% of the Thai population is active on a social network, each of which spends roughly 3 h daily and the number shoots up to 9 h 11 min when the scope is the Internet, not just social media. In terms of devices, the number of mobile subscriptions in Thailand is over 130%. Despite an obvious double-counting problem, it implies that any information potentially sent through mobile phones may be able to reach the whole population of Thailand in a split second. In a nutshell, Thailand has among the most widespread data-driven technology adoption societies in the world. What is interesting, yet worrisome, is that most users are almost fully passive. The research has shown that most users have almost no information on how these technologies may affect their lives.[51]

[50] Taylor (2019).

[51] Leesa-nguansuk (2019).

4.1 *The Powerful State and the Priority of Public Interests*

In this section we explore the current playing field in terms of how these lines separating between private and public interests are drawn in Thailand.

At the very beginning, it is useful to understand the role of the state in Thailand. The brief background in terms of the size or power of the state is that Thailand has had twelve successful and seven attempted coups during her 87 years after the revolution in 1932. The incidence saw Thailand switching her regime from an absolute monarchy to a constitutional monarchy. During the past 30 years, Thailand has had 3 coups in 1991, 2006, and 2014 in succession. Almost all coups during the span of a century were done by the military, including the three most recent ones. It is not unreasonable to state that the military would need to strengthen the public order to ensure the stability during the post-coup transition period.[52] Most laws for the purpose definitely prioritize public interests over private interests. For example, after the 2015 coup, the most recent one led by General Prayuth Chan-ocha and his junta under the National Council for Peace and Order, the martial law was immediately enacted which extended the military court jurisdiction to civilians committing crimes against the crown and state. Moreover, some other repressive measures were introduced such as public demonstrations were prohibited and media freedom was restricted, most of which were justified by the public order. The most extreme measure, especially in the most recent coup, was the introduction of Article 44 of the 2014 interim constitution under which the junta may take any action deemed necessary for the preservation of the country, i.e. security.[53] Therefore, the dominance of military in Thai politics plays a crucial role when it comes to the weight being put on public interests, especially public securities, vis-à-vis private interests.[54] Another piece of evidence worth considering is the nature of laws being legislated during this recent period, which suggests that public interests are seemingly winning their fight against private interests.

Up until now, there are only two laws on the side of privacy protection. The 2017 Constitution of the Kingdom of Thailand Article 32 paragraph one was written "A person shall enjoy the right and liberty in his life and person," while its third paragraph was written "Search of person or any act affecting the right and liberty under paragraph one shall not be made except by virtue of law." The other law is the Thai PDPA enacted in 2019, which its effects have been postponed until June 2021 at the very least. Despite having most provisions resemble those in the GDPR of the European Union, we can still observe some potentially problematic exemptions such as the Article 4 of the PDPA exempting the cases where data processing is done for the 'security' purpose to not fall under the PDPA. The scope of security is evidently far from clarity.

[52]Christensen (1991).

[53]Haberkorn (2015).

[54]Phongpaichit and Baker (2015).

Quite the contrary, there have been nine laws, most of them being enacted in that past few years, that legalize the privacy violation for the sake of 'public security' as follows:

- Anti-money Laundering Act B.E. 2542 (1999)
- Special Case Investigation Act B.E. 2547 (2004)
- Emergency Decree on Public Administration in Emergency Situations, B.E. 2548 (2005)
- Computer-related Crime Act B.E. 2550 (2007)
- Internal Security Act B.E. 2551 (2008)
- Prevention and Suppression of Participation in Transnational Organised Crime Act, B.E. 2556 (2013)
- Cybersecurity Act B.E. 2562 (2019)
- National Intelligence Act B.E. 2562 (2019).

The aforementioned laws have rationales and contexts to put public interests ahead of private interests. It is fair to argue that, as the principle has been stated in the constitution already, it should be no surprise to observe more laws exempting the principle rather than conforming to it. However, this argument is valid as long as the use of these exemptions has a clear scope and must be strictly limited in scope. The presumption is hardly true in the context of Thailand. Therefore, these pieces of evidence suggest that security is leading the contest by quite some distance in Thailand at the moment.

4.2 *Presumptions 1 and 2 in the Context of Thailand: A Competition Law and Redistribution System Are Not in Place*

When it comes to a specific context, it is hard to discuss competition as a separated concept from redistribution. Quite the contrary, competition and inequality are closely related. As we discussed earlier, a country with ineffective competition law tends to bring about larger inequality and also the other way around.

Despite having had two competition acts in the past 20 years, the development of competition law in Thailand is arguably at its infant stage. Thailand has had two Competition Acts, one came into effect in 1999 and the other in 2017. There have been two cases brought to the court so far, none of which has been finalized. Only after the new act saw another long-awaiting case where the Commission has imposed the administrative fine on the liable business operator. As of mid-2020, there have been six cases investigated, all of which fell under the unfair trade practices in Section 57 of the Trade Competition Act. Among six cases, only one case was found violating the Act and was prohibited by the Commission.[55] Unfortunately, none of the decisions have been published.

[55] Sakda (2020, p. 118).

The facts pretty much imply that competition law has practically not existed in Thailand. Even though the current act has been improved recently, it is less promising that the act will effectively be enforced due to the existing economic and business structures of Thailand which will be discussed subsequently.

When it comes to inequality, Thailand has been considered one of the most unequal economies in the world. Swiss Bank, in their 2018 survey on global wealth, put Thailand at the top of the wealth inequality ranking. The ranking saw that the wealthiest 1% of Thais possess 67.0% of the country's overall wealth.[56] Similarly, a recent study of bank depositors by the Bank of Thailand found that the top 10% of depositors own as much as 93% of all the deposits in commercial banks while 32% (12.2 million people) have less than 500 baht (US$ 17) in their accounts.[57]

The relationship between competition and inequality is best understood under the context of business-politics relationship. The business-politics terrain of Thailand has found a strong development in terms of personal relationship since the twentieth century.[58] The current political economic structure could be best described as the *oligarchy* system composed of different groups of oligarchs including the old elites, the Bangkok and other cities' capitalists, the civil servants, the military, and the monarch. Particularly in recent years, Bangkok's capitalists (a majority of which are Chinese-Thais) has its own entity to negotiate their stakes shoulder to shoulder with other oligarchs.[59] We therefore have witnessed a number of government projects won by a few large firms and a lot of single-industry larger firms have started to penetrate into other industries to enjoy the economies of scale.

4.2.1 The Tale of Two Tycoons: ThaiBev and CP Groups

In 2020, there is an ongoing major merger case in the retail industry which has drawn great attention from the public. In January 2020, Tesco PLC, the UK's biggest retailer, has publicly announced their intention to sell all assets in Thailand and Malaysia. At the last stage of auction, there were two leading bidders: Chareon Sirivadhanabhakdi's TCC Group and Dhanin Chearavanont's Chareon Pokphand Group (CP Group). Coincidentally, these two bidders are also considered two of the richest thais, according to Forbes. TCC Group and CP Group are also two of the largest corporates in Thailand. Even though the auction has been concluded and the CP Group won the race with a bidding value over US$ 10 billion, the deal is still pending subject to the clearance decision yet to be made by the OTCC.[60] The decision will definitely shape how competition law will influence the Thai economy in years to come and, judging from the magnitude of involving parties, it is expected to have an everlasting effect on the structure of the Thai economy. We will briefly

---

[56] Zucman (2019). The figure was 58% in 2016.

[57] Sullivan (2019).

[58] Doner and Ramsay (1997).

[59] Phongpaichit and Baker (2015).

[60] Reuters (2020).

introduce these two bidders with an intention to convince the reader that the decision is not merely just another case of a merger.

The ThaiBev group, who started out as a beer producer under the government concession, has become a conglomerate with 138 companies and over 40,000 employees under the same umbrella. The company is now registered in the Singapore Stock Exchange (SGX) with a market cap of over 13 billion USD.[61]

The government regulations clearly support ThaiBev (and its competitor, Boonrawd) where the government tariffs on beer and wine have been consistently increased and kept at a high level, most of the time using the "moral" reason. At the same time, there is a regulation enacted in 2017 that a liquor producer has to be a registered company with the asset value not below 10 million Thai baht and needs to produce more than 10 million liters per annum. This basically means that a smaller producer will not be able to enter the market.

Having not only beverages, restaurants, and liquors, ThaiBev has started to invest in real estate and infrastructure, where most of the larger projects are either done together with or for the government. One of these projects is the 'Bangkok One' project, which is built on the state's land with over 4 billion USD budget, one of the largest investments by a private sector in Thailand. According to the Department of Land, the owner of ThaiBev and family own over 230,000 acres of land in Thailand, which is roughly 0.15% of the area of Thailand. The Emmerson family is one of the families who control the largest area of lands in the US owning over 2 million acres of land, which is accounted for 0.1% of the area of the US. Holding other things constant, a unit of land should have a greater redistributive impact in the relatively more labor-intensive and agriculture-based economy, like Thailand. Therefore, the fact that one family owns this amount of land seems questionable.[62]

Just recently, the CP group-led consortium had just won the contest in bidding for the 220-kilometre high speed inter-airport trains, which had the investment value of over 7.5 billion USD.[63] The outcome came as a surprise to many experts as the CP group had no previous experience in the industry before. Having had a close relationship with the Chinese government, the CP group has played a big part in mediating the relationship between Thailand and China.[64]

The CP group has businesses across different industries *à la* ThaiBev. The CP group owns two important businesses in two sectors. In the telecommunication industry, the CP group has True Corporation with a turnover above 4 billion USD annually, one of the largest telecommunication service providers in Thailand. True Corporation benefited from the executive order right after the election in April, by which all telecommunication operators' debt periods were extended by five years. In the retail and wholesale industry, the CP group has CP All Plc. who operates

[61] Foo (2015).

[62] Lohsakul and Ungsirikul (2018).

[63] EEC (2019).

[64] CP group's main business in China is run under the company called Ping An which is registered in the Hongkong Stock Exchange and Shanghai Stock Exchange. It now has over 200 billion USD market cap.

over 11,000 branches of "7-eleven" convenience store and Siam Makro Plc. who owns over 100 branches of "Makro" wholesale stores. Both brands have over 90% of market shares in the convenience and cash-and-carry stores respectively. Should the acquisition of Tesco stores be given a clearance by the Office of Trade Competition Commission (OTCC), CP Group will be the owner of over a half of the hypermarket market where another half is owned by BCG, a ThaiBev subsidiary. Therefore, a success of the deal will see Thailand's retail industry owned by two families.

All in all, it would be premature to judge the effectiveness of Thailand's competition law no matter what the decision turns out to be, the enforcement of competition law in Thailand still has a long path ahead. Judging how personal data rights could have been compromised, competition law may remain the only hope that Thailand may push back against inequality and its poisonous offsprings.

4.3 Presumption 3 in the Context of Thailand: The Government's Policies Do Not Always Benefit Individuals

Judging from the fact that there have been only 2 competition cases going to court during the period of over 30 years after the previous Competition Act came into effect,[65] it is hard to see any constraint in terms of this expansion, regardless of how it affects end consumers or, more importantly, long-term economic growth. This ineffectiveness of competition law is quite a concern. If we consider the industries in which these firms are mainly operating (e.g., agriculture, alcohol, food, wholesale, and retail), it is hard to see any innovation being introduced. These industries are relatively labor intensive and benefit the most as long as wages remain low. It is reasonable to claim that having the current structure where rent-seeking systems and disparity in wealth are persistent and wages remain relatively low is more desirable to larger corporations in Thailand, due to the nature of their businesses. So far, we have seen no concrete plan or policy to address the issue in a sustainable or structural way. Most policies were short-term oriented and done in the populist manner. For example, "helicopter money," which has been used repeatedly in the past few years, evidence the violation of the presumption 3 discussed earlier. Given that the industries are far from competitive and no proper welfare or redistribution systems are in place, this money will just end up in the pockets of the rich while the poor are forced to be myopic and may end up having more debts, a cycle which has proven burdensome once the crisis hit.

Meanwhile, at the other end of the political spectrum, the average income of the bottom 40% has declined significantly in the past 5 years, according to the World Bank. Thailand's household debt has increased to 79%of its GDP in 2019, the second highest in Asia. The figure was 42.2% in 2003. Non-performing loans have reached 35% of the GDP in 2018, double the figure of 2012. The NPLs also recently have a larger proportion of young adults who just started out their careers. The characteristic

[65]Nikomborirak (2005).

is very prone to a greater level of systematic risks in the economy. TMB Analytics just published a study on consumption behavior of Gen-Y (ages 23–38 years old). Almost 70% of their income is spent on the "must-have," including mobile phone, clothes, cosmetics, electronic devices, bags, and accessories. After spending the remaining on necessary consumption and bills, most Gen-Y's have less than 10% for savings while a big proportion of them have no savings at all. Even worse, the Bank of Thailand's data show that, out of 14.4 million Gen-Y's in Thailand, half of them have bank loans and 20% of these loans have become non-performing loans (NLP).[66] When it comes to the reason why they spend a good part of their income on these must-haves, the top one is to *follow the trend* which accounted for 42%. Given that this group of the population accounted for over 20% of Thailand's population, they are the most active users of social media and Internet in Thailand.[67]

4.4 The Problem Eventually Goes Back to Politics

It has now become a well-recognized concern the influence of data-driven firms on the political freedom of individuals.[68] Yochai Benkler, together with Robert Faris and Hal Roberts, wrote in their work Network Propaganda that "technology is not destiny. Technology interacts with institutions and ideology to shape how we make meaning, how we organize our affairs across economic, political, and personal domains, and how we make our culture and identity."[69] It is evident that, in the past few years, the mechanism of disseminating political beliefs and news, which has a significant role in shaping beliefs and politically actionable knowledge in society, has been particularly influenced by technologies, especially the network-based technologies like social networks. Some people argue that the influence of these mechanisms, including the ones used further by the data-driven political consulting firms, such as the renowned Cambridge Analytica, are totally difficult to measure and one can hardly claim their contribution in shaping the political beliefs of people. However, if we wait until we can, to a certain level of certainty, measure the impact that data-driven technologies such as micro-targeting advertisement has on electoral results or other political aspects, it might be too late to deal with it once the impact looms too large.[70]

Even though the study does not dismiss the positive contribution of the Internet in general and the data-driven tools in particular on democracy or well-being of citizens, it has stated a precautionary situation where "…a politically significant portion of the population does occupy a hyper-partisan, propaganda rich environment," the social

[66] Banchongduang (2019).

[67] Leesa-nguansuk (2019).

[68] Zuboff (2015).

[69] Benkler et al. (2018, p. 381).

[70] Benkler et al. (2018).

situation particularly groomed by crony capitalism and inequality.[71] Not only in Thailand but many developing democracies, oligarchs have aggressively and consistently used propaganda as one of the main tools[72] in the defense of their wealth against the middle and lower classes.[73] On the other hand, the defense of wealth is likely to be empowered by the government whom the oligarchs are able to control or at least negotiate with and one obvious way to guarantee that is to make sure that such government is in position for as long as possible regardless of the measure. When we consider the misalignment of incentives between the government and the citizens and the fact that citizens, especially Thais, have been heavily influenced by the Internet, the fact that micro-targeting techniques can influence voters. These facts raised quite a concern.

Should the situation continue, the problems regarding privacy may come from two sources. On the one hand, governments who rely little on votes or public opinion have relatively little incentive to align their incentives with individuals in the country. On the other hand, firms who need not to compete against each other to win customers find little incentive to treat customers or provide what is best for them. They also have little incentive to treat individuals in such a way that the government may punish them for mistreatment. These two sources of problems may lead to the situation where the lines drawn between public and private interests are being overly pushed towards the private interest side rather than the right balance between them.

5 The Merger Between Personal Data Protection and Competition Laws

Judicial bodies worldwide are still inconclusive when it comes to the inclusion of data protection in competition cases.[74] Such disagreement can be seen from two cases in the EU involving the largest social network, Facebook. In a nutshell, German courts have exhibited a strong position in considering data protection law under the realm of competition case by arguing that a dominant position can be abused through the violation of personal data rights. Meanwhile, the Italian competition authority (AGCM) did not follow the same approach but considered the case of misleading *free* services under the consumer protection law. Some scholars support the idea of having cases involving the interaction between personal data protection and competition laws being considered under the consumer protection law because it is less costly for the authority to enforce as some preliminary analyses such as market definition or market power are not required.[75]

[71] Wade (2006).

[72] Phongpaichit and Baker (2002).

[73] Markus and Charnysh (2017).

[74] Botta and Wiedemann (2019).

[75] Ohlhausen and Okuliar (2015).

From what we have discussed so far, the root of many problems lies in the dynamic of competition and personal data protection law. In other words, only if competition law is enforced effectively and considers data-related, including personal data, issues in its realm, an effective enforcement of personal data rights, let alone personal rights, within the society is hard to materialize.

6 The Necessity of Drawing the Lines

Competition and data protection laws are not only closely related, if not inseparable, in a data-driven world. We have seen that the exponential breakthrough in technological advancement in the past decade has allowed firms to penetrate into the privacy of individuals at an unprecedented level. Apart from that, these two laws also share a crucial similarity in terms of interpretation. The application of both laws need the analysis called *balancing rights*.[76] For example, to consider whether data processing is lawful based on the legitimate interests, the data controller has to prove that her legitimate interests outweigh the adverse impacts on the privacy of data subjects. Similarly, competition law is in principle the balance between incentive and capability, where too much competition puts a disproportionate weight on the former and too little competition does on the latter.[77] Therefore, an attempt to ensure the effectiveness of these laws in the data-driven world is essentially an attempt to *strike a balance between two opposite forces*. These two forces can be private and public interests as in the discussion at the very beginning or any subset of the notions.

Two opposite forces also have different "initial values" across different contexts. In other words, some countries, due to geopolitical and socio-economic reasons, have put more weight on a particular side of the opposite forces, such as private interests. If the initial values have been put too heavily on one side, the line separating between these two opposite forces have to take these initial values into account as well. For instance, in the country where the government is less likely to optimize the benefit of its individuals, it means that the initial value of weight on public interests is relatively higher than that being put on private interests. As a consequence, in the implementation process, the weight should be put more heavily on the private interests and the supporting rationale behind forgoing private interests for the sake of public interests has to be particularly strong. So far, we have discussed the balancing rights in relatively broad sense where private and public interests are two opposite forces. To scope down, we can draw two lines separating between individuals and firms and between individuals and the government. We call these two lines the line separating privacy and utility and the line separating privacy and security. We discuss them below to conclude the chapter, yet to a pose further interesting question specifically on how the lines should be drawn.

[76]Custers and Uršič (2016).

[77]Audretsch et al. (2001).

6.1 The Line Separating Privacy and Utility

The first line is the one separating privacy and utility of data. On the one hand, to preserve absolute privacy, data may never be utilized and have no utility. On the other hand, to ensure the maximum utility, individuals may need to give up their privacy and allow firms to collect all the data they wish. It is clear that neither extreme are preferred and the line should be drawn in between. We argue that a position of this separating line heavily relies on how the benefit of data can be relocated in proportionally to the contribution of parties. In general, the redistribution process is orchestrated by the government, which is particularly important when firms have no or trivial legal presence in the jurisdiction, e.g. multinational enterprises. In the past few years, we have witnessed some recent attempts such as the Digital Services Tax introduced in the European Union and other countries worldwide. However, whenever the relocation process is not performing as it should, privacy should gain more weight as opposed to utility by the degree of concentration. It is debatable that this adjustment of the line separating between two notions is more of hacking at the leaves instead of digging at the roots. To elaborate, one may say that the more efficient solution is to directly target the redistribution system to ensure that the benefits of data usage because, once we prohibit firms from utilizing data because we know that the benefits will not proportionately return to individuals, we start to compromise the benefits that the society as a whole may acquire. However, we have to bear in mind that it is dangerous to care only about efficiency based on total welfare improvement without taking into account the distributional system, especially when the government failure problem exists.[78]

6.2 The Line Separating Privacy and Security

The other line that separates private and public interests is the well-known privacy-security tradeoff. Daniel J. Solove proposed that the right solution to reconcile privacy and security is to place "security programs under oversight, limiting future uses of personal data, and ensuring that the programs are carried out in a balanced and controlled manner."[79] Still, It is hard to draw the line in the situation where the redistribution of benefits will not go back to most people who give up their privacy. This constraint is implicitly implied in Solove's book when he discussed the balance between privacy and security and proposed that it should be strong rules and procedures put in place "to ensure that the government doesn't get out of line."[80] From what we have discussed so far, it turns out that healthy competition might play a crucial part in this tradeoff, let alone other political problems including the rent-seeking and crony-nature of capitalism in a country.

---

[78] Clark and Lee (2008).

[79] Solove (2011).

[80] Solove (2011).

7 Conclusion and Future Research

In conclusion, the data-driven world heavily revolves around these two tradeoffs: the tradeoff between privacy and utility and the tradeoff between privacy and security. This chapter has shown that inequality and the business-government relationship play a crucial part in determining the extent and nature of these tradeoffs. Our mission is to find the *sweet spot* or at least the tuning toolkits by which these opposite forces could be made well-balanced. The tuning toolkits proposed are competition and data-related laws.

Good news is that most developing countries, including Thailand, have laws of these genres enacted already. Bad news is that most of these laws are not yet fully functional or even misused as a discriminatory tool by one party against another. In today's data-driven world, enforcing these laws has become even more complicated. Therefore, this chapter tries to point out how the feedback loop of inequality and market dominance have undermined the effectiveness of both types of law.

The *endogenous* nature of the problem makes it hard to allow the system to unravel itself. Further research should be conducted to address at least two topics. The first topic is to identify factors determining how these laws can be effectively enforced across different contexts. The second topic is the suggestion on how laws and policies should be implemented to make sure that the dysfunctional equilibrium will not persist and the mutual benefit of data is realized among all stakeholders. This chapter has shown that Thailand, among many other developing countries, appears to be an attractive subject to be explored further.

References

Acquisti A, Taylor C, Wagman L (2016) The economics of privacy. J Econ Lit 54(2):442–492
Allcott H, Braghieri L, Eichmeyer S, Gentzkow M (2019) The welfare effects of social media. Working Paper No. 25514. National Bureau of Economic Research. https://www.nber.org/system/files/working_papers/w25514/w25514.pdf. Accessed 15 Dec 2020
Audretsch DB, Baumol WJ, Burke AE (2001) Competition policy in dynamic markets. Int J Ind Organ 19(5):613–634
Banchongduang S (2019) Millennials mired in shopping debts. The Bangkok Post. https://www.bangkokpost.com/business/1802209/millennials-mired-in-shopping-debts. Accessed 15 Dec 2020
Benkler Y, Faris R, Roberts H (2018) Network propaganda: manipulation, disinformation, and radicalization in American politics. Oxford University Press, Oxford
Botta M, Wiedemann K (2019) The interaction of EU competition, consumer, and data protection law in the digital economy: the regulatory dilemma in the Facebook odyssey. Antitrust Bull 64(3):428–446
Cate FH (1994) The EU data protection directive, information privacy, and the public interest. Iowa L Rev 80:431
Chakravorti B (2020) Why it's so hard for users to control their data. https://hbr.org/2020/01/why-companies-make-it-so-hard-for-users-to-control-their-data. Accessed 15 Dec 2020
Chaloupka FJ, Tauras JA, Grossman M (2000) The economics of addiction. In: Jha P, Chaloupka F (eds) Tobacco control in developing countries. Oxford University Press, Oxford, pp 107–129
Choi JP (2010) Tying in two-sided markets with multi-homing. J Ind Econ 58(3):607–626

Christensen S (1991) Thailand after the coup. J Democracy 2(3):94–106
Clark JR, Lee DR (2008) Government transfers and inequality: an anatomy of political failure. Public Finance Manage 8(2):265
Cui W (2019) The superiority of the digital service tax over significant digital presence proposals. https://papers.ssrn.com/sol3/papers.cfm?abstract_id=3427313. Accessed 15 Dec 2020
Custers B, Uršič H (2016) Big data and data reuse: a taxonomy of data reuse for balancing big data benefits and personal data protection. Int Data Priv Law 6(1):4–15
Diker VA, Ünver MB (2017) The right to data portability in the GDPR and EU competition law: odd couple or dynamic duo? Eur J Law Technol 8(1):1–22
Dolnicar S (2002) A review of data-driven market segmentation in tourism. J Travel Tour Mark 12(1):1–22
Doner RF, Ramsay A (1997) Competitive clientelism and economic governance: the case of Thailand. In: Maxfield S, Schneider BR (eds) Business and the state in developing countries. Cornell University Press, Ithaca, pp 237–276
Drahokoupil J, Fabo B (2016) The platform economy and the disruption of the employment relationship. ETUI Policy Brief 5:1–6
Duffy J, Feltovich N (2002) Do actions speak louder than words? an experimental comparison of observation and cheap talk. Games Econ Behav 39(1):1–27
EEC (2019) SRT and CP group signed the PPP agreement to develop the high-speed rail linking three airports project. https://www.eeco.or.th/en/news/signing-ceremony-program-of-public-private-partnership-ppp-agreement-the-high-speed-rail-linking-three-airports-project. Accessed 15 Dec 2020
Esayas S (2019) Data privacy in European merger control: critical analysis of commission decisions regarding privacy as a non-price competition. Eur Compet Law Rev 40(4):166–181
European Commission (2008) Case No Comp/M.4731—Google/Doubleclick. https://ec.europa.eu/competition/mergers/cases/decisions/m4731_20080311_20682_en.pdf. Accessed 15 Dec 2020
European Data Protection Supervisor (2016) Privacy and competitiveness in the age of big data: the interplay between data protection, competition law and consumer protection in the digital economy
Evans DS (2003) The antitrust economics of multi-sided platform markets. Yale J Reg 20:325–381
Evans DS (2011) Platform economics: essays on multi-sided businesses. Competition Policy International. https://papers.ssrn.com/sol3/papers.cfm?abstract_id=1974020. Accessed 15 Dec 2020
Farrell J (2012) Can privacy be just another good? J Telecomm High Tech L 10:251–265
Foo J (2015) Consumer sector: macro headwinds remain. OCBC Securities, 15 December https://research.sginvestors.io/2015/09/consumer-sector-ocbc-securities-2015-09-02-petrafood-thaibev-shengsiong.html. Accessed 15 Dec 2020
Furman J, Stiglitz J (1998) Economic consequences of income inequality. https://www.kc.frb.org/publicat/sympos/1998/s98stiglitz.pdf. Accessed 15 Dec 2020
Gal MS, Aviv O (2020) The competitive effects of the GDPR. J Competition Law Econ. https://ssrn.com/abstract=3548444. Accessed 15 Dec 2020
Gal MS, Rubinfeld DL (2019) Data standardization. N Y U L Rev 94:737–770
Gregg P (1996) It takes two: employment polarisation in the OECD. CEP Discussion Papers No. 304. Centre for Economic Performance, London School of Economics
Haberkorn T (2015) Repression, resistance, and the law in post-coup Thailand. Curr Hist 114(773):241–243
Hayek FA (1945) The road to serfdom. Reader's Digest, New York
Houser KA, Voss WG (2018) GDPR: the end of Google and Facebook or a new paradigm in data privacy? Rich JL Tech 25(1):1–109
Kenney M, Zysman J (2016) The rise of the platform economy. Issues Sci Technol 32(3):61–69
Kerber W (2016) Digital markets, data, and privacy: competition law, consumer law and data protection. J Intell Prop L Pract 11(11):856–866

Krzepicki A, Wright JD, Yun JM (2020) The impulse to condemn the strange: assessing big data in antitrust. Competition Policy International
Langheinrich M (2001) Privacy by design—principles of privacy-aware ubiquitous systems. In: Abowd GD, Brumitt B, Shafer S (eds) International Conference on Ubiquitous Computing 2001: Ubiquitous Computing. Springer, Heidelberg, pp 273–291
Leesa-nguansuk S (2019) Thailand tops global digital rankings. The Bangkok Post. https://www.bangkokpost.com/business/1631402/thailand-tops-global-digital-rankings. Accessed 15 Dec 2020
Lohsakul P, Ungsirikul N (2018) Thailand's top five family-owned businesses: future beyond the decades in Thailand. SPEEDA. https://asia.ub-speeda.com/en/thailands-top-five-family-owned-businesses-future-beyond-decades-thailand/. Accessed 15 Dec 2020
Longo DL, Drazen JM (2016) Data sharing. N Engl J Med 374(3):276–277
Markus S, Charnysh V (2017) The flexible few: oligarchs and wealth defense in developing democracies. Comp Political Stud 50(12):1632–1665
Mata FJ, Fuerst WL, Barney JB (1995) Information technology and sustained competitive advantage: a resource-based analysis. MIS Q 19(4):487–505
Mena J (2003) Investigative data mining for security and criminal detection. Butterworth-Heinemann, Oxford
Mourby M, Mackey E, Elliot M, Gowans H, Wallace SE, Bell J, Smith H, Aidinlis S, Kaye J (2018) Are 'pseudonymised'data always personal data? implications of the GDPR for administrative data research in the UK. Comput Law Secur Rev 34(2):222–233
Newman JM (2015) Antitrust in zero-price markets: foundations. U PA L REV 164:149–206
Nicholas G, Weinberg M (2019) Data portability and platform competition: is user data exported from facebook actually useful to competitors? NYU School of Law. https://www.law.nyu.edu/centers/engelberg/pubs/2019-11-06-Data-Portability-And-Platform-Competition. Accessed 15 Dec 2020
Nikomborirak D (2005) The political economy of competition law: the case of Thailand. Northwest J Int L Bus 26:597–618
OECD (2020) Consumer data rights and competition—background note. https://one.oecd.org/document/DAF/COMP(2020)1/en/pdf. Accessed 15 Dec 2020
Ohlhausen MK, Okuliar AP (2015) Competition, consumer protection, and the right [approach] to privacy. Antitrust L J 80(1):121–156
Pepper R, Gilbert P (2015) Privacy considerations in European merger control: a square peg for a round hole. CPI Antitrust Chronicle, Competition Policy International
Phongpaichit P, Baker C (2002) Power in transition: Thailand in the 1990s. In: Hewison K (ed) Political change in Thailand. Routledge, Oxford, pp 36–56
Phongpaichit P, Baker C (2015) Unequal Thailand: aspects of income, wealth and power. NUS Press, Singapore
Pitruzzella G (2017) Big data and antitrust enforcement. Antitrust Public Policies 4(1):77–86
Posner EA, Weyl EG (2018) Radical markets: uprooting capitalism and democracy for a just society. Princeton University Press, Princeton, NJ
Reuters (2020) Tesco considering Thai bids for Asian assets. The Bangkok Post. https://www.bangkokpost.com/business/1874749/tesco-to-consider-thai-bids-for-asian-assets-on-sunday. Accessed 15 Dec 2020
Robinson N, Graux H, Botterman M, Valeri L (2009) Review of EU data protection directive: summary. https://ico.org.uk/media/about-the-ico/documents/1042349/review-of-eu-dp-directive.pdf. Accessed 15 Dec 2020
Rodwin MA (2010) Patient data: property, privacy & the public interest. Am J Law Med 36(4):586–618
Sakda T (2020) Competition law in Thailand: in transition to an operational law. In: Van Uytsel et al. (eds) Research handbook on Asian competition law. Edward Elgar, Cheltenham, pp 118–133
Šidlauskas A (2019) Video surveillance and the GDPR. Soc Transform Contemp Soc 2019(7):55–65
Solove DJ (2008) Understanding privacy. Harvard University Press, Cambridge, MA

Solove DJ (2011) Nothing to hide: the false tradeoff between privacy and security. Yale University Press, New Haven

Stiglitz JE (2012) The price of inequality: how today's divided society endangers our future. WW Norton & Company, New York

Stucke ME, Grunes AP (2016) Big data and competition policy. Oxford University Press, Oxford

Sullivan B (2019) 33% of Thais have less than 500 Baht on their bank account—banking. https://www.thailand-business-news.com/banking/77384-33-of-thais-have-less-than-500-baht-on-their-bank-account.html. Accessed 15 Dec 2020

Sutter M, Strassmair C (2009) Communication, cooperation and collusion in team tournaments—an experimental study. Games Econ Behav 66(1):506–525

Taylor A (2019) Global protests share themes of economic anger and political hopelessness. The Washington Post. https://www.washingtonpost.com/world/2019/10/25/global-wave-protests-share-themes-economic-anger-political-hopelessness/. Accessed 15 Dec 2020

Tepper J (2018) The myth of capitalism: monopolies and the death of competition. Wiley, Hoboken, NJ

Vock M, Dolen WV, Ruyter KD (2013) Understanding willingness to pay for social network sites. J Serv Res 16(3):311–325

Wade RH (2006) Should we worry about income inequality? Int J Health Serv 36(2):271–294

Zuboff S (2015) Big other: surveillance capitalism and the prospects of an information civilization. J Inf Technol 30(1):75–89

Zucman G (2019) Global wealth inequality. Annu Rev Econ 11:109–138

Ride Hailings Apps Enter in Competition with *Ojek*: Indonesia's Response to the Impact of Disruptive Innovation

Ningrum Natasya Sirait, Mohammad Reza, Angayar Kanni Ramaiah, and Aria Suyudi

Abstract The Indonesian government has long been struggling with transportation. It has been conceded that Indonesia is lagging behind its neighbor ASEAN member states in providing modern mass transportation. Nevertheless, the demand for affordable, available and safe transportation is huge in a country with more than 250 million people. In response to this demand, drivers of motorcycles have gradually stepped up efforts to fill the gap. Being small and flexible, motorcycles proved to be the ultimate mode of transportation compared to cars, buses, or taxis. Motorcycle drivers started to provide, in an informal way, transport to the public. Often these drivers were unemployed people owning a motorcycle that was largely unused during daytime. As this kind of opportunity offered a source of income, this kind of offering transport became a reliable business opportunity for unemployed people. Informally offering transport to consumers is commonly referred to as *Ojek*. *Ojek*, however, is being challenged. Smartphone technology made it possible to start organizing the transportation provided by *Ojek* online. The advantage of moving *Ojek* online: increased consumer choice, security, tariff clarity, etc. One of the forerunners in this field is Go-Jek. As Go-Jek gradually increased its services, to include for example courier, food

N. N. Sirait (✉)
Faculty of Law, Universitas Sumatera Utara, Jalan Abdul Hakim no. 4
Campus USU, Medan, Sumatera Utara 20154, Indonesia
e-mail: ningrum.sirait@gmail.com

M. Reza
Faculty of Law, Universitas al Azhar Indonesia, Jalan Sisingamangaraja no. 2
Kebayoran Baru, Jakarta, DKI Jakarta 12110, Indonesia
e-mail: moh.reza@ymail.com

A. K. Ramaiah
Faculty of Law, University Teknologi MARA (UiTM), Cawangan Pulau
Pinang Permatang Pauh, 135000 Pulau Pinang, Malaysia
e-mail: kanni844@uitm.edu.my

A. Suyudi
Faculty of Law, STIH Indonesia Jentera, Puri Imperium Office Plaza UG 11-12
Jalan Kuningan Madya Kav 5-6, Jakarta, DKI Jakarta 12980, Indonesia
e-mail: aria.suyudi@jentera.ac.id

S. Van Uytsel (ed.), *The Digital Economy and Competition Law in Asia*,
Perspectives in Law, Business and Innovation,
https://doi.org/10.1007/978-981-16-0324-2_5

order, house cleaning and even massage services, the ability to attract consumers to the ride hailing app improved. The fast growing expansion of Go-Jek and the entry of companies offering similar online services has impacted *Ojek*, the conventional motorcycle transportation. The demand for their business declined. Moreover, the conventional taxi services also felt the negative impact of the ride hailing apps. Both identified ride hailing apps as a menace that can destroy the well-established practice of *Ojek* and the business of conventional taxi companies. This chapter details the friction, caused by disruptive innovation in the telecommunication sector, between *Ojek* and the drivers using ride hailing apps. This friction has several dimensions. Socially, the *Ojek* face economic hardship and even unemployment. This is partly due to Internet illiteracy, but also the lack of financial means to afford smartphones needed to make the shift from *Ojek* to an online one. Policy wise, the government has taken an ambiguous stance towards *Ojek*. While holding that *Ojek* does not fit within the category of public transport, the government has taken steps to regulate the use of ride hailing apps used by the conventional taxi business and so discriminate against the motorcycles offering transport. Businesswise, the companies offering ride hailing apps are able to cross-finance between different services and therefore offer promotions on their transportation services that are exclusionary towards *Ojek* and conventional taxi companies.

Keywords Disruptive innovation · Transportation · Ride hailing · *Ojek*

1 Introduction

The history of civilization shows that humans are creatures that always move around to get essential goods for their livelihood. Humans moved from one point to another on foot carrying all their needs. Then, humans tried to tame animals, such as horses, donkeys, and camels, to be used as a mode of transportation. A next step was the motorization of the vehicles that were pulled by the animals. Transportation has been so important for humans that they have always tried to seek better and faster means of transportation. To respond to the transportation needs of everyone, different types of transportation developed. Some people owned vehicles. Other people did not or could not use them. Services developed to offer transportation to the latter category of people. All these different means and types of transportation integrated into a transportation system. It is expected that such transportation system would realize the availability of transportation services in accordance with the level of traffic needs. The system should also be orderly, convenient, efficient and, if possible, low-cost.[1]

The Indonesian government has been long struggling with the organization of an integrated transportation system. Indonesia, with a population of more than 250 million people, has several big cities, such as Jakarta, Surabaya and Medan. These

[1]Muhammad (1998, p. 7).

cities have a dense population. When such a population starts to move, tremendous road congestion could be seen.[2]

It has been conceded that Indonesia is lagging behind its neighbor ASEAN member states in providing modern public transportation. Public transportation is being orgnanized with cars, buses, and taxis. However, this was not sufficient. Motorcycles, even though not able to function as public transportation, were increasingly used to fill a gap in the demand for transportation. As legislation did not follow, the motorcycle transportation business operated in the informal economy.

When smartphones and the ride hailing apps on these smartphones started to challenge the organization of transport, the traditionally organized public transport, mainly taxis, and informal transport, mainly motorcycles, saw their business decline. This caused social unrest, sometimes even leading to physical fights. Regulatory intervention followed, but often unsatisfactory. This chapter will detail the regulatory intervention and how the regulation has been challenged in the court and by the competition authorities.

The chapter is structured as follows. Section 2 introduces the development of transportation offered by motorcycles in Indonesia. The transportation by motorcycles has increasingly been challenged by technological innovation. The impact of this innovation on the transportation by motorcycles is elaborated in Sect. 3. Section 4 highlights the requests to reconsider the conceptualization of the traffic law in the light of constitutional provisions. Arguments have been made that divergent approaches towards different transport modes may deprive some of the actors of their constitutional rights. Around the same time as the constitutional review, the government initiated regulatory reform. The attempts to regulate the innovation and how each of these attempts has failed is subject of Sect. 6. In Sect. 7, the role of the competition authority in this debate is clarified. Section 8 concludes.

2 *Ojek*, a Flexible but Unregulated Mode of Transportation with Motorcycles

Government Regulation No. 74 of 2014 concerning Road Transportation (Regulation 74/2014) defined transportation as the tool to transfer people and/or goods from one place to another using a vehicle.[3] Indonesia has recognized two modes of transportation: private and public transportation. Private transportation refers to a vehicle that operates for the person who owns the vehicle. Public transportation is the service of offering transportation to the general public against a fee.[4] The latter is divided into vehicles that are rented (paratransit) and ordinary public vehicles (transit). Paratransit

[2] Azzuhri et al. (2018, pp. 59–67).

[3] Government Regulation No. 74 Year 2014 on Road Transportation (State Gazette Indonesia year 2014 No. 260 Additional State Gazette Indonesia No. 5594).

[4] Article 1 (10) of Law No. 22 of Year 2009 concerning Traffic and Public Transportation. (State Gazette No. 96 Year 2009 and additional State Gazette No. 5025) (Law 22/2009).

is a mode of transportation in which route and schedule can be changed according to the demands of the passenger.[5] Furthermore, Article 47 (1) of Law No. 22 of Year 2009 concerning Traffic and Public Transportation (Law 22/2009) divides vehicles into motorized and non-motorized vehicles. In Article 47 (2) of Law 22/2009, motorized vehicles are further divided into motorcycles, passenger cars, buses, freight cars and special vehicles. Motorized vehicles, except motorcycles, can be both private or public.

In Indonesia, motorcycles are included in the classification of private motorized vehicles.[6] However, there are many motorcycles that transport goods and/or people for a fee. This type of transportation is known as *Ojek*.[7] The definition of *Ojek*, according to the Indonesian Dictionary, is broader than only motorcycles. It includes motorcycles and vehicle that is rented by a passenger.[8] *Ojek* provides a travel route according to the customer's demand and, in this context, *Ojeks* are actually functioning as paratransit.[9]

Ojeks have been developing since 1969 in rural Central Java. The conditions of village roads make it difficult for cars to pass. Due to this situation, *Ojek* used bicycles to offer transport to the villagers. The strong and sturdy bicycles, produced before World War II, were able to carry both passengers or goods. In Jakarta, *Ojek* developed as new job opportunity for taking people to and from the port of Tanjung Priok. The port area was closed for motorized vehicles, and thus were bicycle *Ojek* the solution for entering the port while carrying goods deposited by passengers.[10] When the citizens of Jakarta began to recognize the convenience of bicycle *Ojeks*, the villagers in Central Java, being innovative, introduced Japanese-made motorcycles with 90 cc engines to operate as *Ojek*.[11] Now motorized *Ojek* is very well-known and familiar to the public. The public accepts the *Ojeks* as part of public transportation in various regions of Indonesia.

Despite the public's opinion of *Ojek* being part of public transportation, no regulation is treating it like that. Bayti's research found that the *Ojek Pangkalan Association* in Surabaya stated that there is no regulation concerning motorcycle transportation

---

[5]Muhammad (1998, p. 86).

[6]Vuchic (1992, p. 79).

[7]The word *Ojek* is derived from the word "object" which is then made into a verb with Javanese accent and so becoming *Ngobjek*. *Ngobjek* is contracted to *NGojek* and eventually reduced to the commonly used *Ojek*. The name *Ojek* itself is different in each Indonesia region, for example in Medan or in North Sumatra Province is known as RBT or *Rakyat Banting Tulang* (People Work Very Hard), a quiet social cynical term to criticize the economic condition. In this article, RBT will further refer to the term *Ojek*.

[8]Ministry of Eduction and Culture Indonesia (2016). Law 22/2009 does not provide a definition of transportation. Article 1 (general provisions) of Law 22/2009 holds that public transportation or public transportation companies are legal entities that provide transportation services for people and/or goods by public motor vehicles.

[9]Vuchic (1992, p. 86).

[10]Available at: https://www.boombastis.com/sejarah-ojek/45601. Accessed 15 December 2020.

[11]Available at: https://historia.id/urban/articles/mengorek-sejarah-ojek-DB9B6. Accessed 15 December 2020.

of people and goods.[12] Hendraru confirmed this view. In his article discussing the history of *Ojek*, he referred to Brigadier General Karamoy, Director of the Police Headquarters Traffic in 1974, who said that the use of motorcycles as a means of transportation was contrary to traffic regulations. The same opinion was conveyed by Ali Sadikin, Governor of Jakarta in that era. Sadikin argued that *Ojek* does not belong to public mass transportation in Jakarta. Jakarta's public mass transportation is only provided by buses, trains, taxis, and mini cars (*bajaj*, *bemo*, and *helicak*).

Even though *Ojek* was considered an infringement on the traffic regulation, neither the police nor the local government acted against them. When it was assessed that the development of *Ojek* was out of control, the police finally held a raid on *Ojek* in 1979. However, it did not have an impact on stopping the operation of *Ojek* transportation service.[13]

Today, *Ojeks* are still seen throughout Indonesia, not least in big cities. *Ojek* remains the ultimate choice for people willing to break through traffic jams in the city or even navigate the steep roads in rural Indonesia. Throughout its existence, though, *Ojek* has been illegal. There is no legal basis, neither from the central nor the local government.[14]

3 Ride Hailing Apps Change the Transportation Scene in Indonesia

A tremendous evolution in the communication technology allowed the commercialization and marketing of a new type of device that could be positioned somewhere between a mobile phone and a computer. As this device, which we now refer to as smartphone, became more popular, new businesses developed. One of the business innovations was a platform to which both owners of a vehicle and people looking for transportation could subscribe. The application aims to connect the owner of the vehicle, who is offering a ride, with customers, who wants to move to another point. The positions of the drivers and the customers are determined by the Global Positioning System. This model, first developed in the United States, got local variations in many countries. In Indonesia, this was Go-Jek.

Go-Jek, originally developed in 2010 as a ride hailing call center for motorcycles in Indonesia, embraced the online ride hailing app in 2015.[15] At present, Go-jek has partnered with around 200,000 motorcycle drivers in almost all regions in Indonesia. The services of Go-Jek, both available on Android and iOS, have expanded as well. Besides the ride hailing app, Go-Jek is offering a variety of services, including house cleaning, running errands, ordering meals, and various fintech services.

---

[12]Bayti (2018).

[13]State History (2014).

[14]Ridwan (2016).

[15]Available at: https://www.gojek.com/about/. Accessed 15 December 2020.

The ride hailing apps do not restrict themselves anymore to motorcycles. Also, cars can be hailed by the ride hailing apps. At present, several ride hailing apps are competing for their share of the market in Indonesia. Besides Go-Jek, Grab and Bluebird have ride hailing apps in the Indonesian market. Uber left the market in 2018 when it merged with Grab.

Ride hailing apps have been developed to improve the quality of human life. The technology facilitates the connectivity between people who need transportation and people offering transportation. The technology allows people to quickly get a vehicle at the exact location where they notified to the driver.[16] The service is more cost effective compared to conventional modes of transportation. Moreover, as there are various types of vehicles, the ride hailing apps can also offer the advantage of the motorcycle *Ojek*. Motorcycles are sometimes much more convenient to reach places. Improved security is another factor motivating people to switch to transport organized by the ride hailing apps.[17]

The just described innovation proved to be a double-edged sword. On one hand, the innovation facilitates transport, saves time, and is cost efficient. On the other hand, the innovation is disrupting the transportation industry.[18] The ride hailing apps erode the long existing businesses with something that is not a real substitute. Khasali exemplifies this by referring to Blue Bird taxi, one of the transportation companies that has dominated the market for many years but that is defeated by cars that are not branded as taxis but operate like taxis. The result? *Ojek* is facing trouble to sustain its existence.

4 The Impact of Ride Hailing Apps on *Ojek* and Beyond

The rollout of the ride hailing apps started to marginalize *Ojek*. *Ojek* used to be active and had almost never free time in between the transportation of two customers. Since the ride hailing apps, the waiting time for customers started to become long for *Ojek*. Even regular *Ojek* customers started to switch to the ride hailing apps to book their transportation. It goes without saying that such a situation has an impact was on the daily income. The presence of ride hailing apps is said to have reduced the income by half. The drivers are the financial backbone of the family. Unpredictable income made them struggle to survive.

For most of the conventional *Ojek,* their driving work is their main job. In general, the drivers do not have any other job experience. Many enjoyed only lower education. This results in limited opportunities to work in other fields. *Ojek* drivers realize that offering transportation by motorcycle is, as a job, the best alternative. Thus, they feel that there is no other way but to survive in the midst of the fierce competition with ride hailing apps, such as the one offered by Go-jek.

[16] Kasemin (2015, p. 10).

[17] Wahyusetyawati (2017).

[18] Malau (2017).

The competition between the *Ojek pangkalan*, or conventional *Ojek*, and ride hailing apps is widely discussed in the media, especially the competition between the informally organized *Ojek* and the information technology-driven Go-jek. The media's focus is on social but also physical conflicts. The latter often result from the conventional *Ojek* trying to maintain their working area - commonly called base. The drivers using the ride hailing apps often wait around the same area as the conventional *Ojek* for orders of customers. This situation has often ended in the destruction of conventional *Ojek* base facilities, and so reducing the opportunity for a job for the conventional *Ojek*.

Of course, the social unrest is fed by the switch of the public to use the ride hailing apps. There are several reasons for this switch. The rates offered are nominal, without the need for bargaining as is commonly done with conventional *Ojek*. Ride hailing apps also allow promos. The price discount could be as much as the whole amount, thus the customer not paying anything at all. Another incentive to use a ride hailing app is security, because the customer knows the identity of the driver and has certainty about the route traveled.

Because of the social unrest and the popularity of the ride hailing apps, companies working with the ride hailing apps posted job openings in various cities. There were opportunities for everyone to get a new job. The offer was also addressed to conventional *Ojek* drivers. Their response was mainly negative. Many conventional *Ojek* drivers refuse to join, and become a kind of online *Ojek*. Some of the reasons to refuse the switch include the inability to own and operate a smartphone. Further, it is burdensome and difficult to become an online *Ojek*. The requirements for an online *Ojek* driver include having a motorcycle that is technically checked, an up-to-date smartphone, a registration, and work equipment such as helmets, jackets, masks, and rain coats. All of these requirements are perceived as a burden because it is unnecessary to become a conventional *Ojek* driver.

The reality is thus not directly reflecting the opinion that the presence of ride hailing apps and the ride hailing apps providing companies are able to absorb a high workforce and so reduce unemployment in Indonesia. The Director of the Institute for Development of Economics and Finance, Enny Sri Hartati, indicated that, based on the data released by AlphaBeta in 2017, about 43% of the total 5000 partners joining the companies using the ride hailing apps were previously unemployed. There is further an argument that the digital technology will be necessary for the economy, especially in cities. This technology will encourage an increase in economic activity. Enny argues that "[a]ccording to the economic outlook, surely, innovation will increase direct increase of labor and create economic efficiency which later may increase national productivity."[19] In line with this, the Indonesian Ministry of Communication and Information has been targeting a contribution of the digital

[19]INDEF (research institute) stated that 43 percent Ojek driver are unemployed. See Ningrum (2017).

economy to gross domestic product (GDP) in 2020 of 11%. The increasing number of unicorn companies,[20] such as Go-Jek, had to contribute to this target.[21]

Despite the vision of the government, it turned out that ride hailing apps were only able to provide jobs for those that had the ability to operate smartphones. This is not the case for most conventional *Ojek* drivers. The social imbalance so arising between the conventional *Ojek* and the online *Ojek*, resulting in loss of livelihoods of conventional *Ojek*, can probably only be restored through a legal umbrella for business people in the field of motor cycle based transportation.

5 The Traffic and Road Transportation Law Under Constitutional Court Review

One way to force the government to establish a legal umbrella for the transportation services, the Law 22/2009 was taken to the Constitutional Court for a review in context of the 1945 Constitution of the Republic of Indonesia (1945 Constitution). A constitutional review was asked twice. The Constitutional Court rendered the following decisions: Decision Number 97/PUU-XV/2017 dating May 31, 2018[22] and Decision Number 41/PUU-XVI/2018 dating June 28, 2018.[23]

The decision 97/PUU-XV/2017 of the Constitutional Court concerns a petition of online transportation drivers from Grab and Go-Jek for a constitutionality review of Article 151 (a) of Law 22/2009[24] with Article 27 (2) and Article 28D (1) of the 1945 Constitution. Both constitutional provisions relate to the right to work, earn livelihood and receive appropriate remuneration for work. The petitioners argued that these constitutional rights were impaired by Article 151(a) of Law 22/2009, which application advocated for public transport on non-designated routes to occur by taxis. The petitioners held that this would exclude the use of the ride hailing apps or other online taxis from being a legitimate means of taxi transportation and thus infringe the constitutional rights. Therefore, the petitioners claimed that Article 151 (a) should have the phrase "technology-based taxis or online taxis" added next to the current word "taxis."

The Constitutional Court rejected the claim. One reason is that a lack of regulation does not render a norm unconstitutional. It is not the role of the Constitutional

---

[20]Privately held startups valued over 1 billion US dollar.

[21]Tempo Daily Newspaper (2019).

[22]Constitutional Court No. 97/PUU-XV/2017 on the judicial review of the Law. No. 22 Year 2009 Article 151 (a) on the Traffic and Public Transportation Toward Indonesian Constitution 1945, dated 31 May 2018.

[23]Constitutional Court Decision No. 41/PUU-XVI/2018 on the judicial review of the Law. No. 22 Year 2009 Article 47(3) on the Traffic and Public Transportation Toward Indonesian Constitution 1945, dated on 28 June 2018.

[24]Article 151(a) of Law 22/2009 ("People transportation services with public motor vehicle which are not included in designated routes as stated in Article 140(b), are: a. People transportation by Taxi").

Court to fill a gap in legislation. The formulation of the norm in Article 151 (a) of Law 22/2009 does not cause legal uncertainty either. The Constitutional Court is of the opinion that the purpose of Article 151(a) of Law 22/2009 is clearly the transportation of people using taxis as public transportation. Such a stipulation should also not be interpreted to prevent anyone from working or doing business in the public transport sector. Moreover, the existence of Article 151(a) of Law 22/2009 does not cause the vulnerability to the work of the information technology-based application taxis. Technology-based applications are not something that indicate the type of transportation. Rather, they are a means of customers to obtain access to the transportation services. As a means to obtain transportation services, it can hardly be argued that separate regulation is required. Today's reality shows that the transportation of people using conventional taxis, as referred to in Article 151(a) of Law 22/2009, has also applied and used technology-based applications.

The Decision 41/PUU-XVI/2018 of the Constitutional Court is a petition, again from online transportation drivers (Go-Jek) for constitutionality review of Article 47(3) of Law 22/2009 under Article 28(D)(1) of the 1945 Constitution. The constitutional provision aims for people being recognized and protected by the law, and thus to provide equal treatment. The petitioners contend that this is not the case because Article 47(3) of Law 22/2009 holds that only cars, buses, and cargo cars can be categorizes as either private motorized vehicles or public motorized vehicles. This article does not allow motorcycles to be categorized as either private or public motorized vehicles. Therefore, the provision is said to organize difference in the treatment or discrimination based on the type of transportation. Motorcycles are excluded to get a fair recognition, guarantee, protection, and legal certainty when the motorcycle drivers transport people along a non-designated route. It does not matter whether, for example, the motorcycle driver uses a ride hailing app or not. This stands in contract to the cars, busses and cargo cars, which can act as public motorized vehicles, and in this capacity, they are protected by the Ministry of Transportation Regulation No. PM 108 of 2017 concerning the Implementation of Transportation of People with Public Motor Vehicles on Non-Designated Routes. This is even so when they are using ride hailing apps to offer transportation on non-designated routes.

The Constitutional Court rejected the petition. The Constitutional Court is of the opinion that Article 47(3) of Law 22/2009 is a legal norm aiming at social engineering. The norm is aiming at guaranteeing that citizens use transportation that prioritizes security and safety. This applies to both private and public motorized vehicles. Since there is no distinction in terms of security and safety, Article 47(3) of Law 22/2009 is not contravening the constitutional provisions. The Constitutional Court also stated that it does not reject the fact that there is a motorcycle taxi phenomenon. The existence of such a phenomenon has nothing to do with the (un)constitutionality of Article 47(3) of Law 22/2009. The fact is that when an online application that provides motorcycle services does not yet exist or is available as it is today, motorcycle taxis, such as *Ojek*, continue to run their business on their own way. Article 47(3) of Law 22/2009 does not prevent the petitioners from obtaining decent work and livelihoods. In fact, *Ojek*, even without ride hailing apps, continue to run even though Article 47(3) 22/2009 does not have a specific regulation to cover that kind of transportation.

Moreover, the Constitutional Court explains what is meant by different treatment. Different treatment is when treating different things for the same thing or treating the same for different things. In the current context, security and safety issues for motorcycle vehicles transporting people and goods is different than for public motor vehicles. Therefore, the Constitutional Court cannot but hold that different things require different treatment. If not, the Constitutional Court would be violating the 1945 Constitution.

The constitutional review did not impose a duty to act on the legislator. The conceptualization of public transport and the existence of the informal *Ojek* practice were not affected, neither in the negative nor in the positive sense.

6 The Difficult Birth of Regulatory Approaches Towards Ride Hailing Apps in Indonesia

6.1 Ride Hailing Apps, but also Ojek, Declared Illegal

The ride hailing app business has been contested in Indonesia. The dispute stems from the allegations that their presence is illegal. Just like with *Ojek*, the operation of the ride hailing apps does not satisfy the rules of the public transportation administration. The drivers using ride hailing apps are not organized under a legal personality. Neither do these drivers have a have a public transportation business permit. As a consequence, it is no possibility to conduct due diligence on these drivers.[25] Also, the drivers have no obligation to pay taxes as their services are located in the informal economy. Therefore, the price setting of the ride hailing apps can be lower than the conventional public transport.

The advantages of the ride hailing apps caused the conventional transportation market to collapse. The dramatic decline in market share resulted in strong resistance from the *Ojek* and conventional public transport firms, especially the dominant taxi companies.[26] Over time, the presence of ride hailing apps caused social jealousy. They have been blamed as the culprit of the declining income of the *Ojek* and conventional public transport drivers. There were large-scale demonstrations against the presence of drivers using ride hailing apps from companies like Go-Jek,[27] Uber, and Grab.[28]

The government tried to respond to this situation. At first, the Ministry of Transportation (MOT) started to count the number of taxis registered on the ride hailing apps of Grab Car and Go Car. The number registered on these ride hailing apps totaled 91,953 vehicles, this in 14 Provinces. The largest quota was in the Greater

---

[25] Safitri (2019).

[26] Safitri (2019).

[27] Gojek's history, available at: https://www.go-jek.com/about/. Accessed 15 December 2020.

[28] Wahyusetyawati (2017).

Jakarta area, where 36,510 vehicles were registered.[29] Confronted with the numbers, the MOT issued Letter Number UM.302/1/21/Phb/2015 on November 9, 2015 prohibiting the operation of *Ojek*, Uber taxis, and other services offered through ride hailing apps.[30] The reason? All of them do not meet the requirements of Law 22/2009 and Regulation PP 74/2014.

Ojek and businesses operated by ride hailing apps are considered to violate Article 138 (3), 139(4) and 173(1) of Law 22/2009. Article 138(3) of Law 22/2009 regulates that public transportation of people and/or goods should be carried out only by public motorized vehicles. Private motorized vehicles, that can be identified by a black registration plate, cannot be used for public transportation. Article 139(4) of Law 22/2009 stipulates that the provision of public transportation services should be is carried out by state-owned enterprises, regionally-owned enterprises, and/or other legal entities in accordance with statutory provisions. Furthermore, Article 173(1) of Law 22/2009 states that public transport companies are required to have a permit to operate transportation.

The public reacted strongly against the ban. The public believed that the ride hailing apps assisted their daily lives.[31]

6.2 The Supreme Court Forces the Government to Reconsider Its Regulatory Attempts

In a response to the public reaction, the MOT issued a Ministerial Regulation, called *Peraturan Menteri Perhubungan/Permenhub* No. 32 of 2016 concerning the Implementation of Transportation of People with Public Motor Vehicles along a Non-Designated Route (*Permenhub* 32/2016).[32] This regulation provides a more transparent legal umbrella to regulate the categories of taxi, rental transportation, charter, and online transportation services (which include the ride hailing apps).[33] *Permenhub* 32/2016 was replaced with the Ministry of Transportation Regulation No. 26

[29] Available at: https://www.cnbcindonesia.com/news/20190606082835-4-76928/mau-jadi-driver-taksi-online-maaf-jumlahnya-dibatasi. Accessed 15 December 2020.

[30] Putra (2015).

[31] Jumat (2015).

[32] Ministry of Transportation Regulation No. 32 Year 2016 on the Implementation of Public Transportation with Public Motorcycle for Non-Designated Routes (State Gazette Indonesia Year 2016 No. 494).

[33] Available at: http://dephub.go.id/post/read/permenhub-32-tahun-2016-payung-hukum-taxi-aplikasi-yang-transparan. Accessed 15 December 2020 (in Indonesian).

of 2017 concerning the Implementation of Transportation of People with Motorized Vehicles along Non-Designated Routes (*Permenhub* 26/2017).[34] The Permenhub 26/2017 explicitly recognized that the reservations could be done through information technology-based applications, here referred to as ride hailing apps.

The *Permenhub* 26/2017 regulates the special rented-transport of public motor vehicles, thus not motorcycles. Among the changes that introduced by this regulation are the recognition that information technology based-transportation, or in short ride hailing apps, can be a special form of rental transportation as of April 1, 2017. Many other requirements are formulated, some with different implementation deadlines as others and this to allow for the companies to adjust to the new regulatory scheme. To operate as a ride hailing app provide, a legal entity under Indonesian law needs to be established and this entity needs to comply with the laws of Indonesia, among which the tax law seems to be one of the most important. For the pricing, these providers have to follow minimum and maximum tariffs. If the ride hailing provider wants to operate as a public transport company, a Public Transportation Services Operation License is required or cooperation with a company that has such a license. The latter license demands that the company has 1) at least 5 public vehicles with a minimum required cylinder capacity of 1,000 cc and that have a Vehicle Registration Certificate; 2) a vehicle storage area; 3) ownership of or cooperation with workshops that can maintain the vehicles. It is further required to have 1) periodic roadworthy testing of the vehicles, and 2) special stickers on the vehicles using the ride hailing apps. The government must also be given access to the a digital dashboard, which allows the government to check, among others, (1) the details of the ride hailing app providers used, (2) the data of all public transportation companies cooperated with, the data of all vehicles and drivers, (3) the tariffs and vehicle movement, and (4) the consumer complaints.[35]

The *Permenhub* 26/2017 was reviewed by the Supreme Court at the request of drivers using ride hailing apps. The Supreme Court discussed several elements regarding the presence of ride hailing apps in its Decision Number 37P/HUM/2017 of June 20, 2017 (Decision MA 37P/HUM/2017), among which the following[36]:

a. Special rental services based on ride hailing apps are a logical consequence of the development of information technology in the transportation sector to offer better services, guarantee travel security, and apply relatively cheap and timely prices;
b. The facts show that the recognition of ride hailing apps as a special rental services resulted in changing the market from a monopoly to competitive one. The technological advantages of ride hailing apps incentivized micro and small

---

[34]Ministry of Transportation Regulation No. 26 Year 2017 on the Implementation of People Transportation with Public Motor Vehicles for Non-Designated Routes (State Gazette 2016 No. 494), Article 71.

[35]Available at: http://dephub.go.id/post/read/pm-26-tahun-2017-tentang-revisi-aturan-angkutan-sewa-online-diberlakukan-dengan-masa-transisi. Accessed 15 December 2020 (in Indonesian).

[36]Available at: http://dephub.go.id/post/read/pm-26-tahun-2017-tentang-revisi-aturan-angkutan-sewa-online-diberlakukan-dengan-masa-transisi. Accessed 15 December 2020 (in Indonesian).

business communities to partner with these app providers and this to share mutually economic benefits and this without neglecting the principle of affiliation or kinship as mandated by Article 33 (1) of the 1945 Constitution of the Republic of Indonesia;

c. The preparation of regulations for information technology-based transportation should be based on the principle of consensus. It should involve all stakeholders in the field of the transportation services so that they can jointly develop micro, small and medium-sized businesses, without leaving the principle of affiliation or kinship acid.

The Supreme Court stated that there are 14 articles in *Permenhub* 26/2017 that contradict two higher laws and regulations,[37] namely Law Number 20 of 2008 concerning Micro, Small and Medium Enterprises (Law 20/2008)[38] and Law 22/2009 on Road Traffic and Transportation. Being contrary to higher statutory regulations, these 14 articles were annulled and declared to have no binding legal force.[39]

The Supreme Court ruling that online application-based transportation to run their operational again. The decision may trigger a return of unrest between conventional transport and online application-based transportation. The legal reasoning of Supreme Court Decision 37P/HUM/2017 was based on the consideration that the entry of online transportation is the consequence of technology development and able to change the market to be more competitive. Sharing economy provides better partnership with micro and small medium business. The Supreme Court considered that the Ministry of Transportation Regulation is contrary to several laws such as: Law No. 20/2008 on Micro, Small Medium Business and Law No. 22/2009 on Traffic and Road Transportation and put heavy burden on the online transportation drivers to bear operational cost. In fact, sharing economy change the idle asset to become productive assets. To end the judicial review, Ministry of Transportation revoked the 14 articles annulled by the Supreme Court.[40]

[37] Supreme Court Decision 37P/HUM/2017. The second consideration of Decision declares that Article 5(1)(e), Article 19(2)(f) and (3)(e), Article 20, Article 21, Article 27(a), Article 30(b), Article 35(9)(a)(2) and (10)(a)(3), Article 36(4)(c), Article 37(4)(c), Article 38(9)(a)(2) and (10)(a)(3), Article 43(3)(b)(1sub b), Article 44(10)(a)(2) and (11)(a)(2), Article 51(3), and Article 66(4) Regulation of the Ministry of Transportation of the Republic of Indonesia Number PM. 26 of 2017 concerning the Implementation of Transportation of People with Public Motor Vehicles not in Route contrary to the higher laws and regulations, namely: Law Number 20 of 2008 concerning Micro Business, Small and Medium Enterprises; and Law Number 22 Year 2009 concerning Road Traffic and Transportation.

[38] Law No. 20 Year 2008 on Micro, Small Medium Entrepreneurship (State Gazette No. 93 Year 2008 and additional State Gazette No. 4866).

[39] Supreme Court Decision 37P/HUM/2017. The third consideration of the decision stated that Article 5(1)(E), Article 19(2)(F) and (3)(E), Article 20, Article 21, Article 27(A), Article 30(B), Article 35(9)(A)(2) and (10) (A) (3), Article 43(3)(B)(1 sub B), Article 44(10)(A)(2) and (11)(A)(2), Article 51(3), and Article 66(4) Ministry of Transportation Regulation No. 26 Year 2017 on the Implementation of Public Transportation with Public Motorcycle for Non-Designated Routes will have no binding power anymore.

[40] Supreme Court Decision 37P/HUM/2017. The fourth consideration of the decision ordered the government, in specific the Ministry of Transportation to decline application of Article 5(1)(E),

Because having no legal umbrella was not an option, the MOT, in a response to the considerations of Decision 37P/HUM/2017, issued Ministerial Regulation No. 108 of 2017 concerning Transportation Services for Non-Designated Routes (Regulation 108/2017). Many of the provisions of *Permenhub* 26/2017 were repeated in Regulation 108/2017. After repeating that a legal entity must be established, the Regulation 108/2017 required a license to run a taxi service. In order to be active online, through ride hailing apps, the Regulation 108/2017 imposed that at least five cars must be used as taxi, that the cars have a certificate motor vehicle number in name of the legal entity, that motor vehicle tests are regularly passed, that a car storage is available, that there is a workplace for car maintenance, that drivers have a driver licence, that prices were within the scope determined. Ride hailing app providers could not organize public taxi services, unless they comply with these requirements. Otherwise, they could only offer their service to recognized public taxi companies. Equally, individual drivers could only operate as taxi if they act within the legal entity scheme. The tight restrictions on ride hailing app providers made them in reality conventional taxi companies but using a ride hailing app to adMinistry the reservations.

The Supreme Court also annulled Regulation 108/2017 for similar reasons as it annulled *Permenhub* 26/2017. The MOT responded with yet another regulation: Regulation Number 118 of 2018 on the Provision of Special For-Hire Transportation Services (Regulation 118/2018). Unlike the previous regulations, Regulation 118/2018 specifically applies to information technology-based ride hailing services and neither to motorcycle based ride hailing services nor to conventional taxi companies. Regulation 118/2018 makes a distinction between ride hailing providers, i.e. drivers of a car, and an app provider. For the first time, it is allowed that the ride hailing providers do not incorporate, thus opening business operations for micro and small businesses. Besides setting out the requirements for a licence and the operating area, Regulation 118/2018 still upholds minimum and maximum tariffs. It is to be seen whether the latter is a ground to go to court, just like in the previous regulations.

In a country where there are many micro and small businesses, this regulation is expected to encourage the growth of the national economy based on a just economic democracy. Micro and small businesses are empowered by providing them legal certainty on aspects of safety, security, comfort, equality, affordability, and order. At the same time, the regulation is an effort to respond to people's demand for good public transportation services, safety protection, and, altogether, law enforcement.[41] Motorcycle *Ojek* have been kept outside the regulation. *Ojek* operating with a car have been given a first recognition.

Article 19(2)(F) and (3)(E), Article 20, Article 21, Article 27(A), Article 30(B), Article 35(9)(A)(2) and (10)(A)(3), Article 36(4)(C), Article 37(4)(C), Article 38(9)(A)(2) and (10)(A)(3), Article 43(3)(B)(1 sub B), Article 44(10)(A)(2) and (11)(A)(2), Article 51(3), and Article 66(4) Ministry of Transportation Regulation No. PM 26 Year 2017 on the People Transportation with Public Motor on Non-Designated Routes.

[41]Supreme Court Decision 37P/HUM/2017.

7 *Ojek*, Ride Hailing Apps and Competition Law

Government competition policy must determine whether it supports competition in the market by taking into account developments in a specific industry. Fair competition could be reached in two ways.[42] First, the government could set policies encouraging competition in the market by removing barriers to entry or reducing government intervention. Second, the government could pursue the enforcement of Law No. 5 Tahun 1999 on the Prohibition of Monopolistic Practices and Unfair Business Competition (Law 5/1999) by the Commission for the Supervision of Business Competition (KPPU). When emphasis is put on policy, it is more than just making rules or laws.[43] Competition policies need to ensure the objectives of market regulation in order to compete fairly.[44]

7.1 Competition Advice on Legislation Related to Transport Services

Indonesia's economic system is based on Article 33(1) of the 1945 Constitution, which stipulates that "the economy shall be organized as a common endeavor based upon the principle of a family system." After the fourth amendment of the 1945 Constitution, Article 33(4) stipulates that "the national economy shall be organized based on economic democracy with the principles of solidarity, efficiency along with fairness, sustainability, keeping the environment in perspective, self-sufficiency, as well as based on maintaining balanced progress and the unity of the national economy." The principle of kinship, affiliation, or family system has developed and shaped the business atmosphere to be less competitive. This can be especially noticed in the traditional way of doing business. In light of the foregoing, the controversy between conventional *Ojek* and online *Ojek* can not approached simply by citing one or the other law or regulation. The conflict needs to be put into a bigger policy framework.

One possible response to the controversy surrounding conventional and online *Ojek* is to revert to Law 5/1999. The law envisions the enforcement of the rule of law and the guarantee of equal protection for every business actor in an effort to create a fair business competition. Law 5/1999, in Article 2 and Article 3, states that the objective of business competition policy in Indonesia is to guarantee the public interest, improve national economic efficiency, improve people's welfare, create a conducive business climate through the regulation of fair business competition so as to ensure

[42]World Bank Group and OECD (2017, p. 5).

[43]Eleanor Fox (1999) Memorandum to the Indonesian Policy Makers, Unpublished: 'there is a distinction between "policy and the "law". In a general sense, policy is the set of goals and objectives one formulates to deal with particular matters, and laws are instruments used to carry out policy. Governments, of course, can take policy actions beyond enacting laws.

[44]World Bank Group and OECD (2017).

equal business opportunities for large, small and medium business actors, preventing monopolistic practices and unfair business competition caused by business actors and the creation of effectiveness and efficiency in business activities.[45]

To achieve the above goals, the Law 5/1999 is enforced by the KPPU. Among the broad scope of enforcement powers, the KPPU has the competence to overlook and analyze anti-competitive conduct, including the ones that are part of the government policy. Based on the provisions of Article 35 (e) of Law 5/1999, KPPU is given the task of providing advice and considerations on government policies. KPPU can play a role in providing input through policy papers on government policies without having to directly make this dispute a case of unfair business competition.[46] The other role of the KPPU lies in providing tools for checking draft legislations, draft regulations, draft policies for the economic sector and this against the substance of Law No. 5/1999. The tool to check the government regulation and policy is provided by KPPU Regulation No. 4 of 2016 concerning Guidelines for the Use of the Checklist of Competition (Regulation 4/2016). To evaluate whether a government regulation or a policy is hindering innovation, Regulation 4/2016 roughly looks at the ability of the regulation or policy to limit the number of companies, what the companies can do, or the capacity of the companies. Another element that will be evaluated is the potential reduction of the incentive to compete or of the choice for the consumers.

One example of the above task of the KPPU is the recommendation that Syarkawai Rauf, then head of the KPPU, gave in relation to *Permenhub* 32/2016. *Permenhub* 32/2016 created an environment in which the transportation with the ride hailing apps would be restricted. The restrictions are not imposed by competitors, but by the legislative initiative of the MOT. Three recommendations were formulated. First, KPPU was not satisfied with setting a lower level on the transportation tariff than the one applicable to conventional taxis. The recommendation is thus to either lower the base tariff for conventional taxis or to increase the one for online taxis. Second, imposing a minimum number of vehicles is, according to the KPPU, also too restrictive. The recommendation is not to set a number for vehicles, neither for the conventional taxis nor for the online taxis. Third, KPPU also recommended to abolish the requirement of having vehicle number certificates on behalf of the legal entity for online taxis.

The above recommendations relate to market access. Regulation 118/2018 is the first regulation that has responded to some of the concerns of the KPPU. However, it should be noted that the KPPU's recommendations only applied to the legislation concerning the use of cars as conventional and online taxis. The unequal status of the motorcycles, thus the conventional and online *Ojek*, is not addressed by these recommendations. If the indeed relates to the security and safety, the KPPU may not consider itself the appropriate agency to advice the government on appropriate legislation.

---

[45]Law No. 5 Year 1999 on prohibition of Antimonopoly and Unfair Business Practices, Section II on Principles and Objectives of Article 2 and Article 3 (Law 5/1999).

[46]Law 5/1999, Article 35.

7.2 *Enforcement of the Competition Law*

The second task of the KPPU is to enforce Law 5/1999. The question is to what extent Law 5/1999 can be applied to the technological innovations that are changing the structure of the conventional transportation industry.[47] Disruption has been felt among taxi companies and, especially, *Ojek*. Normal cars, not registered as taxi, could now be ordered and paid through ride hailing apps, and so creating competition for taxis. *Ojek*, already operating outside the scope of the law, saw a part of their business being taken by motorcycle drivers who could operate ride hailing apps. It is not because the technology has been disruptive, that competition law can be applied. For that, several other issues need to be addressed.

Competition law can only be applied when there is an anti-competitive conduct originating from the market participants. At present, there are a few complaints floating around in the literature. One relates price fixing, the other one to predatory pricing. The former requires an answer to whether the drivers using ride hailing apps are independent undertakings or employees from the ride hailing firms. The latter demands an analysis of the market to determine whether the company implementing the predatory pricing had the power to do so.

The KPPU has not taken an investigation into the issue of whether the drivers using ride hailing apps are independent undertakings or employees. Guidance could be found in the European Union (EU). The Court of Justice decided in the Poucet et Pistre case that Uber is not a digital application company but a transportation providing company. The consequence is that drivers cannot be considered as undertakings independent from Uber, but rather employees. Employees cannot be held liable for fixing prices.[48] Indonesia may consider the decision of the EU Court, but cannot deny the various indigenous regulations and agencies related to road traffic, including: Ministry of Public Works Regulation Number 01/PRT/M/2012 concerning Guidelines The Role of the Community in Operating the Road,[49] Law 22/2009 (police for traffic control),[50] Regulation 118/2018, the agency in charge for the registration and identification of motorized vehicles, tax agency on motorized vehicles, Law Number 64 of 1963 concerning Compulsory Contribution of Traffic Accidents Fund System, and Presidential Regulation No. 5 of 2015 concerning the Administration of the One-Stop Motor Vehicle Administration System.[51] Policies need to be harmonized well in order to be effectively implemented and generate legal certainty. A first indication may, however, be drawn from Regulation 118/2018. This regulation differentiates two actors, each of them with their own duties and obligations: 1) the ride hailing provider and 2) the application provider. Besides, if price fixing were

[47]Rusydi (2017).

[48]Rizqa (2017).

[49]Ministry Regulation of Public Labour Number 01/PRT/M/2012, concerning Guidelines for Community Roles in Road Operation (State Gazette No. 72 Year 2012).

[50]Law 22/2009, Article 260.

[51]Presidential Regulation No. 5 Year 2015, on the Implementation Administration System on Online Single Submission (State Gazette 2015 No. 6).

to be proven, it most likely has to be between the minimum and maximum tariff imposed by the relevant regulation.

Equally, KPPU has not yet made an investigation on the relevant market. Despite the existing guidelines on the definition of relevant market,[52] KPPU will have to take consider various elements. First, Law 22/2009 has strict requirements for public transport permits. Based on Article 173(1) of Law 22/2009, application providers cannot be categorized as a public transport provider company because it does not have a permit: a) for carrying out transportation of people on designated routes; b) for conducting transportation of people on nondesignated routes; or c) for the operation of special goods or heavy equipment transportation. Information technology-based transportation can be performed by recognized public transport companies, but it is not required. Second, ride hailing providers, i.e. the ones driving a car, and application providers have been considered as separate actors in Regulation 118/2018. Separate obligations are imposed on the ride hailing providers compared to application providers. Third, unlike in previous MOT regulations, the ride hailing services are separated from the motorcycle ride hailing-based services and other for-hire transportation services, such as taxis. Fourth, besides the official public transportation companies, *Ojek* is offering transportation on non-designated routes. Also *Ojek* is now divided between the conventionally operated *Ojek* and *Ojek* seeking to offer services online through ride hailing apps. If a relevant market can be defined and a company with market power identified, the finding of predatory pricing will also mean an infringement of the then applicable regulation upholding the minimum tariffs.

Once a relevant market has been defined, an infringement needs to be identified. One of the alleged infringements was predatory pricing. Predatory pricing is prohibited by Article 20 of Law 5/1999, and requires the following elements to be present: (1) supply of goods or services, (2) without profit or a very low price, (3) with the intention to eliminate or end the competitor's business. Even though promotion actions, the court has cleared Go-jek from committing the infringement of predatory pricing. Equally, it has not been proven that Go-jek used its market power to induce suppliers to sell goods and services at lower than normal market prices. If it were proven, the practice of squeezing suppliers could have also explained the lowe prices of the drivers using the ride hailing apps.

Is any of this helpful for *Ojek*? Yes, and no. *Ojek* would benefit from a successful competition law case against the ride hailing app providers for low price setting. Such a conviction would drive up the prices offered through the ride hailing apps and thus benefit the conventional *Ojek*. However, a competition law case does not affect the status of conventional *Ojek*. They will still be operating in the informal economy, without any kind of protection that is offered to other public transportation service providers. Of course, protection, as we have indicated above, comes with requirements. These requirements are often a hurdle for *Ojek* to take the step from the informal to the formal economy.

---

[52]Commission Regulation No. 3 Year 2009, Guidelines Article 1 (10) on the Relevant Market Definition.

8 Conclusion and Recommendation

Technological innovations have an impact on the lives of consumers. The once very popular mode of transport in Indonesia, *Ojek*, has been challenged by technological innovation. *Ojek*, a mode of transport organized outside of the law by owners of a motorcycle, feel an increasing competition of mainly motorcycles and cars of which the owners started to use ride hailing apps for attracting customers. For various reasons, customers found the ride hailing apps attractive, negatively impacting the worklife of *Ojek* and other conventional public transport. Constitutional review of the law regulating public transport has not made the position of *Ojek* any better. In response, the government should immediately re-consider existing legislation comprehensively to create fair and equal competition between conventional *Ojek* and other public transport and the service provided by ride hailing apps.

The government, however, did initially nothing, except declaring that *Ojek* and ride hailing apps are not in compliance with the law and should be forbidden. Reactions from the public and the ride hailing apps providers made the government reconsider its position. Not more than four regulations followed to recognize the presence of the ride hailing apps. The first three regulations were annulled by the Supreme Court for reasons, among others, that micro and small businesses were not given appropriate opportunities. The latter is explicitly considered in the last regulation. However, the regulation applies to every motorized vehicle on the road except motorcycles. Hence, motorcycle *Ojek* was left outside the scope of regulation.

The KPPU, as the authority to safeguard fair competition, is another agency that could consider what is going on in the transportation sector. The KPPU has two ways to intervene. On the one hand, the KPPU has the authority to provide advice and considerations to government regulation and policies. On the other hand, the KPPU is the authority to enforce the competition law. The former requires from KPPU to examine the substance of regulations and policies on their appropriateness in the light of the principle of fair business competition. The advice given so far is to make market entrance as easy as possible. The latter demands the KPPU to investigate whether there is an infringement of the competition law. Up until now, no infringement has been found. Hence, innovation should be considered as the initiator of low price setting.

All of this shows that the government, and more in specific the legislator, has not yet reacted appropriately towards the problems created by ride hailing apps for *Ojek* and conventional taxis. Special policies are required for *Ojek* and conventional taxis, especially if the social impact is taken into consideration.

References

Azzuhri AA, Syarafina A, Yoga FT, Amalia R (2018) A creative, innovative, and solutive transportation for indonesia with its setbacks and how to tackle them: a case study of the phenomenal GOJEK. RIBER 7:59–67

Bayti RN (2018) Paguyuban Ojek Pangkalan studi kasus tindakan sosial Paguyuban Ojek Pangkalan dalam menghadapi persaingan dengan Ojek on line. Doctoral dissertation, University of Airlangga (one file with the author)
Choirul Marati N (2016) Influence of the service quality and price toward the customer Ojek online—study on the Gojek consumers in Surabaya. JPTN 3(3):1–12
Hotana MS (2018) Industri e-commerce dalam menciptakan pasar yang kompetitif berdasarkan hukum persaingan usaha. Jurnal Hukum Bisnis Bonum Commune 1(1):28–38
Julianto PA (2017) Rhenald: the world is watching the downfall of big companies. https://ekonomi.kompas.com/read/2017/02/17/194118226/rhenald.dunia.tengah.saksikan.runtuhnya.perusahaan-perusahaan.besar. Accessed 15 Dec 2020
Jumat (2015) Menhub ralat larangan beroperasi Ojek online dkk!. http://mastel.id/menhub-cabut-larangan-untuk-go-jek-dkk/. Accessed 15 Dec 2020
Kasemin K (2015) Agresi perkembangan teknologi informasi-sejarah bunga rampai hasil pengkajian dan pengembangan penelitian tentang perkembangan teknologi informasi, 1st edn. PT Fajar Interpratama, Jakarta
Malau B (2017) Online transportation conflict. http://wartakota.tribunnews.com/2017/03/15/konflik-transportasi-online-dan-konvensional-akan-terus-terjadi-jika-aturan-tidak-ditegakkan. Accessed 15 Dec 2020
Ministryy of Eduction and Culture Indonesia (2016) Kamus besar bahasa Indonesia (KBBI). https://kbbi.kemdikbud.go.id/entri/penelitian. Accessed 15 Dec 2020
Muhammad A (1998) Hukum pengangkutan niaga. Citra Aditya Bakti, Bandung
Najichah (2012) Biografi tokoh ilmuwan dunia. PT Balai Pustaka, Jakarta
Ningrum DA (2017) Indef sebut 43 persen driver ojek online berasal dari pengangguran. https://www.merdeka.com/uang/indef-sebut-43-persen-driver-ojek-online-berasal-dari-pengangguran.html. Accessed 15 Dec 2020
Nurhidayah F, Alkarim F (2017) Domination of transportation network companies (tncs) in indonesia: an indonesian case. IJBEL 12(3). ISSN: 2289-1552
Putra YMP (2015) Kemenhub resmi larang Gojek dan sejenisnya beroperasi. https://www.republika.co.id/berita/nasional/umum/15/12/18/nziml1284-kemenhub-resmi-larang-Gojek-dan-sejenisnya-beroperasi. Accessed 15 Dec 2020
Ridwan (2016) Penggunaan sepeda motor sebagai sarana angkutan umum di Kota Malang perspektif Undang-undang nomor 22 tahun 2009 tentang lalu lintas dan angkutan jalan dan maqhasid syari'ah. Doctoral dissertation, Universitas Islam Negeri Maulana Malik Ibrahim (one file with the author)
Rizqa H (2017) Uni Eropa: Uber perusahaan transportasi bukan aplikasi. http://www.republika.co.id/berita/ekonomi/bisnis-global/17/12/21/p1aid3408-uni-eropa-uber-perusahaan-transportasi-bukan-aplikasi. Accessed 15 Dec 2020
Rusydi I (2017) Disruptive Innovation dalam Kajian Hukum Persaingan Usaha. Juristek 5(2):192–205
Safitri M (2015) Tinjauan hukum persaingan usaha terhadap konflik antara taksi konvensional dan taksi online. Keadilan Progresif 6(2):138–148
Safitri M (2019) Tinjauan Hukum Persaingan Usaha terhadap Konflik antara transportasi konvensional dan transportasi online. Jurnal Keadilan Progresif 6(2):138–148
State History (2014) Development and progress of road transportation progress in indonesia since the occupation era. https://www.sejarah-negara.com/2014/09/perkembangan-transportasi-darat.html. Accessed 15 Dec 2020
Tempo Daily Newspaper (2019) Digital economy reach and contribute 11% in 2020. https://en.tempo.co/read/1258313/govt-eyes-11pct-digital-economy-contribution-to-gdp-in-2020. Accessed 15 Dec 2020
Vuchic VR (1992) Urban passenger transportation modes. In: Gray GE, Hoel LA (eds) Public transportation, 2nd edn. Prentice Hall, New Jersey
Wahyuningtyas SY (2016) The online transportation network in Indonesia: a pendulum between the sharing economy and ex ante regulation. Competition Regul. Netw. Ind. 17(3–4):260–280

Wahyusetyawati E (2017) Dilema pengaturan transportasi online. https://rechtsvinding.bphn.go.id/jurnal_online/TRANSPORTASI%20ONLINE_ENDANG.pdf. Accessed 15 December 2020
Wijaya (2016) Aspek hukum bisnis transportasi jalan online. Sinar Grafika, Jakarta
Windasari IP, Uzzi FN, Satoto KI (2017) Sentiment analysis on Twitter posts: an analysis of positive or negative opinion on Gojek. In: 4th International Conference on Information Technology, Computer, and Electrical Engineering (ICITACEE), 2017. IEEE, pp. 266–269
World Bank Group and OECD (2017) A step ahead, competition policy for shared prosperity and inclusive growth. The World Bank, Washington, DC
Yusron M (2010) Tinjauan Tentang Dasar Hukum Transaksi Elektronik di Indonesia. Jurnal Hukum 19:63–77

Part III
Algorithms, Coordinated Price Setting, and Competition Law

Algorithmic Collusion and Indian Competition Act: Suggestions to Tackle Inadequacies and Naivety

Nikita Koradia, Kiran Manokaran, and Zara Saeed

Abstract The debate around algorithmic collusion has gained substantial momentum leading to divergent views amongst economists. While some have expressed serious concerns over the menace of algorithmic collusion and its adverse impact on the competition, others have disregarded it as an unlikely threat. The common scepticism that emanates in any discourse concerning the regulation of the unique forms of algorithmic collusion is the inadequacy of the anti-trust legal framework to effectively tackle issues of detection, investigation and evidence-collection that is incumbent in the process of proving such collusion. Much of these apprehensions are attributable to the inconsistencies in the Indian jurisprudence concerning the elements of 'hub-and-spoke', 'tacit collusion' and the acceptable 'plus factors' required to establish the same. Further, the restrictive approach adopted by the anti-trust authorities in pronouncing judicial decisions impede the scope of the Competition Act, 2002 to address the algorithm problem in its present form. The paper reconnoitres the rise of algorithmic collusion and expounds on how algorithms in disguise of maintaining competitive balance can destroy competition. It further expounds how traditional notions of tacit collusion and hub-and-spoke should be reconstrued in the context of digital markets to bring algorithmic collusion within the sweep of Section 3 of The Indian Competition Act. It further offers an array of reforms and recommendations to adapt the Competition Law and to better equip the Antitrust Authorities to suit the changing needs of the digital market.

Keywords Agreement · Price fixing · Algorithms · Concerted practice · Hub-and-spoke · Tacit collusion · India

---

N. Koradia (✉)
Institute of Law, Nirma University, Ahmedabad 382481, India
e-mail: nikita.koradia@nirmauni.ac.in

K. Manokaran
Kasthuri & Sundar Associates, Chennai 600020, India

Z. Saeed
Shanghai Electric Group, Karachi 75200, Pakistan

S. Van Uytsel (ed.), *The Digital Economy and Competition Law in Asia*,
Perspectives in Law, Business and Innovation,
https://doi.org/10.1007/978-981-16-0324-2_6

1 Introduction

The existence of algorithms is not new to economies worldwide. They have been in existence for thousands of years. However, it is very recently that with digitalization, economies have started becoming mindful to it from competition law perspective. Digitalization has not only changed the perspective of consumers towards businesses, but it has also impacted the ideology of businesses on how to conduct business. The change in the ideology of business can be seen from the change in importance attached to the data which has become the new currency. Digitalization has brought the issues faced due to algorithms on the forefront.

Algorithms have become an inevitable part of the modern economy. Their importance in today's world cannot be understated. Some scholars consider algorithms to have a windfall effect on economies for the advantages that they offer in terms of automation, predictive analysis, increased efficiency and better quality. Alternatively, some scholars contend the impact automation of human-decision making might have on competition in the market. This narrative was evidenced when two competitors selling the second-hand copies of the book 'The Making of a Fly' entered into a price war by way of algorithms shooting the price of the book to $23,698,655.96.[1] The situation gave a sneak-peak into what can happen when algorithms are left alone or unsupervised. This issue has not been left unaddressed and various reports and interdisciplinary research has been conducted on the effect/dangers of algorithms on competition in the market more so where they can be used actively by companies to distort competition in the market.

One of the biggest concerns that was raised was of algorithms as facilitators of collusion. The concerns highlighted how algorithms could be used to collude in innovative and unusual ways which do not fit within the contours of the definition of agreement as we understand in traditional antitrust sense. The digital markets have made it conducive to collude through algorithms as there is more transparency in the market, the frequency of communication is higher and the price fluctuations are so frequent that it is highly improbable to detect anti-competitive activity in the market. Researches have pointed out how algorithms can lead to collusion through hub-and-spoke or tacitly. The other scenario that has been debated about is the collusion reached by deep learning algorithms without any human intervention.

The Chapter shall highlight how algorithms can be used to collude in novel ways in the competition landscape of India. Section 2 deals with the definition of agreement under the Indian Competition Act 2002 (Competition Act) and whether the definition needs to be revisited to address algorithmic collusion. This Section deals with how tacit collusion can be an inevitable consequence of price setting through algorithms and can get aggravated with differing market structures and how a perfectly competitive market can imitate an oligopoly market. The third Section deals with the developing jurisprudence of hub-and-spoke in India with special emphasis on the case against Uber for price fixing. It also emphasizes on the recent amendments proposed under the Competition Act with respect to hub-and-spoke and how can

[1] Roozendaal (2018).

the Competition Commission of India (CCI) deal with hub-and-spoke through algorithms differently. The third Section also deals with the digital eye scenario and questions whether such circumstances can raise competition concerns in the near future. The chapter, towards the end in Section 4, makes recommendations that can be adopted by the CCI in line with developed jurisdictions to address the problem of algorithmic collusion. Section 5 concludes.

2 Anti-Competitive Agreements Under the Indian Competition Law

In India, the regulation of competition was formerly governed by the Monopolies and Restrictive Trade Practices Act, 1969 (MRTP Act) which was rather narrow in its ambit. Even the definition of 'agreements' in the erstwhile MRTP Act simply defined the term to include any arrangement or understanding, whether or not intended to be enforced by legal proceedings.[2] However, pursuant to the wave of liberalization in the country since the early 1990's[3] and the ever-changing market conditions as a consequence of rapid economic development, it was felt that the MRTP Act was becoming obsolete.[4] Consequently, the High Level Committee on Competition Policy and Law (also known as the Raghavan Committee) was constituted to examine and suggest reforms to the existing Competition Law regime in light of the growing liberalization and globalization.[5] Pursuant to the Raghavan Committee's recommendations, the Competition Act was legislated with a much greater scope so as to tackle emerging issues in the Competition Law and it provides for one of the widest definitions for 'agreements' when compared with the antitrust laws of other jurisdictions.

2.1 The Definition and Scope of Anti-Competitive Agreements

The Competition Act defines an 'agreement' to include any arrangement, understanding or action in concert, whether or not, such arrangement, understanding or action in concert is formal or in writing or is intended to be enforceable by legal

[2] Section 2(a) of the MRTP Act 1969: "agreement" includes any arrangement or understanding, whether or not it is intended that such agreement shall be enforceable (apart from any provision of this Act) by legal proceedings.

[3] Banga and Das (2012).

[4] The Finance Minister on 27 February 1999 declared in the budget speech that MRTP Act has become obsolete in light of international economic developments relating to Competition Law.

[5] Raghavan Committee (2013).

proceedings.[6] In comparison with the erstwhile definition of agreement in the MRTP Act, it can be seen that Section 2(b) of the Competition Act provides for a wider scope by including in its ambit 'action in concert' which is akin to the concept of 'concerted practice' in EU and 'collusion' in the US

It further clarifies that there is no requirement as to the form of agreement.[7] As the CCI observed in Re: Alleged Anti-Competitive Conduct by Maruti Suzuki India Limited that agreements restraining competition are generally made in smoke filled rooms and therefore it is difficult to find formal/written agreements.[8] Thus, the definition is a wide one as it is inclusive and non-exhaustive. The understanding required by the definition may even be tacit and the definition covers situations where the parties act on the basis of a nod or a wink. The Competition Act further widens the scope while addressing 'anti-competitive' agreements. It prohibits enterprises and persons (including association of enterprises and persons) from entering into any agreement with respect to the production, supply, distribution, storage, acquisition or control of goods or provision of services which causes or is likely to cause an appreciable adverse effect on competition within India.[9] Any agreement entered in contravention of the same is void.[10] In addition to the same, the act specifically addresses agreements between enterprises engaged in identical or similar trade of goods or provision of services (horizontal agreements)[11] and agreements between enterprises at different stages of the production chain in different markets (vertical agreements).[12]

Section 3(3) of the Competition Act, in particular, has been given a large sweep by the language used in the same. The Section reads as,

> Any agreement entered into between enterprises or associations of enterprises or persons or associations of persons or between any person and enterprise or practice carried on, or decision taken by, any association of enterprises or association of persons, including cartels, engaged in identical or similar trade of goods or provision of services…

This Section also expressly provides an illustrative and non-exhaustive list of such agreements.

As can be seen from the language used in the provision, in addition to including 'agreements' as defined under Section 2(b) of the Competition Act which includes any arrangement, understanding and action in concert, the provision also includes

---

[6]Section 2(b) of the Indian Competition Act 2002 (Competition Act): "agreement" includes any arrangement or understanding or action in concert: (i) whether or not, such arrangement, understanding or action is formal or in writing; or (ii) whether or not such arrangement, understanding or action is intended to be enforceable by legal proceedings.

[7]Technip S.A. vs. S. M. S. Holding Pvt. Ltd. (2005) 5 SCC 465.

[8]Competition Commission of India (CCI), Suo Motu Case No. 01 of 2019, in Re: Alleged Anti-Competitive Conduct by Maruti Suzuki India Limited (MSIL) in implementing discount control policy vis-à-vis dealers.

[9]Section 3(1) of the Competition Act.

[10]Section 3(2) of the Competition Act.

[11]Section 3(3) of the Competition Act.

[12]Section 3(4) of the Competition Act.

practices carried on or decisions taken by any association of enterprises or persons, and cartels. The Competition Act defines a 'practice' to include any practice relating to the carrying on of any trade by a person or enterprise.[13] Trade has been defined to mean any trade, business, industry, profession or occupation relating to the production, supply distribution, storage or control of goods and includes the provision of any services.[14] The term 'decision' has not been defined and thus it follows the ordinary English meaning. In the Kerala Cine Exhibitors Association,[15] the joint decision taken by the opposite parties to boycott the films which were displayed in the theatres of the members of the informant was held to have resulted in restricting the distribution of film in the market.

Although the terms 'practice carried on' and 'decision taken' exists in addition to the term 'agreements' in Section 3(3) of the Competition Act, which could provide for a wider interpretation so as to include practices and decisions independent of an agreement, the CCI has rather restrictively interpreted the provision by holding that mere existence of a practice or decision among enterprises without an underlying agreement or understanding would not be covered in the provision's sweep. A practice to be covered under Section 3(3) of the Competition Act should be the result of an agreement, express or implied.[16] It would be noteworthy to extract the observations of Mr. R. Prasad, Member of CCI in his dissenting order in M/s. Metalrod Ltd vs. M/s. Religare Finvest Ltd, in this regard:

> … there is a feeling of some different inference on the term "agreement". There is a view that Section 3(3) Indian Competition Act 2002 is wider in scope than Section 3(1) Indian Competition Act 2002 as Section 3(1) Indian Competition Act 2002 deals only with any agreement whereas Section 3(3) Indian Competition Act 2002, in addition to any agreement, also covers practises carried on or decision taken by which results in [appreciable adverse effect on competition (AAEC)]. The fact that the Indian Competition Act 2002 uses, these three terms also indicates that "agreement", "practises carried on" and "decision taken" are envisaged as distinct and distinguishable. A "follow the leader" syndrome may lead to anti-competitive "practises carried on" and "decision taken" without being an "agreement". But these would still be actionable under Section 3(3) if they result in acts covered under sub-clauses (a) to (d). The inference drawn cannot be subscribed to. Section 3(1) Indian Competition Act 2002 is the covering Section of the entire Chapter on "Prohibition of agreements" and it is the broader provisions which covers both Section 3(3) and Section 3(4) Indian Competition Act 2002. In fact, in Section 3(1) Indian Competition Act 2002 two situations i.e. 3(3) and 3(4) have been envisaged. It means that any contravention of Sections 3(3) and 3(4) Indian Competition Act 2002, the contravention of Section 3(1) Indian Competition Act 2002 has to be there. Section 3(1) Indian Competition Act 2002 is inherent and implicit in Section 3(3) and 3(4) Indian Competition Act 2002. It also cannot be concluded that "practises carried on" or "decision taken by" as provided in Section 3(3) Indian Competition Act 2002can be without any "agreement". Agreement is a necessary element in all the Sections provided under Section 3. It is the crux of the Chapter "Prohibition of agreements".

---

[13]Section 2(m) of the Competition Act.

[14]Section 2(x) of the Competition Act.

[15]CCI, Case No. 45 of 2012, Kerala Cine Exhibitors Association vs. Kerala Film Exhibitors Association.

[16]CCI, Case No. 5 of 2009, Neeraj Malhotra vs. Deustche Post Bank Home Finance.

> Unless there is an agreement, there can't be prohibition of agreements. Thus, a contravention of Section 3(3) Indian Competition Act 2002 without having an agreement cannot be visualized. This presumption is further strengthened by the fact that in Section 19(3) Indian Competition Act 2002 also it is clearly mentioned that 'while determining whether an agreement has an AAEC under Section 3, have due regard to all or any of the following factors, namely (a) to (f).[17]

Thus, for the application of Section 3(3) of the Competition Act, it is necessary to establish the existence of an agreement in any form between the enterprises. The use of different phraseology merely reflects the legislature's intention to provide a very wide definition of the term agreement in contrast to how agreements are understood under civil law.[18] Even if one were to take a view that the specific use of the words 'practice' and 'decision' in addition to a predefined term 'agreement' is to be construed as independent categories, the provision uses those terms only in relation to 'association of enterprises or persons' and not enterprises and persons individually. Thus, independent business conduct would not be covered under Section 3(3) in any event.

A crucial feature of Section 3(3) of the Competition Act is that it, upon establishing the existence of a horizontal agreement, the provision presumes the agreement to have an appreciable adverse effect on competition (AAEC), thereby shifting the burden of proof on the accused enterprises to prove that their agreement is not anti-competitive in terms of the factors listed in Section 19(3) of the Competition Act.[19] The presumption as to the AAEC is a rebuttable one and the accused enterprises must be given the opportunity to rebut the same.[20] The Indian jurisprudence on the law of presumption is well settled such that the terms 'shall presume' as found in Section 3(3) of the Competition Act would only raise a rebuttable presumption.[21] The Supreme Court of India has held that "a presumption not in itself evidence but only makes a prima facie case for the party in whose favour it exists. It indicates the

[17]CCI, Case No. 28 of 2010, M/S Metalrod Ltd vs. M/S. Religare Finvest Ltd—Dissenting Order of Mr. R. Prasad, Member.

[18]CCI, Case 59 of 2011, Shri Jyoti Swaroop Arora vs. M/S Tulip Infratech Ltd. & Ors.

[19]Section 19(3) of the Competition Act: 'The Commission shall, while determining whether an agreement has an appreciable adverse effect on competition under Section 3, have due regard to all or any of the following factors, namely: —

(a) creation of barriers to new entrants in the market;
(b) driving existing competitors out of the market;
(c) foreclosure of competition by hindering entry into the market;
(d) accrual of benefits to consumers;
(e) improvements in production or distribution of goods or provision of services; or
(f) promotion of technical, scientific and economic development by means of production or distribution of goods or provision of service.'

[20]CCI, Case No. 20/201, M/s Santuka Associates Pvt. Ltd. vs. All India Organization of Chemists and Druggist &3 ors, at para. 28.3.

[21]Sodhi Transport Co. & another vs. State of UP and another, 1986 AIR 1099.

person on whom burden of proof lies."[22] Thus, upon establishing the existence of a horizontal agreement, the onus is on the accused enterprise to demonstrate that the pro-competitive effects of the agreement outweigh the anti-competitive effects. The position in India is, thus, different from the US's per se rule where further enquiry as to the anti-competitive effects are ceased upon establishing the presence of a horizontal agreement.[23]

2.2 *The Section 3 Prohibition: Tacit Collusion and Action in Concert*

As seen from the definition, the presence of an agreement can also be through its more elusive form of 'action in concert'. The Raghavan Committee consciously included 'action in concert' to cover situations of tacit and informal arrangements between enterprises. The Committee observes the following in its report:

> In principle, any kind of agreement (including oral and informal agreements and arrangements) could be illegal, if it violates the law. In the case of written or formal agreements, there can be no legal controversy. On the other hand, in the case of oral or informal agreements, it is necessary to prove the existence of an agreement. Proof will generally be based on circumstantial evidence, and parallelism of action between firms can indicate this. It follows that any prohibitions should also apply to what in the U.K. law are known as "concerted practises". Although the distinction between these and agreements are often imprecise, a concerted practice exists when there is informal cooperation without a formal agreement.[24]

Thus, even an informal co-operation can be construed as an agreement for the purpose of Section 3 of the Competition Act through the devise of 'action in concert'. The exact scope and ambit of 'action in concert' has been the subject of scrutiny and deliberation in several cases. It is well known that parallel behavior in markets, particularly in oligopolistic markets,[25] can occur as a natural reaction to market factors even in the absence of any agreement to not compete. Therefore, discourse as to the full reach of the notion of 'action in concert' has always run its course bearing caution to not trample on independent prudent behavior of businesses that reflects parallelism. The CCI has time and again held that mere parallel behavior would not fall within the scope of 'action in concert' and emphasized the need for circumstantial evidence (in the form of plus factors) establishing that there is meeting of minds.[26] Thus, the CCI relies on the existence of certain 'plus factors' to infer 'meeting of minds' and establish collusion.[27] Plus factors, as defined by

---

[22] Sodhi Transport Co. & another vs. State of UP and another, 1986 AIR 1099, para. 3. Also see AR Antuley vs.RS Nayak, 1984 SCR (2) 495; Noor Aga vs. Union of India CA No. 1034 of 2008.

[23] United States vs. Socony-Vacuum Oil Co., Inc., 310 U.S. 150 (1940).

[24] Raghavan Committee (2013).

[25] Posner (1968).

[26] CCI, Case 7 of 2013 in Re: Chief, Materials Manager—I.

[27] CCI, MRTP Case: RTPE No. 20 of 2008, All India Tires Dealers Federation vs. Tire Manufacturers (MRTP Case: RTPE No. 20 of 2008).

the commission, "are economic actions and outcomes, above and beyond parallel conduct by oligopolistic firms, that are largely inconsistent with unilateral conduct but largely consistent with coordinated action."[28] The CCI has also held that particular actions of competitors can be construed as evidence of concerted practice where there is no plausible alternative.[29]

The emphasis on 'meeting of minds' again takes the test under Section 2(b) and Section 3 of the Competition Act to whether there was some kind of understanding or arrangement between the enterprises that appear to be acting in co-ordination. Thus, an attempt to prove an 'agreement' through the devise of 'action in concert' would boil down to establishing 'meeting of minds' between the enterprises exhibiting parallelism.

While CCI has been conscious in avoiding overreach under 'action in concert' it has also been vigilant in scrutinizing those that seek to escape the clutches of Section 3 of the Competition Act through the guise of 'conscious parallelism'. In Re M/s Sheth & Co,[30] while adjudicating allegations of collusive bidding, the commission noted that price parallelism coupled with peculiar market conditions like few enterprises with same owners, stringently standardized product, predictable demand, and other such plus factors point towards collusive tactics adopted by accused enterprises and held their actions to be in violation of Section 3(1) read with Section 3(3)(a) and Section 3(3)(d) of the Competition Act.[31] Therefore, in ensuring that the protective mantle of 'conscious parallelism' does not clothe culpable enterprises with immunity,[32] the CCI has examined carefully any joint behavior with the varying facts and circumstances of each case which could potentially contribute as a plus factor in determining the existence of 'meeting of minds.'

However, the approach to determining the adequacy of plus factors in holding parallel behaviors as collusive and not conscious has somewhat been inconsistent. The frequently cited examples to demonstrate the inconsistence are the Cement Manufacturers Case[33] and the Tire Manufacturers Case.[34] In the Cement Manufacturers Case, the CCI decided that a group of cement manufacturers were involved in forming a cartel which attributed in a significant increase in cement prices. It further held that the cement manufacturers had transgressed the limits in sharing of sensitive information pertaining to price, production and supply, through the platform created by their trade association which had facilitated in price and production parallelism in a concerted manner.[35] Although it recognized that the relevant market

[28]MRTP Case: RTPE No. 9 of 2008, para. 123.

[29]MRTP Case: RTPE No. 20 of 2008.

[30]CCI, Suo Motu Case No. 04 of 2013, In Re: M/s Sheth and Co, and Others (Suo Motu Case No. 04 of 2013).

[31]Suo Motu Case No. 04 of 2013, para. 38.

[32]Theatre Enterprises Inc. vs. Paramount Film Distributing Corp, 346 U.S. 537 (1954).

[33]CCI, Case No. 29 of 2010, Builders Association of India vs. Cement Manufacturers' Association.

[34]MRTP Case: RTPE No. 20 of 2008.

[35]CCI, Case No. 29 of 2010, Builders Association of India vs. Cement Manufacturers' Association, para. 284.

had an oligopolistic setup, it rejected the defense of consequential interdependence and decided against the cement manufacturers by relying on the minutes of their trade association meeting to support a finding of collusion.[36]

Curiously, the Tire Manufacturers case, which was decided in the same year,[37] had near similar fact and yet witnessed a different verdict from the CCI. Even in this case, the CCI categorized the tire market to be an oligopolistic market in nature, as in the Cement Manufacturers case. However, the Commission was of the opinion, that by taking the conduct of the tire companies into consideration, there wasn't enough proof that the tire companies acted together in limiting the production and increasing the price of tires in the market.

While it is pertinent to note, that the Commission had applied the same principles to determine the merits of both the cases, in the Tire Manufacturers case, the CCI took a view that there was 'no specific pattern' to conclude a formation of an agreement between the parties.[38] Despite the visible parallelism among the tire manufacturers in terms of pricing and production, and the recorded exchange of information[39] among the manufacturers through the platform created by their trade association, the CCI, while conceding that the actions of the tire manufacturers does display some characteristics of a cartel, held that the evidences were inadequate to establish the existence of a cartel.[40] This is in stark contrast to the approach adopted by the CCI in the Cement Manufacturers case.

In a more recent case of Rajasthan Cylinders and Containers Limited vs. Union of India and another,[41] the CCI had ruled that suppliers of Liquefied Petroleum Gas (LPG) Cylinders to the Indian Oil Corporation Ltd had been involved in cartelization, thereby influencing and rigging the prices, and subsequently, violating the provisions of Section 3(3)(d) of the Competition Act. However, the Supreme Court of India (Supreme Court), set aside the CCI's findings and the Competition Appellate Tribunal's (COMPAT) decision which up-held the CCI's order. The Supreme Court was of the view that, the CCI's conclusions were based on the plus factors including but not limited to market conditions, presence of the number of players, and submission of identical bids (with varying costs) that it had taken into account[42] and that

[36]CCI, Case No. 29 of 2010, Builders Association of India vs. Cement Manufacturers' Association, para. 285.

[37]The Cement Manufacturer Case was decided on 20 June 2012 whereas the Tire Manufacturer Case was decided on 30 October 2012.

[38]Urs and Shroff (2007).

[39]The CCI, like in the Cement Case, referred to the minutes of the meeting of the Tire Manufacturers Trade Association (ATMA).

[40]CCI, Case No. 29 of 2010, Builders Association of India vs. Cement Manufacturers' Association, para. 365.

[41]Rajasthan Cylinders and Containers Limited vs. Union of India and another, Civil Appeal No. 3546 of 2014.

[42]Rajasthan Cylinders and Containers Limited vs. Union of India and another, Civil Appeal No. 3546 of 2014.

these factors were "only one side of the coin"[43] and had to be evaluated by keeping the ground realities in place. Both the COMPAT and, subsequently, the Supreme Court accepted the theory of oligopolistic interdependence[44] and held the parallel conduct to be a consequence of the structure of the market.

Therefore, despite the broad language of Section 2 and 3(3) of the Competition Act which is capable of capturing a wide range of anti-competitive conduct within its ambit, the inconsistency with respect to the acceptability of evidence in order to establish plus factors, and the zealous differences to the oligopolistic defense somewhat muddles the true practicable scope of the provision.

2.3 *Standard of Proof*

The CCI has also been mindful of the difficulties in proving the existence of such agreements and has held that the standard of proof is 'preponderance of probability' while observing that "[i]n most cases, the existence of an anti-competitive practice or agreement must be inferred from a number of coincidences and indicia which, taken together, may, in the absence of another plausible explanation, constitute evidence of the existence of an agreement."[45] Preponderance of probability is the standard of proof required mostly in civil and administrative proceedings.[46] It simply refers to the greater weight of evidence required to decide in favor of one side[47] If the holistic appreciation of all the evidence makes the existence of a fact more probable than the other possible versions of fact, then the standard has been said to have been met with respect to the existence of that probable fact.[48] It is often contrasted with the more stringent standard of 'beyond reasonable doubt' followed in criminal proceedings which requires a fact to be established beyond any reasonable doubt and if there are two possible versions of the fact that can be inferred from the evidence, the courts would accept the version favoring the innocence of the accused.

An attempt was made in challenging this standard in Re: Western Coalfields Limited.[49] It was contended that since the proceeding under the Act have penal consequences, the standard of proof under Section 3 ought to be beyond reasonable

[43]Rajasthan Cylinders and Containers Limited vs. Union of India and another, Civil Appeal No. 3546 of 2014, para. 88.

[44]Whish and Bailey (2018).

[45]The CCI in *Director General (Supplies & Disposals) vs. M/s Puja Enterprises Basti and Ors.* [(2013) Comp. L. R. 714 (CCI)]. The standard has also been affirmed by the Supreme Court in Rajasthan Cylinders and Containers.

[46]Union of India and Others vs. Hindustan Development Corporation and Others, (1993) 3 SCC 499.

[47]Black's Law Dictionary, 11th Edition.

[48]Some have defined the standard as requiring at least 51% probability as to the existence of a fact. Available at: https://www.legalmatch.com/law-library/article/preponderance-of-the-evidence-vs-beyond-a-reasonable-doubt.html. Accessed 15 December 2020.

[49]CCI, Case No. 34 of 2015, Re: Western Coalfields Limited.

doubt and not preponderance of probability.[50] The Commission rejected the argument by relying on the decision of COMPAT in International Cylinder (P) Ltd Vs. Competition Commission of India which justified adopting the more liberal standard of preponderance of probability in light of the difficulty in establishing the existence of such agreements in reality. COMPAT observed as follows:

> The burden in this behalf cannot be equated with the burden in the criminal cases where the prosecution has to prove the allegation beyond the reasonable doubt. A strong probability would be enough to come to the conclusion about the breach of the provisions of the Competition Act. Some of the learned counsel argued that their participation or the preconcerted agreement would have to be proved beyond doubt. We do not think so. It is obvious that an agreement cannot be easily proved because it may be a wink or a nod or even a telephone call. What is required to be proved is a strong probability in favour of a pre-concerted agreement and the factors which we have highlighted go a long way in that direction and as plus factors…

Thus, the CCI has struck a balance in terms of adopting a lesser threshold of proof considering the practical difficulties in proving agreements. In fact, the Indian Courts have been more inclined to endorse the test laid down by the European Court of Justice in Imperial Chemical Industries Ltd vs. Commission of the European Communities[51] in tackling the issue of concerted practice.[52] *T*he Supreme Court, reflecting on the observations made by the European Court of Justice in Dyestuffs,[53] rejected the oligopolistic defense of the appellants in a bid-rigging setup and further emphasized the need to consider the plus factors as a whole and not in isolation.[54]

2.4 Agreements and Concerted Practice's Under the European Union

It would be of relevance to compare and contrast how different jurisdictions interpret the formation of agreements in line with their laws. For the purpose of this discussion, we will analyze the decisions pertaining to concerted practices under Competition law in European Union (EU).

---

[50] CCI, Case No. 34 of 2015, Re: Western Coalfields Limited, para. 13.5.

[51] Case 48–69, [1972] ECR 619.

[52] See also, CCI, Case 1 of 2014 In Re: Alleged Cartelization in Supply of LPG Cylinders.

[53] "By its very nature, then, the concerted practice does not have all the elements of a contract but may inter alia arise out of coordination which becomes apparent from the behaviour of the participants. Although parallel behaviour may not itself if identified with a concerted practice, it may however amount to strong evidence of such a practice if it leads to conditions of competition which do not respond to the normal conditions of the market, having regard to the nature of the products, the size and number of the undertakings, and the volume of the said market. Such is the case especially where the parallel behaviour is such as to permit the parties to seek price equilibrium at a different level from that which would have resulted from competition, and to crystallise the status quo to the detriment of effective freedom of movement of the products in the [internal] market and free choice by consumers of their suppliers."

[54] Excel Corp Care Ltd. vs. CCI, (2017) 8 SCC 47.

Article 101 of the Treaty on the Functioning of the European Union (TFEU) is the relevant provision that identifies different types of agreements and can be said to be similar to the provision of Section 3(3) of the Competition Act. It prohibits "all agreements, decisions by associations of undertakings and concerted practises"[55] which lead to an anti-competitive market. Article 101 TFEU provides not only for explicit agreements but also ensures that all coordinated conduct leading to anti-competitive market outcome is prohibited.[56]

Both the Indian Competition Act and the EU laws on competition include the phrase 'actions in concert' and 'concerted practices' respectively in order to widen the scope of an agreement. However, the aforementioned laws do not define or describe what concerted practices are. In the case of ICI v Commissioner (Dyestuffs),[57] the European Court of Justice (ECJ) for the first time defined a concerted practice is as follows:

> form of coordination between undertakings which, without having reached the stage where an agreement properly so-called has been concluded, knowingly substitutes practical cooperation between them for the risks of competition.[58]

It can be highlighted that, the ECJ tried to draw a fine line between agreements and concerted practices by forming a view that a concerted practice must have adverse effects on competition in the market to fall under the purview of Article 101 TFEU, while mere existence of an agreement would be sufficient to prove that it attracts Article 101 TFEU.[59] To that extent, the Competition Act considers concerted practices within the definition of agreement under Section 2(b) and hence raises a presumption of illegality for both agreements and concerted practices making the scope of that Section stricter.

While the Dyestuffs case had set the foundation of concerted practices, in the case of Suiker Unie UA and others vs. Commission of the European Communities,[60] the ECJ had elaborated the concept of concerted practice as

---

[55] Article 101 (1) of Treaty of the Functioning of the European Union (TFEU).

[56] Nicholls (2018).

[57] ICI vs. Commissioner, [1972] ECR 619.

[58] ICI vs. Commissioner, [1972] ECR 619, para. 64.

[59] Article 101(1) TFEU and Article 101(2) TFEU: Article 101(2) TFEU does not mention the word concerted practices and hence this could be attributed either to the legislatures neglect or a purposeful omission to not include concerted practices under the category of presumed void. Case T-411/08 R, Artisjus vs. Commission, [2008] ECR II-270. The President of the General Court ruled, first, that 'nullity under Article 101(2) TFEU does not apply to prohibited concerted practices'. Available at: http://curia.europa.eu/juris/document/document.jsf?text=&docid=136267&pageIndex=0&doclang=en&mode=lst&dir=&occ=first&part=1&cid=2129811. Accessed 15 December 2020; 'As a matter of EU law, neither anticompetitive concerted practices nor consequential agreements resulting from such practices can be declared null and void under Article 101(2). If at all, consequential agreements can only be impacted by national civil law applicable to the contract.' Available at: http://competitionlawblog.kluwercompetitionlaw.com/2013/04/23/why-does-article-1012-tfeu-not-list-concerted-practises/?doing_wp_cron=1590764105.5379240512847900390625. Accessed 15 December 2020.

[60] *Suiker Unie*, [1975] ECR 1663.

> a form of coordination between undertakings, which, without having been taken to the stage where an agreement properly so-called has been concluded, knowingly substitutes for the risks of competition, practical cooperation between them which leads to conditions of competition which do not correspond to the normal conditions of the market, having regard to the nature of the products, the importance and number of the undertakings as well as the size and nature of the said market.

In the aforementioned case, the ECJ determined that sugar producers in certain areas of Europe had communicated with each other and concerted together by abolishing uncertainties about their future market behavior, which could be evident from their letters, telex and notes.[61]

The ECJ further explained that there was no requirement of a plan to prove the existence of a concerted practice.[62] However, this requirement does not prevent the companies from adapting existing market conditions and every market player should take decisions independently without any form of contact with other players in the market.[63]

The definition and application of concerted practice was further clarified in the Polypropylene case[64] and T-Mobile case,[65] in which the ECJ formed a view that a concerted practice can be the result of undertakings concerting with each other, forming a subsequent conduct on the market and the presence of a causal link between the act of concerting and the conduct.[66] This is also the position followed in India. Even though there is a difference in treatment of concerted action, which, unlike in the EU, is expressly declared as void in India, the scope of the principle is the same.

For a developing jurisdiction with a fairly nascent competition regime, the Competition Act is quite wide and ahead in its scope when compared to the laws of most other jurisdictions. The language and ambit of the provisions are adequately sophisticated to tackle the vice of algorithmic collusion in digital markets, be it in terms of the broad inclusive definition of agreements, legal recognition and prohibition of 'action in concert' or the presumption as to the AAEC of certain agreements. However, there is room for improvement and further clarity in terms of enforcement of the provisions and better equipping the enforcement agencies to identify contraventions in the digital market and effectively apply the provisions to prosecute the transgressors. While these improvements can be effected through minor amendments to the Act, there is no necessity to revisit the definition of 'agreements' since it already covers the situations of algorithmic collusions.[67]

---

[61] *Suiker Unie*, [1975] ECR 1663, para. 269.

[62] *Suiker Unie*, [1975] ECR 1663, para. 173.

[63] *Suiker Unie*, [1975] ECR 1663, para. 174.

[64] Case C-199/92P, Huls v Commission, [1999] ECR I-4287.

[65] C-8/08, *T-Mobile Netherlands and others*, [2009] ECR p. I-4529.

[66] C-8/08, *T-Mobile Netherlands and others*, [2009] ECR p. I-4529, para. 51.

[67] See infra [this chapter] 4 Recommendations.

3 Involving Algorithms in Anti-Competitive Agreements

Ariel Ezrachi and Maurice E. Stucke have raised four major concerns from a competition law perspective that can arise due to algorithms.[68] They distinguish between four scenarios: messenger, hub-and-spoke, tacit collusion and digital eye. Among these scenarios, there are ones that use the algorithms to implement or give effect to an explicit agreement which shall fall within the definition of agreement in contravention of Section 3(3) of Competition Act. There are equally scenarios in which there is a unilateral use of pricing algorithms which could result in coordinated outcomes not explicitly barred by the Competition Act.[69] For the purpose of this chapter, hub-and-spoke, tacit collusion and digital eye will be discussed. In the end, the messenger scenario, in which algorithms are used to give effect to an explicit agreement, can be easily dealt with under the Competition Act.

3.1 Algorithms in a Hub-and-Spoke Scenario

In most jurisdictions, direct communication between market players with an intention to behave in an anti-competitive manner and consequently disrupting welfare of the consumers can be categorized as collusion. However, in most circumstances, these market players do not directly exchange information but rather adopt sophisticated forms of collusion. One such form of collusion is known as hub-and-spoke arrangement where an entity at a different level of supply chain (hub) coordinates a horizontal conspiracy amongst competitors (spoke) (together hub-and-spoke) at a different level of supply chain by way of a series of vertical agreements.[70] From a competition law perspective, such arrangement can raise concerns due to indirect information exchange amongst the competitors without any direct communication which can lead to collusive outcome.[71]

While analyzing the hub-and-spoke scenario, Ezrachi and Stucke raise a legitimate challenge in detecting algorithm collusion where the collusion may be facilitated amongst the competitors by way of a hub or a third-party facilitator.[72] While the hub-and-spoke scenario is in itself anti-competitive in nature, the presence of pricing algorithms[73] and repricing software,[74] supporting the hub-and-spoke arrangement

[68]Ezrachi and Stucke (2017a).

[69]Competition & Markets Authority (2018).

[70]Falls and Saravia (2015).

[71]OECD (2019b).

[72]Ezrachi and Stucke (2017a).

[73]An algorithm that uses price as an input, and/or uses a computational procedure to determine price as an output.

[74]Price adjustments implemented by an algorithm in response to changes in demand, inventory, or competitors' prices.

may likely cause the anti-competitive output in a technologically governed market, to exacerbate.

Even though the existence of hub-and-spoke is inherently counterintuitive,[75] it still exists and poses a challenge specifically in less mature jurisdictions where detection could be difficult owing to the sophistication required by the authorities to deal with such arrangements. It becomes a serious concern, specifically in India, owing to the absence of jurisprudence and cases that have addressed the issue of hub-and-spoke except for the case of Samir Agrawal vs. ANI technologies (Uber case).[76] The reluctance by the authorities in recognizing the hybrid model of vertical and horizontal agreements is attributable to the negligible amount of cases present on the subject matter in India.

This reluctance stands testified from the recent proposed amendment to the Competition Act, the Competition Bill 2020,[77] wherein they have acknowledged that such conduct exists in the market. Most of the developed jurisdictions such as the US[78] and the EU[79] do not have detailed guidelines on whether and under what circumstance hub-and-spoke conspiracy should come under a per se or a rule of reason approach. India, after Britain,[80] remains one of the only jurisdictions that has explicitly proposed a combination of horizontal and vertical agreements, thus hub-and-spoke, to have a presumed appreciable adverse effect in the market through the Competition Bill 2020. In terms of certainty of legal test on how hub-and-spoke must be treated (whether it should have presumed AAEC under Section 3(3) of the Competition Act or judged under rule of reason under Section 3(4) of the Competition Act), the Competition Bill 2020 has laid a very clear stance. Despite these new suggestions, this Section shall recognize the limited jurisprudence developed

[75] Falls and Saravia (2015) (the reason is no party at different level of distribution chain would want to give a higher bargaining power by increasing the market power of either upstream players or downstream players in the market. It follows the same analogy to why vertical agreements might not raise anti-competitive concerns usually owing to the parties having counter incentives in a negotiation unlike a horizontal agreement where the incentives are aligned. This is specifically true where the hub or the third-party facilitators does not have any interest in the functioning of the upstream or downstream suppliers. E.g., where a person merely provides the same pricing algorithms to the competitors. Hence, the algorithm provider's interest is independent to the functioning or the working of the companies situated at different level of production/distribution chain).

[76] Competition Appeal (AT) No. 11 OF 2019.

[77] The Bill proposes to add a proviso to Section 3(3) of the Act providing that any Enterprise or Association, though not engaged in identical or similar trade will be presumed to be a part of the Horizontal Agreement/Cartel if it actively participates in the furtherance of such an agreement.

[78] The only Section dealing with horizontal collusion is Section 1 of the Sherman act. The courts through decisional practices have widened the scope by including hub-and-spoke as a per se offence where horizontal coordination could be proved. However, there isn't any guidelines on what shall constitute.

[79] Article 101 TFEU does not mention about hub-and-spoke instead there is a mention of this in the guidelines for information exchange under Guidelines on the applicability of Article 101 of the Treaty on the Functioning of the European Union to horizontal co-operation agreements. Available at: https://eur-lex.europa.eu/legal-content/EN/TXT/HTML/?uri=OJ:C:2011:011:FULL&from=EN. Accessed 15 December 2020.

[80] Odudu (2011).

in India pertaining to hub-and-spoke and investigate how far the Competition Act is equipped to deal with hub-and-spoke arising in digital markets by way of algorithms.

The difference between hub-and-spoke in a traditional sense and a new kind of hub-and-spoke in the algorithm driven world has gained much relevance in the debate of how far algorithms can ease collusion.[81] The traditional understanding of hub-and-spoke needs to be slightly more expansive when dealing with algorithms. The hub-and-spoke scenario in cases involving algorithms does not necessarily deal with a hub who is either at the upstream or downstream supply chain but rather a common intermediary or an algorithm developer (third-party facilitator) who is entirely unrelated to the colluding parties.[82] It is important to differentiate between the two elusive and intertwined concepts of hub-and-spoke as it determines the liability to be foisted on the third-party and/or hub. This Section will presume that there is a difference between a hub and a third-party facilitator.

3.1.1 Potential Scenarios Under Hub-and-Spoke

There are broadly two main umbrella functions that an algorithm performs: first is to collect information and second is to analyze the information (data). All the other functions flow from these two main functions. The function of an algorithm is like any human brain where after they analyze the information they make pricing decisions keeping in mind that the product is priced above the marginal cost but below a competitor cost.[83] This leads to a dynamic competitive market where algorithms determine prices for commodities after collecting the information from the market and then analyzing it in their favor independently. However, where they do not follow the norms mentioned above it can lead to unsolicited outcomes for the market as well as for themselves. The making of a fly case was one such unwanted outcome that was a result of a poorly documented algorithm.[84]

The unsolicited outcomes to the market can also be a result of information sharing amongst these algorithms which limits their capability of determining prices independently. The other issue that can arise from a competition policy perspective is where businesses who do not have the resources or do not wish to make their own algorithms outsource it from a third party.

The above issue can raise four kinds of scenarios from a competition law perspective:

---

[81] In traditional a hub-and-spoke cartel, the hub is usually at the upstream or downstream level of the supply chain and coordinates the agreement amongst the spokes at a different level of the same supply chain.

[82] OECD (2019b).

[83] The optimal pricing decisions by a company must be a price above its own marginal cost but below the competitors cost. Hence, the competitors cost must be above their marginal cost.

[84] Both the parties had set an algorithm to match the competitors price which led to an upward spiral in prices. The result was a result of a poorly documented algorithm wherein in order to match the prices of its competitor the algorithm started calling the shots and led to upward spiral of prices, the book being priced at $23,698,655.93. Demetis and Lee (2018).

1. First, where the competing businesses outsource the algorithm to the same third party which might provide the same pricing algorithms to all the competing companies.[85] This will lead to the algorithms reacting in the similar manner to any change in the market conditions and therefore determining the pricing decisions in parallel, which can inevitably result in price parallelism assuming the products are homogenous and the input feed is similar across the competitors.[86] This scenario presumes that the competing businesses were not aware of each other's decisions but the third party was aware of it. The first sub-issue is how far a third party can be made liable for providing the same algorithm to competing parties where it is a prudent commercial and cost-saving decision though it has resulted in a perverse outcome in the market.[87] The second sub-issue is how far the competing business ought to have been aware that the algorithms so outsourced could have possibly resulted in anti-competitive outcomes. The answer to the first sub-issue is quite straightforward. The third party is under no obligation to not provide the same algorithm to the competing companies. Even if they are not allowed, it shall not be within the purview of the Competition Act and raises a bigger question of corporate governance and contracts. The second sub-issue could point towards the fact that where there is no strategic communication or exchange of information that reduces uncertainty in the market between the parties, it shall not come within the definition of concerted practices under Section 3(3) of Competition Act.[88] The second sub-issue could also point to the solution that antitrust by compliance could be

---

[85] OECD (2017).

[86] OECD (2017).

[87] This is a commercial decision making as they will not have to build different algorithms for each of the party.

[88] 'Any agreement entered into between enterprises or associations of enterprises or persons or associations of persons or between any person and enterprise or practice carried on, or decision taken by, any association of enterprises or association of persons, including cartels, engaged in identical or similar trade of goods or provision of services, which—

(a) directly or indirectly determines purchase or sale prices;
(b) limits or controls production, supply, markets, technical development, investment or provision of services;
(c) shares the market or source of production or provision of services by way of allocation of geographical area of market, or type of goods or services, or number of customers in the market or any other similar way;
(d) directly or indirectly results in bid rigging or collusive bidding, shall be presumed to have an appreciable adverse effect on competition: Provided that nothing contained in this sub-Section shall apply to any agreement entered into by way of joint ventures if such agreement increases efficiency in production, supply, distribution, storage, acquisition or control of goods or provision of services. Explanation. — For the purposes of this sub-Section, "bid rigging" means any agreement, between enterprises or persons referred to in sub-Section (3) engaged in identical or similar production or trading of goods or provision of services, which has the effect of eliminating or reducing competition for bids or adversely affecting or manipulating the process for bidding'.

imposed on the companies and the algorithm providers.[89] It shall be discussed in the latter part of the chapter.

2. The second scenario that can arise is where the third-party platform fixes prices between the competing parties who can be imputed to be aware or unaware of the collusion. This argument can draw parallels with the concept of unified price setting model for all service providers by the platform.[90] The first sub-issue is the incentive behind the third party in setting the prices in a totally unrelated market or at a different level of the supply chain which will essentially benefit the downstream or the upstream parties. While the second sub-issue that can arise is how far the act of the third party can be considered an imputed knowledge to the competing companies to be indicted under concerted practises in violation of the Competition Act or can it be considered imputed knowledge inevitably on them signing up for the services of the third-party. This scenario can be illustrated by way of the Uber business model wherein Uber as a platform fixes the prices using algorithms that can be charged by the drivers (service providers) without the drivers having an agreement with each other.[91] This can be specifically seen in the surge pricing phenomenon.[92] The incentive behind Uber doing this is straightforward. Uber charges a certain percentage of fixed commission[93] from the drivers on each trip.[94] The higher the price charged by the drivers to the consumers the higher the commission that will be received by Uber. From the competition law perspective, one argument could be that this unilateral act by the third party shall not come within the definition of collusion to be indicted under Section 3(3) of Competition Act at present even though the outcome is undesirable to consumer welfare.[95] This situation can draw parallels to the fourth scenario mentioned below. However, the answer could vary where the third-party is a platform and the service providers sign up with cognizance of such a unified price setting model. In this situation, the defense of a unilateral act by the platform might not hold good. The second sub-issue on whether the drivers shall be considered to have imputed knowledge shall be answered in the latter part while dealing with Samir Agrawal vs. ANI Technologies case.[96] The third sub-issue that can arise in this context is what if the platform is unable to provide differential pricing due to the oligopolistic nature of the market where the best price is the common price set by the platform. Can a pricing scheme

---

[89]OECD (2017).

[90]Nowag (2018a).

[91]Competition Appeal (AT) No. 11 OF 2019.

[92]Under this phenomena prices adjust in response to demand and supply in real time; Castillo (2019).

[93]Chen et al. (2015).

[94]Ezrachi and Stucke (2017b).

[95]In this scenario, the author presumes that the parties who are signing up are unaware of collusion amongst themselves, and the knowledge through signing up for a unified price setting mechanism shall not be imputed on them. In that situation, if Uber fixes prices on behalf of them without their knowledge it becomes a unilateral act.

[96]Competition Appeal (AT) No.11 OF 2019.

which is more consumer-welfare enhancing even though it is achieved through a hard-core restraint be considered to rebut the presumption of AAEC under Section 3(3) of Competition Act.

3. The third scenario that can arise from a competition law perspective is where the competing parties collude with each other on prices by way of a facilitator (algorithm provider).[97] In this particular setting, the competing parties by way of vertical agreements with the third-party/hub exchange information through hub with each other to facilitate collusion between them. This is the traditional form of hub-and-spoke conspiracy.[98] The question in this is where there are a series of vertical agreements facilitating a horizontal agreement amongst the competitors, how shall the competition law in India deal with it. The second sub-issue that can arise is what is the incentive in this case for the third-party to coordinate the agreement amongst the competitors in an unrelated market.
   An extension to the third scenario is a situation where, though the competing parties are not explicitly colluding with each other,[99] they are aware or may be aware that all of them are using a similar algorithms from the same third party.[100] This is also called the predictable agent scenario.[101] This will help them to predict the competitors pricing decisions and adjust their pricing strategically. This scenario shall have the effect of information exchange with reduced uncertainty and more transparency which might give rise to a tacit collusion outcome.[102] The question that can arise is how far the algorithm provider can be called a hub. The second sub-issue this scenario advances is, if there is a difference between a hub who plays a more intervening role in the hub-and-spoke conspiracy and a third party provider who is merely providing an algorithm without playing an interventionist role in the entire collusive strategy. This particular issue is raised even in the first concern where the third party is the only one who is aware of all competing businesses using the similar algorithms and nothing more. Using similar algorithms might inevitably result in parallel prices in the market but without any interventionist role in bringing out the collusive equilibria by the third party. The question once again is can a third-party provider who falls short of being a hub be liable for being a party to the anti-competitive agreement which is seminal in tying the liability to a hub or a third-party facilitator in prompting collusion amongst competitors. It is important to address the difference between the hub and third party facilitator as, if it is considered a hub with an interventionist role the antitrust liability encircling it, would be graver vis-à-vis a third-party facilitator where he might not be considered a party to the anti-competitive agreement. The predictable

[97] OECD (2017).

[98] Rutten and Buts (2019).

[99] It differs from the first situation as in the first situation the competing parties were not aware of all of them using the similar algorithms from the third party.

[100] Competition & Markets Authority (2018).

[101] Ezrachi and Stucke (2018).

[102] Competition & Markets Authority (2018).

agent scenario will be dealt with under the heading of tacit collusion.[103] The difference between a hub and a third-party facilitator shall be dealt in later part of this chapter.[104]

4. The fourth scenario could be where the third-party acts as an invisible hand and determines the prices amongst the competing parties without them knowing. There hasn't been a case on this scenario, but it is likely possible that such a situation can arise and can produce unwarranted outcomes in the market.[105] The incentive behind the third-party acting invisibly to determine prices could be to make its services more profitable by allocating more profits to the software users. This can happen in a situation for instance in ETURAS case where the operator of booking system got in place a discount control mechanism wherein the operators could not give discount beyond 3%.[106] In this case ETURAS informed all the operators to adhere to the maximum discount, however if in a situation, he would have not informed them regarding the maximum discount but would have set the algorithm to not provide a discount beyond 3% he would have been able to fix prices as an invisible hand without knowledge of the affecting firms. Such unilateral conduct of the invisible hand shall not fit within the contours of Section 3(3) of Competition Act for the lack of agreement/concert amongst the competing parties.

3.1.2 Applying the Competition Act to Hub-and-Spoke Scenarios

The concept of hub-and-spoke is novel to the jurisprudence under the Indian Competition Law 2002. There are only three very few Indian cases that mention of hub-and-spoke. Out of the three cases those few, it was only in the case of Samir Agrawal v ANI Technologies[107] that the hub-and-spoke arrangement allegation actually went to trial. The other two cases, revolving on a hub-and-spoke arrangement which was effectuated by way of RPM, were never pursued by the CCI and hence never investigated. Even though there is limited jurisprudence developed in India with regards to hub-and-spoke, CCI recently came up with the Competition Bill 2020 which mentioned hub-and-spoke agreements being covered under the anti-competitive agreements under Section 3 of the Competition Act.

The chapter shall first discuss the various cases that raised the allegation of hub-and-spoke under the Indian Competition Law 2002. The case of Fx Enterprise Solutions Pvt. Ltd and Anr. vs. Hyundai Motor India Pvt. Ltd and the case of Uber in India, shall illustrate the position of India on hub-and-spoke arrangements. After, the chapter shall elaborate on how far the amendment, the Competition Bill 2020, shall equip the commission to deal with complex hub-and-spoke scenarios.

---

[103] See infra [this chapter] 3.3 Predictable Agent.

[104] See infra [this chapter] 3.1.2.3 Legislative Gap under Section 3(3) of Competition Act.

[105] Liability for outsourced algorithmic collusion—A practical approximation.

[106] Case C-74/14, Eturas and other vs. Lietuvos Respublikos konkurencijos taryba [2016] OJ C 98/3 ECLI:EU:C:2016:42.

[107] Competition Appeal (AT) No.11 OF 2019.

Fx Enterprise Solutions Pvt. Ltd and Anr. vs. Hyundai Motor India Pvt. Ltd

(1) The CCI, in Fx Enterprise Solutions Pvt. Ltd and Anr,[108] passed a judgement against Hyundai holding them liable for RPM, which was overturned by NCLAT,[109] on the premise of lack of evidences to substantiate the claim. The NCLAT, while reversing the judgment, reasoned that the CCI failed to undertake an independent investigation into the claims and relied solely on the Director General's (DG) investigation report. Despite the reversal of the CCI's decision, it is pertinent to discuss the CCI's stand in the Hyundai case in order to throw light on the Commission's approach in tackling an allegation of hub-and-spoke. In this case the claimants instituted proceedings before the CCI against Hyundai Motor India Limited (Hyundai) for fixing maximum resale price and maximum discount that could be charged by the dealers of Hyundai to its customers.

(2) Maximum resale price maintenance, coupled with the maximum discount fixed by Hyundai effectively acted as a minimum price floor "including the dealer's margin" which stripped away any price competition amongst the dealers. Hyundai admitted that they had mechanisms in place through which they could keep a check on dealers trying to undercut the prescribed prices or who had a discount scheme. If caught, they were to be penalized and it could also result in termination of dealership of Hyundai. The arguments of Hyundai in support of appointing mystery shopping agencies to keep a check on dealers deviating from the price so mandated was to put in line those dealers who were secretly jeopardizing the financial health of other dealers. The data was collected on discounts being given by all the dealers and shared with each of them in an email thread. The violating dealer's information was shared with other dealers and the penalty so charged which ranged from Indian Rupees Two Hundred Thousand (INR 200,000) per violation up to Indian Rupees Eight Million) (INR 8,000,000) which was extremely high and hence acted as a deterrent for all dealers to not deviate from the price mandate given by Hyundai.[110]

(3) From the facts, the CCI inferred that the dealers would have essentially competed on discounts, if not for the discount control mechanism in place. The email thread which communicated to all the dealers the discounts offered by other dealers was a commercially sensitive information exchange wherein the dealers exactly knew what their competing dealers are charging implying that the dealers were conscious of the prices being charged by their competing businesses. The penalty so collected from dealers who did not adhere to the discount mandate were distributed amongst the non-violating dealers. It was also evidenced that Hyundai use to meet with its dealers on a monthly basis to

[108]CCI, Case no. 36 and 82 of 2014, Fx Enterprise Solutions Pvt. Ltd. and Another. vs. Hyundai Motor India Pvt. Ltd.

[109]Competition Appeal (AT) No. 06 of 2017.

[110]Higher penalty in itself is not conclusive proof of collusion. United States vs. Parke, Davis & Co, 362 US 29 (1960).

discuss prices charged and discount offered by the dealer which categorically indicates that all dealers exchanged commercially sensitive information and were aware of the mandate and agreed to carry on such activity in concert.[111] However, the CCI did not pursue the case of horizontal agreement amongst the retailers.

(4) The case can draw parallels to the facts of United States v Parke, Davis & Co.[112] Where in the retailers were suggested the resale prices in advance by way of a retail catalogue that was circulated amongst all of them. The company went ahead to impress upon all the retailers that the prices are being adhered to by all of them and if anyone deviates from the prices or advertises the discounts, he shall be 'put in line'. Each retailor was personally visited to make them cognizant of resale prices. The retailors agreed to adhere to the prices based on a common understanding that everyone else were also adhering to it. The exchange of commercially sensitive information coupled with commitment by the parties to act on it with a common understanding was sufficient to constitute undue restraint of trade.[113]

Information Exchange Under Indian Competition Law

(1) The Competition Act has, under Section 2(b),[114] one of the widest definitions of agreement vis-à-vis any other jurisdiction and includes arrangement, understanding and concerted practices.[115] The provision dealing with horizontal collusion under Section 3(3) of the Competition Act is wide enough to include an "agreement, practices carried on or decision taken" in which practice as defined under Section 2(m) of the Competition Act[116] includes any practice relating to the carrying on of any trade by a person or an enterprise; and is of wide amplitude to include the practice of exchanging commercially sensitive information which can have AAEC in the market. Information exchange under competition law has not been defined nor has the commission issued any

---

[111]The SIA 'VM Remonts' (formerly SIA 'DIV un KO') and Others vs. Konkurences padome (2016) highlighted conditions to prove a concerted action: (1) The undertaking knew about the anti-competitive intention and intended to contribute; (2) The undertaking could have reasonable foreseen and was prepared to accept the risk.

[112]United States vs. Parke, Davis & Co, 362 US 29 (1960).

[113]United States vs. Parke, Davis & Co, 362 US 29 (1960).

[114]"(b) 'agreement' includes any arrangement or understanding or action in concert (i) whether or not, such arrangement, understanding or action is formal or in writing; or (ii) whether or not such arrangement, understanding or action is intended to be enforceable by legal proceedings."

[115]"The concept of concerted practice comprises an informal cooperation between undertakings, without the conclusion of an agreement, substituting the risks of competition "[S]uch a practice is a form of coordination between undertakings by which, without it having been taken to the stage where an agreement properly so-called has been concluded, practical cooperation between them is knowingly substituted for the risks of competition." Case C-8/08—T-Mobile Netherlands v Raad van Bestuur van de Nederlandse Mededingings Autoriteit [2009], para. 26.

[116]Section 2(m) of the Competition Act states that "practice" includes any practice relating to the carrying on of any trade by a person or an enterprise.

guidelines. However, it has been found to be anti-competitive through various judicial decisions under Section 3(3) of the Competition Act.

(2) In a recent judgement,[117] the CCI held that the exchange of commercially sensitive information in itself shall not amount to anti-competitive activity but it may be considered as a plus factor and the Commission must establish the test of commitment[118] amongst the colluding parties to prove collusion. The test of commitment as laid down in EU jurisdiction states that it must be proved by the commission that the colluding parties not only received that information but also acted upon it.[119] However, this test has been diluted post the ETURAS case[120] wherein the regulator held that the dispatch of information to all travel agents through a platform shall be anti-competitive and that parties must show they have done some overt act to distance themselves from such message. In this case where the burden was shifted onto the parties to prove that they did not read the email or they tried in all capacities to distance themselves from the conduct which is very different from all the other cases involving hub-and-spoke where the burden still remains on the plaintiff to prove agreement amongst the spokes. It was held in this case that "the presumption of innocence in primary law does not preclude a domestic court from presuming awareness of a message from the date of its dispatch in light of further objective."[121]

(3) The National Company Law Appellate Tribunal (NCLAT) in an appeal in the Cement Manufacturers case[122] held that exchange of commercially sensitive information shall amount to evidence of collusion if it reduces the strategic

[117] CCI, Suo Motu Case No. 01 of 2017 In Re: Alleged Cartelization in Flashlights Market in India.

[118] In that regard, the Court of Justice has held that, subject to proof to the contrary, which the economic operators concerned must adduce, it must be presumed that the undertakings taking part in the concerted action and remaining active on the market take account of the information exchanged with their competitors in determining their conduct on that market. In particular, the Court of Justice has concluded that such a concerted practice is caught by Article 101(1) TFEU, even in the absence of anticompetitive effects on that market. C 8/08, T-Mobile Netherlands and Others, EU:C:2009:343, para. 51, 2015, C 286/13 P, Dole Food and Dole Fresh Fruit Europe v Commission, EU:C:2015:184, para. 127.

[119] Case C-74/14, Eturas and other vs. Lietuvos Respublikos konkurencijos taryba [2016] OJ C 98/3 ECLI:EU:C:2016:42.

[120] Case C-74/14, Eturas and other vs. Lietuvos Respublikos konkurencijos taryba [2016] OJ C 98/3 ECLI:EU:C:2016:42.

[121] Case C-74/14, Eturas and other vs. Lietuvos Respublikos konkurencijos taryba [2016] OJ C 98/3 ECLI:EU:C:2016:42.

[122] Ambuja Cements Limited & Ors vs. CCI, TA(AT) (Compt) No. 22 of 2017, order dated 25 July 2018, sub judiced in Supreme Court.

uncertainty amongst the alleged collusive parties.[123] What information constitutes 'reduced strategic uncertainty' has not been elaborated under Indian Competition law.[124] The fact that the dealers of Hyundai adhered to the discount control mechanism and to the resale prices since the deterrent penalty was really high and the dealers did act on RPM and discount mandate qualified the test of commitment. However nowhere in the judgement is it unequivocally mentioned that the dealers and the manufacturer exchanged price sensitive information which was anti-competitive in nature. But the same could be inferred from the nature of the market,[125] information exchange,[126] the monitoring policy, frequency of information exchange, deterrent penalty which was ignored by the commission absolutely.

(4) As was illustrated in United States v Parke, Davis & Co,[127] it was made clear by Hyundai that all the dealers were impressed upon the same expectation and hence such negotiations were a part of the concerted action to minimize price competition amongst the dealers. The dealers were all informed of each other's prices and any deviations by the violating dealer. It was an attempt to carry on a common understanding that each of them observe the directed prices.[128] It is interesting to note that NCLAT while deciding the appeal completely ignored the admission by Hyundai of impressing upon each dealer the resale price as well the discount control mechanism. Rather than going into the merits of the appeal, the NCLAT chose to reverse the case on the grounds of inability of the CCI to conduct an independent inquiry from the DG's investigation.

---

[123]"In so far as concerns, in particular, the exchange of information between competitors, it should be recalled that the criteria of coordination and cooperation necessary for determining the existence of a concerted practice are to be understood in the light of the notion inherent in the Treaty provisions on competition, according to which each economic operator must determine independently the policy which he intends to adopt on the common market" (judgments of 4 June 2009, C 8/08, T-Mobile Netherlands and Others, EU:C:2009:343, para. 32, and of 19 March 2015, C 286/13 P, Dole Food and Dole Fresh Fruit Europe vs. Commission, EU:C:2015:184, para. 119).

[124]In particular, an exchange of information which is capable of removing uncertainty between participants as regards the timing, extent and details of the modifications to be adopted by the undertakings concerned in their conduct on the market must be regarded as pursuing an anticompetitive object (judgment of 19 March 2015, C 286/13 P, Dole Food and Dole Fresh Fruit Europe vs. Commission, EU:C:2015:184, para.122; see also, to that effect, judgment of 4 June 2009, C 8/08, T-Mobile Netherlands and Others, EU:C:2009:343, para. 41).

[125]Automobile market is an oligopoly market in India and hence information exchange on prices and discounts to be offered by the dealers reduces strategic certainty in the market making it more conducive to concertation.

[126]The nature of information that was exchanged reduced any incentive between the dealers to compete since they could either compete on prices which was fixed through RPM or on discounts that they could offer which was also curtailed. Hence there was no parameter on which the dealers could have possibly competed. The nature of information exchanged was also not taken into consideration. There mere exchange of commercially sensitive information does not amount to conclusive proof of collusion but can used as a plus factor.

[127]United States vs. Parke, Davis & Co, 362 US 29 (1960); Comments: The Parke, Davis case: Refusal to deal and the Sherman Act. Duke L.J. (1961), p. 127.

[128]United States vs. Parke, Davis & Co, 362 US 29 (1960)

(5) It was also contended that the discount control mechanism was implemented on behalf of the dealers, however the contention stopped at that and the commission failed to dwell into the veracity of the claim. The CCI held Hyundai liable for vertical restraint under Section 3(4)(e) together with Section 3(1) of the Competition Act for RPM which was over-ruled by NCLAT. The contention of a hub-and-spoke arrangement between Hyundai and its dealers was not brought to investigation by the CCI under Section 26(1) of the Competition Act, even though it was brought up by the complainant.[129] The Director-General (DG) merely made an investigation on the vertical agreement between the dealers and Hyundai. The question that still remains is whether the DG could have *suo motu* made a case under the horizontal prohibition while investigating vertical anti-competitive agreement. As was held under Grasim Industries Case,[130] the DG does not have the power to go beyond the claim referred to it by the CCI under Section 26(1) of the Competition Act.[131] However, in the Hyundai v CCI Case,[132] the Madras High Court has relied on Section 26(1) of the Competition Act[133] to state that, if the subject matter of information is already known to the CCI, the new information on that same subject matter can be added to the previous information and no *prima facie* case need to be made by the CCI.[134] However, whether the new information could fall under the proviso to Section 26(1), which includes an inquiry into a horizontal agreement while investigating a vertical agreement, remains debatable. According to the author the heading under which both horizontal and vertical agreement fall, is anti-competitive agreements under Section 3 of the Indian Competition Act 2002. Therefore, if the DG finds the presence of a horizontal agreement supported by vertical agreements, the author does not think that the CCI needs to form a separate *prima facie* opinion on that issue and it can be accommodated under the proviso to Section 26(1) of the Competition Act. If so, the DG on various occasions in its report pointed out towards the existence of a horizontal coordination amongst the dealers but did not observe the same to be a case of hub-and-spoke.

(6) The approach by the CCI would have been better suited if the allegation pertained to both the RPM and a claim under Section 3(3) of the Competition Act. The author suggests this as, assuming Hyundai would have been able

---

[129] Procedure for inquiry on complaints under Section 19 of the Competition Act.

[130] CCI, Case No 62/2016, CCI vs. M/s Grasim Industries.

[131] Section 26 of the Indian Competition Act lays down procedure for under inquiry.

[132] WP Nos. 31808 and 31809 of 2012; Hyundai Motor India Limited vs. CCI.

[133] "On receipt of a reference from the Central Government or a State Government or a statutory authority or on its own knowledge or information received under Section 19, if the Commission is of the opinion that there exists a prima facie case, it shall direct the Director General to cause an investigation to be made into the matter: Provided that if the subject matter of an information received is, in the opinion of the Commission, substantially the same as or has been covered by any previous information received."

[134] Hyundai Motor India Ltd vs. CCI, Competition Appeal (AT) No. 6 of 2017, decided on 19 September 2018.

to give pro-competitive justification for implementing RPM, in case of allegation under Section 3(3) of the Competition Act the reversal in burden of proof would have shifted the onus on Hyundai to prove that its act did not have AAEC in the market. The author does not suggest over-regulation by the CCI. However, where it was *prima facie* evident that a horizontal conspiracy existed, the CCI should have brought the claim under Section 3(3) of the Competition Act.

(7) If either the CCI or the NCLAT had positively determined the arrangement between Hyundai and its dealers to be a case of hub-and-spoke, it would have been a classic example of Type II hub-and-spoke under the three-pronged taxonomy[135] proposed by Craig Nicholls in his article titled *Analysing Incentives and Liability in "Hub-and-spoke" Conspiracies*. The Type II hub-and-spoke consist of reduced competition at the level of horizontal participants which could be either at the upstream or downstream level which is given effect by vertical agreements with the third party at the different level of supply chain. This is usually effected by way of RPM wherein the manufacturer's downstream dealers conspire amongst themselves to remove intra-brand competition by asking the manufacturer to impose RPM.[136]

There were clear evidences produced during investigation, that all dealers were aware of each other's conduct and consciously continued to adhere to the RPM policy, it met the requirement of the definition of agreement under Section 2(b) and of horizontal conduct under Section 3(3) of Competition Act raising the presumption of AAEC in the market. However, the CCI chose not to pursue the case under Section 3(3) and the NCLAT did not even go into the merits of Hyundai's admission of adherence to such policy by all the dealers, which shows the sluggishness and inability of the commission to evolve and acknowledge the existence of hub-and-spoke. The OECD report mentions:

> Opting for an RPM case instead of a full-blown hub-and-spoke investigation could serve as a shortcut, at least under legal frameworks where RPM is considered an infringement by object, like in the EU.[137] Since RPM is the commonly used tool to implement hub-and-spoke arrangements, a competition agency that puts an end to the RPM will also disrupt the underlying hub-and-spoke arrangement. It cannot function without. The legal requirements for an RPM case are certainly lower. An agency needs to prove that a price related communication between a supplier and a retailer amounted to RPM, but no more than that. This would constitute an object violation of Art. 101 (1) TFEU and its national equivalents, without

[135] Nicholls (2018).

[136] Callery (2011).

[137] RPM is currently listed as one of the hard-core violations that make any vertical agreement ineligible for an exemption from Art. 101 (1) within the framework of the Vertical Block Exemption Regulation, Art. 4 (a) VBER—Commission Regulation No 330/2010. The European Commission has started the process of the review of the VBER, and the debate about the correct placement of RPM as a hard-core, object infringement can be expected to be one of the main discussion topics for the years to come. Also available at: http://ec.europa.eu/competition/consultations/2018_vber/index_en.html. Accessed 15 December 2020.

> the need for further analysis of effects or efficiencies or of complicated tri- or multilateral relationships.[138]

It could be seen that the CCI had an opportunity to establish the precedent for hub-and-spoke but chose not to do so either due to its inability to deal with such complex arrangements or due to the lack of investigative tools to decipher horizontal collusion or merely because it wanted to opt for a short-cut.

Hub-and-Spoke and Algorithm Collusion: The Recent Case of Uber in India

India was one of the only jurisdictions, after the US,[139] to institute a suit against Uber for price fixing and facilitating a cartel between the drivers by acting as a hub/third-party provider.

The private ride hailing services essentially function on the machine learning model wherein it seeks to match the demands of the passengers to the drivers by taking real time, real demand, distance of the passenger to the driver, the length of the journey etc. into account while deciding the fares to be charged.[140] It operates in real time and changes the price charged at each moment depending on the demand and other factors.[141]

The allegation against Uber pertained to it acting as a platform in the form of a third-party intermediary to exchange commercially sensitive information amongst the drivers who have been held to be independent contractors.[142] The claim was that Uber fixed prices on behalf of the drivers and hence constituted a hub-and-spoke conspiracy where the drivers acted as spokes. However, for the claim of hub-and-spoke to succeed it has to be proved that there was a horizontal agreement amongst the Uber drivers. The fact that the drivers signed up to Uber knowing that other drivers shall also follow the price determined by the common platform and hence element of understanding for constituting agreement under Section 2(b) of the Competition Act can be inferred. The question then remains whether the commission and, the NCLAT and the Supreme Court of India (SC) belittled the anti-competitive business model or once again showed its incompetence to deal with such an arrangement. It is ironic that Indian competition law is one of the most expansive and flexible laws compared to other jurisdictions and yet decisional practice nullifies the scope of the law.

The argument by the CCI as well as, NCLAT and SC while dismissing the case against Uber rested on lack of evidence of conspiracy between the drivers.[143] The commission expounded that the application of hub-and-spoke mandatorily requires collusion amongst the parties at the horizontal level. The mere accession of drivers

---

[138]OECD (2019a).

[139]Meyer vs. Uber Technologies, Inc., No. 16-2750 (2d Cir. 2017).

[140]Wang and Yang (2019).

[141]Lee (2018).

[142]Competition Appeal (AT) No.11 OF 2019.

[143]Section 2(b) of the Competition Act.

to a common unified price setting mechanism is not a proof of agreement amongst the drivers inter-se. The mere allocation of pricing power to a common third-party does not prove agreement between the drivers and hence there is no substance to the allegation of price fixing by Uber through hub-and-spoke.[144] The conservative approach of the CCI and, NCLAT and SC in deciding this case could also be due to the inability to interpret Section 3(3) of the Competition Act to include enterprise or association of enterprises who might not be in a similar/identical trade and hence could not be presumed to be a part of the agreement.

The Uber case in India missed the whole essence of hub-and-spoke. The Uber case in India points out to the second scenario mentioned above wherein the third party provides the purpose and also the method to reach to that purpose. However, one set of arguments could be that the knowledge among the competitors to settle on the same algorithm could not be inferred to mean existence of agreement amongst them. The drivers are so widespread that it is impossible for them to agree with each other for there to be a horizontal conspiracy, rather they have no say in the business model adopted by Uber. The problem if at all one exists is of the business model of Uber and not the fact that knowledge can be wrongfully attributed to the drivers for using Uber in parallel. The case was merely based on assumptions and, unlike the US case against Uber for price fixing,[145] where in order to get the petition admitted the plaintiff did give proofs of meetings held between the drivers and the representatives of Uber, such evidences were never raised in the case against Uber in India.[146] Moreover, for the hub-and-spoke concept to be applied the competition authorities have to strictly prove an agreement between the competitors as per the United States position.[147] This position however seems to have got a little diluted in the European Union after the ETURAS case[148] where the knowledge amongst the competitors was presumed and they had to discard the burden that they did an overt act to distance themselves from such agreement. India has yet not settled on its approach to dealing with algorithm price setting.

The other set of arguments could be where the service providers are competitors and not agents or do not form one single economic entity with the platform, theoretically the platform fixing prices on their behalf through algorithms could very well come within the prohibition under Section 3(3)(a) of Competition Act by way of hub-and-spoke.[149]

If the second set of arguments hold true which the author thinks they should as the service providers and the platform does not form a part of one single economic

[144]Section 2(b) of the Competition Act.

[145]Meyer vs. Uber Technologies, Inc., No. 16-2750 (2d Cir. 2017).

[146]Competition Appeal (AT) No.11 OF 2019

[147]The evidence must prove defendants had the intent to adhere to an agreement that was designed to achieve an unlawful objective; specific intent to restrain trade is not required; Meyer vs. Uber Technologies, Inc., No. 16-2750 (2d Cir. 2017).

[148]Case C-74/14, Eturas and other vs. Lietuvos Respublikos konkurencijos taryba [2016] OJ C 98/3 ECLI:EU:C:2016:42.

[149]OECD (2019b).

entity since the service providers and the platform nor the service providers amongst themselves shared the cost nor pursued a common economic goal.[150] In the Indian Context, there is no sufficient control[151] that Uber exercise over the service providers and lack of central decision-making power[152] takes them out of the purview of single economic entity defense.[153] In the Honda case,[154] it was held that "the exemption of single economic entity stems from the inseparability of the economic interests[155] of the parties to the agreement."[156] The closest Uber model could come to is the structure of a membership organization.[157] One argument could be that if Uber resembles a membership organization, in the USA context, Uber could be treated under rule of reason if they offer a new product or in the absence of such uniform price fixing they wouldn't have been able to offer this product at all.[158] This could be a convincing defense that could be used by Uber to justify its business model, however it is unlikely that this argument shall succeed as Uber does not necessarily fit in the contours of a membership organization. This is so as sellers do not come together to make Uber nor do sellers have any autonomy or say in the price fixed by the platform which is usually the case in membership organizations. Also, there are instances where the interest of Uber and sellers may not be aligned[159] and hence nullifying the argument of Uber being a membership organization.[160] Uber's Business model might not even fit the joint venture defense since there needs to be a sharing of risk and pooling of assets amongst the parties which in this present case is absent.[161] Uber's relationship with the sellers cannot categorically be put under the vertical

---

[150] Anderson and Huffman (2017).

[151] If there is 'real autonomy in determining their course of action in the market [or] carry out the instructions issued to them.' Case T-102/92, Viho vs. Commission, [1995] ECR II-17 para. 47, see also Case 48/69, ICI vs. Commission, [1972] ECR 619 para. 134; Case 66/86, Ahmed Saeed Flugreisen and Others, [1989] ECR 803 para. 35, Joined Cases T-68/89, T-77/89 and T-78/89 SIV and Others, [1992] ECR II-1403 para. 357.

In this examination of autonomy, legal, organizational and economic links between the entities are examined with a particular focus on whether control can legally and factually be exercised. Case C-521/09, P Elf Aquitaine v Commission [2011] ECR I-8947 para. 54–72. Case C-217/05, Conferacion Espanola de Empresarios de Estaciones de services EU:C:2006:784, para. 44. Nowag (2018b).

[152] *Copperweld* Corp. *vs. Independence Tube* Corp., 467 U.S. 752 (1984).

[153] CCI, Case No. 52 of 2012, Exclusive Motors Pvt. Limited Informant vs. Automobili Lamborghini S.P.A. Opposite Party.

[154] CCI, Case No. 03/2011.

[155] The economic interests pursued by Uber and their drivers are substantially different; Uber acts as a market place where buyers meet the seller.

[156] Gupta (2019).

[157] Nowag (2018b).

[158] Broadcast Music, INC. vs. Columbia Broadcasting System, 441 US 1 (1979).

[159] Nowag (2018b). "if there is an increase in the overall number of transactions, the platform might accept a reduction in the prices. On the other hand, sellers pay negligible attention to the number of transactions, and pay heed to the number and price of transactions conducted by them."

[160] Nowag (2018b).

[161] Texaco Inc. vs. Dagher, 547 U.S. 1 (2006).

agreements as we understand under Section 3(4) of the Competition Act since there is no product that is being sold by Uber to its sellers which could be resold by the seller to the consumers. Section 3(4) of the Competition Act covers agreement amongst enterprises at different stages of the production chain in different markets in relation to the trade of goods or provision of services. Firstly, Section 3(4) of the Competition Act talks about presence at different stages of the production chain to mean that the goods produced by one enterprise acts as an input for the other enterprise. In this particular scenario, there are no goods or services that are being sold by Uber to the sellers for it to act as an input. Instead they are acting like a marketplace where consumers come and buy the goods or services from the sellers who are present on the marketplace.

The closest model through which Uber could be indicted is by categorizing it as a hub-and-spoke through agency. In hub-and-spoke, through brokerage/agency,[162] a hub acts as broker/agent who can fix prices on behalf of their client to receive higher commission or reward payments or fees. For instance, in Re Insurance Brokerage Antitrust Litigation the dual role of insurance brokers who acted as consultants to the customers taking insurance and producers for the insurers.[163] The Uber model could be slightly differentiated from the above case wherein Uber the agent fixes prices on behalf of the principal (the sellers) and bears no risk of transaction between the principal and the final consumer.[164] This is different from the traditional agency relationship wherein the agency also bears the risk of acting on behalf of the principal. The traditional agency agreements are outside the scope of competition law.[165] However, a hub-and-spoke through agency represents in essence a typical hub-and-spoke conspiracy, wherein the hub does not bear the risk of performance of the principal to the consumers. Rather it merely acts as a platform for the sellers and the buyers to interact. The problem commences where the agent who fixes the price for one principal starts doing it for multiple principals eventually leading to a cartel behavior amongst the principals situated at the same level of the supply chain. The incentive for the platform to do so is very straightforward.[166] The higher the aggregate transactions of all the principals with their consumers the higher the fees of the platform.[167] The platform does not care about individual principal's transaction rather it is more concerned the aggregate transaction of all the principals just like in a typical hub-and-spoke cartel where the facilitator benefits when the entire cartel becomes profitable.[168]

[162] Agency as we understand traditionally must be distinguished from what we understand under antitrust since agency would be a defense for antitrust as agent acts on behalf of the principal and therefore they cannot be considered two separate entities for the purpose of agreement.

[163] Kolasky and McNeece (2015).

[164] Guidelines on Vertical Restraints, [2010] OJ C130/01, para 6.

[165] Nowag (2018a).

[166] Nowag (2018a).

[167] Nowag (2018a).

[168] Nowag (2018a).

The conscious and simultaneous signing up of drivers to unified price setting by the platforms should be considered an imputed knowledge. Hence, the business model of Uber must be presumed to have AAEC in the market. The act of Uber where drivers knowingly sign up for an invisible hand determining the prices for all of them commonly is presumed to have appreciable adverse effect on the market and thus, under Section 3(3) of Competition Act, reversing the burden of proof to Uber. Uber should prove that its price setting strategy did not have AAEC in the market. It was not for the CCI or the NCLAT to determine the AAEC in the market, rather, the business model, if elaborated extensively or understood extensively, it could have per se acted as a proof of collusion and the burden of proof should have been reversed. It was for Uber to prove that it was consumer welfare enhancing and rebut the presumption under Section 3(3) of the Competition Act.

A similar case was instituted by the Luxemburg Competition Commission against Webtaxi,[169] which worked with the same business model as Uber.[170] The Luxembourg Competition Authority presumed that the agreement restricted competition by object and is void under Article 101(2) TFEU. However, it was rebutted on account of efficiency justification mentioned under Article 101(3) TFEU.[171] This result was reached by seeking answers to the following questions. First, would in absence of an Uber like business model consumers be charged more or less, i.e. will the model increase consumer welfare? Second, could such a business model exist without prices being coordinated centrally? Third, what impact will the business model have on competition in the market? Fourth, could an is alternative business model offer the same services but be less restrictive?[172] A similar approach by CCI could have brought more clarity in deciphering the competitive constraints posed by such business models.

Could Uber Case Have Said to Miss the Existence of Section 3(1) of Competition Act

The Competition Act has given the widest amplitude to anti-competitive agreements under Section 3, by bifurcating it into three segments: Section 3(3)[173] deals with horizontal agreements, Section 3(4)[174] deals with vertical agreements and, as per the interpretation of CCI in the case of Ramakant Kini,[175] Section 3(1) deals with commercial agreements between enterprises which cannot be categorized either under horizontal

[169]Conseil de la Concurrence, (Luxembourg Competition Authority), Decision of 7 June 2018 no. 2018-FO-01, Webtaxi Sarl.

[170]Available at: http://webtaxi.mobi/business-model. Accessed 15 December 2020. The Webtaxi Model resembles the Uber Model in its functioning as a platform where sellers and buyers meet and hence an analogy can be drawn on the case being decided on same principle.

[171]The commission said that the service will be of no use to the consumers without the unified price setting and hence it met all the requirements under efficiency justification.

[172]OECD (2019b).

[173]Section 3(3) of the Competition Act.

[174]Section 3(4) of the Competition Act.

[175]CCI, Case no. 39 of 2012, Hiranandani and Ramakant Kini vs. CCI.

or vertical agreements as defined under Section 3(3) or 3(4) respectively, but have AAEC in the market nonetheless.

This interpretation came in the background of an agreement between a stem cell bank and a hospital wherein anyone who wanted to enroll for stem cell banking procedure could only do it with the Cryobank with which the hospital had an agreement to the exclusion of any other stem cell banking services.[176] The CCI held that this type of agreement shall not fall within the wording of Section 3(4) of the Competition Act since the stem cell bank and the hospital were not operating at different levels of the same production chain which is a pre-requisite for vertical agreements to fall under Section 3(4) of the Competition Act. However, since it did have appreciable adverse effect it could be brought within Section 3(1) of the Competition Act. The CCI stated that "Section 3(3) of the Indian Competition Act 2002 and Section 3(4) are expansion of Section 3(1) but are not exhaustive of the scope of Section 3(1) of the Indian Competition Act 2002."[177] Though the case was appealed and the penalty was reversed by the COMPAT,[178] the standalone applicability of Section 3(1) of Competition Act by the CCI as recognized in this case could bring any agreement between enterprises irrespective of their horizontal or vertical relations, if the agreement has AAEC in the market, within Section 3 infringement.

The Uber case brought in front of the CCI and, NCLAT and SC a different type of agreement that necessarily did not fit within the contours of Section 3(3) the Competition Act as they were not present at the same level of supply chain and 3(4) the Competition Act as Uber and the service providers were not present at different levels of the same production chain as well.[179] However, it is undebatable that the business model in itself did not allow the service providers to offer its services for a price lesser than what was fixed by the platform, i.e. Uber, even if they wanted. Hence, the business model did not allow the service providers to compete with each other on prices which is essentially the goal of competition law. Hence it was a commercial agreement that should have been brought under Section 3(1) of the Competition Act to assess the appreciable adverse effect it had on competition by basing itself on its own jurisprudence. The argument that it could be consumer welfare enhancing could be assessed while determining appreciable adverse effect factors mentioned under Section 19(3) of the Competition Act. However, the commission failed to take cognizance of the jurisprudence of Section 3(1) of the Competition Act to bring Uber under the purview of competition law. Also, its wavering mind-set to rely on standalone applicability of Section 3(1) the Competition Act post the Ramakant

176 CCI, Case no. 39 of 2012, Hiranandani and Ramakant Kini vs. CCI.

177 CCI, case no. 39 of 2012, Hiranandani and Ramakant Kini vs. CCI, p. 135.

178 Competition Appellate Tribunal New Delhi appeal no. 19 of 2014 Under Section 53-B of the Competition Act, 2002 against the order dated 05 February 2014 passed by the CCI in Case No.39/2012.

179 As was held in a dissenting judgement by Gita Gouri, member of commission, in the case of CCI, Case no. 39 of 2012, Hiranandani and Ramakant Kini vs. CCI. She held the hospital as a platform which puts the doctors, stem cell banks and other services provided in the hospital etc. in contact with the patients who are provided these services through the hospital as a platform, hence it is a two sided market.

Kini Case[180] shows its reluctance in applying such an expansive interpretation of the Section.[181]

Legislative Gap Under Section 3(3) of Competition Act

Under the India's legislative framework, the prohibition of anti-competitive agreements is dealt under Section 3 Competition Act. It is modelled upon Article 101 of TFEU.[182] However, the regulation of an agreement presumed to have AAEC under Indian competition law is stricter than in the European Union.

Article 101(2) TFEU states that any decision taken by or agreement shall be void. The legislators have not mentioned the concerted practices being presumed void.[183] However, under Indian law 'any agreement, decision or practices carried on' shall be presumed to have affected the market adversely. Section 2(b) of the Competition Act defines agreement which include any arrangement, understanding or action in concert. Section 3(3) of the Competition Act states '[a]ny agreement entered

---

[180] CCI, case no. 39 of 2012, Hiranandani and Ramakant Kini vs. CCI.

[181] CCI, case no. 39 of 2012, Hiranandani and Ramakant Kini vs. CCI, p.189.

[182] 1. 'The following shall be prohibited as incompatible with the internal market: all agreements between undertakings, decisions by associations of undertakings and concerted practices which may affect trade between Member States and which have as their object or effect the prevention, restriction or distortion of competition within the internal market, and in particular those which:

(a) directly or indirectly fix purchase or selling prices or any other trading conditions;
(b) limit or control production, markets, technical development, or investment;
(c) share markets or sources of supply;
(d) apply dissimilar conditions to equivalent transactions with other trading parties, thereby placing them at a competitive disadvantage;
(e) make the conclusion of contracts subject to acceptance by the other parties of supplementary obligations which, by their nature or according to commercial usage, have no connection with the subject of such contracts.

2. Any agreements or decisions prohibited pursuant to this Article shall be automatically void.
3. The provisions of paragraph 1 may, however, be declared inapplicable in the case of:

- any agreement or category of agreements between undertakings,
- any decision or category of decisions by associations of undertakings,
- any concerted practice or category of concerted practices,

which contributes to improving the production or distribution of goods or to promoting technical or economic progress, while allowing consumers a fair share of the resulting benefit, and which does not:

(a) impose on the undertakings concerned restrictions which are not indispensable to the attainment of these objectives;
(b) afford such undertakings the possibility of eliminating competition in respect of a substantial part of the products in question'.

[183] Rivas (2013).

into between enterprises or associations of enterprises or persons or associations of persons or between any person and enterprise or practice carried on, or decision taken by, any association of enterprises or association of persons, including cartels, engaged in identical or similar trade of goods or provision of services which shall limit prices or control output shall be presumed to have AAEC in the market.' Section 2(b) read with Section 3(3) raises a presumption, against concerted practices automatically and considers them void.

Further, the scope of Section 3(3) of the Competition Act is extremely wide and does not only prohibit agreements which have been concluded through express communication but also communication that facilitates coordination or cooperation amongst the competing parties in any manner including exchange of commercially sensitive information. However, Section 3(3) of the Competition Act restricts itself to agreements, including exchange of information, amongst enterprises engaged in identical or similar trade of business. A traditional hub-and-spoke where the parties in the upstream level acting as hub are either manufacturer/supplier/dealer and are facilitating a collusion in the downstream level amongst their retailers (spokes) shall be considered to be a part of such agreement and covered under Section 3(3) of the Competition Act. The definite mention of identical or similar trade of goods might not cover within its ambit a third-party provider who is neither in the similar or identical trade of business but is a party absolutely unrelated to the trade.

The problem might arise where the hub is absolutely in an unrelated business to that of spokes or is merely acting as a platform where sellers and buyers meet. This category of hub-and-spoke have become more prevalent wherein competing companies at the same level of supply chain adopt similar algorithms from the same third-party or use the third-party to facilitate collusion amongst them or acts as a platform and fixes prices on behalf of the competitors causing price parallelism and hence needs address.

The Future of Hub-and-Spoke in India, the Competition Bill 2020

The CCI recently proposed its not the CCI, it is the Ministry of Corporate affairs recently proposed, in the Competition Bill 2020, to amend the existing Competition Act. The Competition Bill 2020 recommends to amend Section 3(3) of the Competition Act to include the following proviso:

> Provided further that an enterprise or association of enterprises or person or association of persons though not engaged in identical or similar trade shall be presumed to be part of the agreement under this sub-Section if it actively participates in the furtherance of such an agreement.[184]

[184]Provided further that enterprise or association of enterprises or persons or association of persons though not engaged in identical or similar trade shall be presumed to be part of the agreement under this sub-Section if it actively participates in furtherance of such an agreement.

The new proviso has expressly brought within its sweep hub-and-spoke conspiracies and has categorically stated that such conspiracies shall be presumed to have appreciable adverse effect in the market. This new proviso would bring a lot of clarity to how hub-and-spoke must be treated under the Indian law. The proviso has further clarified the irrelevance of the hub's existence in similar or identical trade and has qualified any party who plays an intervening role in facilitating collusion to be a part of such agreement even if in unrelated business, hence having presumed appreciable adverse effect in the market. India remains one of the only jurisdictions to have mentioned such prohibition emphatically in its legislative mandate and thereby placing hub-and-spoke arrangement under 'restriction by object doctrine.'[185] This is in wide contrast to the US and the EU who have acknowledged the existence of such agreements but have not as yet laid down any detailed guidelines or directives for them to be treated under per se or by object doctrine. The EU indirectly mentions the existence of such arrangement under the guidelines issued on information exchange,[186] where they recognize that the data can be shared through a common agency or a third party which indirectly recognizes the hub-and-spoke.[187]

The proviso has also drawn a difference between an active hub and a third-party who is a mere facilitator. The above discussion is raised in the initial part of the chapter where the author has tried to differentiate between a hub and a third-party facilitator. The proviso states 'if it actively participates in the furtherance of such an agreement' thereby expressly limiting the application of the future Section 3(3) to those third parties who take an active interest in furthering the goal of restricting competition in the market.[188] However, what still remains debatable is when do we say that a third-party has become a hub and/or falls short of becoming a hub.

To answer this question, parallels could be drawn with US and EU practice. It is well-established that a hub/third-party who facilitates, organizes or supports a cartel in any manner shall be equally considered a party to the agreement intending to restrict competition in the market.[189] In AC v Treuhand it was emphatically stated that the word agreement under Article 101 TFEU has a very wide scope and shall include any agreement 'between the undertakings' even though the perpetrator and the other party may not operate in the same relevant market and a joint intention[190] to

[185]It has been brought under Section 3(3) read with Section 3(1) which deals with agreements presumed to have appreciable adverse effect in the market and have the effect of restricting competition by the very purpose of their existence and hence are void.

[186]Guidelines on the applicability of Article 101 of the Treaty on the Functioning of the European Union to horizontal co-operation agreements (2011). Available at: https://eur-lex.europa.eu/legal-content/EN/TXT/HTML/?uri=OJ:C:2011:011:FULL&from=EN. Accessed 15 December 2020.

[187]Secondly, data can be shared indirectly through a common agency (for example, a trade association) or a third party such as a market research organization or through the companies' suppliers or retailers. Available at: https://eur-lex.europa.eu/legal-content/EN/TXT/HTML/?uri=OJ:C:2011:011:FULL&from=EN. Accessed 15 December 2020.

[188]A hub may be considered an active party when it partakes any commercial or economic interest in the activities of the spokes.

[189]United States vs. Apple Inc., 952 F. Supp. 2d 638 (S.D.N.Y. 2013).

[190]The European Commission has held in multiple cases that even though the intention of the parties is not a vital factor to take into consideration for concluding if an agreement between undertakings

behave anti-competitively in a market is sufficient even though the perpetrator is not present in that market.[191] It is not necessary to "being capable to exert a competitive constraint on the affected market."[192]

What remains debatable is what is the nature of a facilitator in organizing the cartel and under what circumstances can he be considered an active party to such agreement. In the Case C-194/14 PAC-Treuhand AG v European Commission, it was stated[193]:

> In order to establish that an undertaking has participated in a cartel and to hold it liable for such conduct, it is sufficient for the Commission to show that the undertaking intended, through its own conduct, even in a subsidiary, accessory or passive role, to contribute to the common objectives pursued, and that the undertaking in question was aware of the substantive conduct planned or implemented by other undertakings or that it could reasonably have foreseen that conduct and that it was ready to accept the attendant risk.[194]

The above case points to the fact that the quality of role does not determine the liability. The reference to 'subsidiary, accessory or passive role' eliminates any difference between a hub and a third-party facilitator. However, under the regulation of EC 2006 guidelines,[195] the European Commission shall determine the liability of imposition of fines taking into consideration 'the context' in which anticompetitive act was conducted and the seriousness of the infringement, how long the infringement continued and the role of each party to the infringement.[196] The European Commission does not give detailed guidelines on the liability to be imposed on a third-party

---

is restrictive, there is no prohibition for g the competition authorities or the European Courts or the national courts to take the aforementioned factor into account. Cf. judgments of 14 March 2013, C 32/11, Allianz Hungária Biztosító and Others, EU:C:2013:160, para, 37; of 11 September 2014, C 67/13 P, CB v Commission, EU:C:2014:2204, para. 54, and of 19 March 2015, C 286/13 P, Dole Food and Dole Fresh Fruit Europe v Commission, EU:C:2015:184, para. 118.

[191] Case C-194/14 P, AC-Treuhand AG vs. European Commission, paras 117 to 122.

[192] Rivas (2013).

[193] Based on the facts mentioned in recitals 356 to 359, AC-Treuhand played a significant role in the organization and conduct of the meetings. AC-Treuhand had a precise knowledge of the anti-competitive arrangements and in fact, drafted and disseminated in a very professional way all the information on prices, quotas and customers. It was entrusted with the power to conduct audits with the cartel participants. Only the data ultimately approved by AC-Treuhand became the basis of negotiations and arrangements. AC-Treuhand made available its location to conceal the cartels. In both cartels, its role was that of preventing the detection of both infringements. As moderator, its role was that of encouraging compromises with a view to concluding the anti-competitive agreements. AC-Treuhand provided its services, its professional expertise and infrastructure to both cartels in order to benefit from them.

[194] Case C-194/14 P, AC-Treuhand AG vs. European Commission. Available at: https://eur-lex.europa.eu/legal-content/EN/TXT/HTML/?uri=CELEX:62014CC0194&from=EN#c-ECR_62014CC0194_EN_01-E0024. Accessed 15 December 2020.

[195] Guidelines on the method of setting fines imposed pursuant to Article 23(2)(a) of Regulation No 1/2003 (2006/C 210/02).

[196] Article 23(2)(a) of Regulation (EC) No 1/2003 (OJ 2006 C 210, p. 2, 'the 2006 Guidelines').

facilitator in a collusion but merely mentions that each party's liability shall be determined on individual basis. In the ICAP case,[197] the European Commission observed that:

> That the 2006 Guidelines provided only limited guidance on the calculation of the fine for facilitators. Since Icap was an operator active on the brokerage services markets, and not on the interest rate derivatives market, the Commission held that it could not substitute brokerage fees for those for the prices of Japanese Yen interest rate derivatives in determining the value of sales and setting the fine, as such substitution does not reflect the gravity and nature of the infringement. It inferred, in essence, that it was necessary to apply point 37 of the 2006 Guidelines,[198] which makes it possible to depart from those Guidelines for the determination of the basic amount of the fine.[199]

The proposed amendment to Section 3 of the Competition Act[200] explicitly mentions the need for active participation in the furtherance of an anti-competitive agreement. This could be interpreted to mean that the law recognizes the difference between the active role of a hub and the passive role of a third party. As per the proviso only the hub, which plays an active role could be considered a party to the agreement, would be indicted under Section 3 of the Competition Act.

Most of the hub-and-spoke cases in various jurisdictions have had a hub who is either active or has more than a passive role in facilitating collusion. The hub has taken up various roles. It was determined the hubs' responsibilities in a collusion has been more than a mere bystander.

The hubs have either acted as retailors/manufacturers/distributors who have actively fixed prices at the downstream level/upstream level. For instance in the Interstate Circuit Case[201] or Toys 'R' Us Case,[202] both Interstate Circuit and Toys 'R' US, respectively at the downstream and upstream level of the supply chain, fixed prices at a different level to facilitate collusion. In some cases, hub acts as a broker who can fix prices on behalf of their client to receive higher commission or reward payments. For instance, in Re: Insurance Brokerage Antitrust Litigation, insurance brokers acted in a dual role. They were both consultants to the customers taking insurance and producers for the insurers.[203] They helped the insurers in bid rigging,

[197]T-180/15-ICAP and others v Commission.

[198]T-180/15-ICAP and others vs. Commission. Although these Guidelines present the general methodology for the setting of fines, the particularities of a given case or the need to achieve deterrence in a particular case may justify departing from such methodology. Guidelines on the method of setting fines imposed pursuant to Article 23(2)(a) of Regulation No 1/2003. Available at: https://eur-lex.europa.eu/legal-content/EN/TXT/HTML/?uri=CELEX:52006XC0901(01)&from=EN. Accessed 15 December 2020.

[199]Guidelines on the method of setting fines imposed pursuant to Article 23(2)(a) of Regulation No 1/2003.

[200]Provided further that enterprise or association of enterprises or persons or association of persons though not engaged in identical or similar trade shall be presumed to be part of the agreement under this sub-Section if it actively participates in furtherance of such an agreement.

[201]Interstate Circuit, Inc. vs. United States, 306 U.S. 208 (1939).

[202]Toys 'R' Us, Inc., **vs.** Federal Trade Commission Seventh Circuit No. 98-4107 (1999).

[203]Kolasky and McNeece (2015).

allocating customers and exchanged commercially sensitive information to receive higher commission. The third type of role that a hub can assume is that of an interested third-party facilitator who though not related to the business in the affected market has some interest in inducing anti-competitive activity in that market. For instance, in the Apple E-Book case, Apple (hub) wanted to launch an iBook store and facilitated collusion by fixing prices amongst book publishers through MFN clauses and exchanged information between the publishers in order to compete with Amazon who had already established Kindle.

In all the above roles assumed by the hub, the hub has always had an incentive to facilitate collusion in a different market. What constitutes an active role of a hub in collusion could be deciphered from the assumption of an incentive theory. The author suggests that what constitutes an active role shall be determined on a case to case basis keeping in mind the incentive for the third-party to involve itself in such an anti-competitive activity and the kind of role it has played in encouraging collusion.[204] Transposing this theory to the situation where the third-party is a mere algorithm provider and no more, if it actively participates in facilitating collusion for receiving kickback payments or some part of the increased joint profit, then the third-party can be assumed to have an interventionist role in the collusion and must be treated similar to horizontal parties. If the algorithm provider does no more than providing algorithm to the competing parties, it is unlikely that the act of the third party shall be considered a part of hub-and-spoke conspiracy. The other standard that could be used to determine the liability of a hub could be inferred from the standard laid down in AC Treuhand Case, which states:

> to contribute to the common objectives pursued, and that the undertaking in question was aware of the substantive conduct planned or implemented by other undertakings or that it could reasonably have foreseen that conduct and that it was ready to accept the attendant risk.[205]

Unlike in the European Union, where guidelines determine that the type, nature and length of infringement should be taken into consideration on an individual basis while imposing fines on the parties,[206] the Competition Act has no such provision in law. However, this way of calculating the fine has been established through jurisprudence. In the case of Dry-Cell Batteries,[207] the CCI levied penalties on individual enterprises keeping in mind their market share and how far they could dictate the terms of the anti-competitive conduct. The same standard can also be followed wherein the fine

---

[204]This shall take into account exchange of commercially sensitive information, through the hub, setting the algorithms by collecting all data from competing companies and using the same input feed, being told to monitor the deviating parties and inform other parties of the deviation if any, sanctioning the deviating parties, imposing discount control mechanisms, consciously facilitating price fixing etc.

[205]Case C-194/14 P, AC-Treuhand AG v European Commission.

[206]Guidelines on the method of setting fines imposed pursuant to Article 23(2)(a) of Regulation No 1/2003 (2006/C 210/02).

[207]CCI, Suo Motu Case No. 03 of 2017, In Re: Anticompetitive conduct in the Dry-Cell Batteries Market in India.

imposed on the third party shall be determined on a case to case basis as per the role of the hub in aiding and easing collusion.

Should India Adopt the Public Distancing Approach as in ETURAS Case to Deal with Indirect Information Exchange?

India's stance on information exchange is the proof of exchange of commercially sensitive information and the 'commitment standard' for it to come within the purview of alleged horizontal agreement.[208] The EU's stance before the ETURAS case was also similar. However, the ETURAS case changed the subtleties for cases involving pricing algorithms. The approach adopted by the commission reiterated the ANIC presumption with more objectivity.[209] The court in the case mentioned various ways in which public distancing can be effected: first, oppose such a concerted move to all the alleged concerting parties; second, inform the administrator and the users of the site; third, inform the competition authorities of such an act; fourth, apply the discount above the cap repeatedly.[210] The effectiveness of the first option is doubtful particularly in platform collusion where the parties might not know the other concerting parties. However, the second and the third option shall help meet the goal of public distancing. The fourth option could be feasible but it might also strictly mean that the party is trying to cheat on the cartel.[211] The second impediment to giving discounts above the mandated cap would also mean additional technical changes to be done by the party which in all circumstances a party might not be willing to undertake.

For public distancing, the burden of proof is often reversed and imposed on the companies present at the meetings. The reversal of burden of proof does not conflict with the presumption of innocence where the parties had reasonable opportunity to rebut the presumption without taking extraordinary steps or was not too difficult.[212] For instance, in Boel vs. Commission,[213] the companies who attended the meetings

[208]Comments: The Parke, Davis case: Refusal to deal and the Sherman Act. Duke L.J. (1961).

[209]Available at: https://eur-lex.europa.eu/legal-content/EN/TXT/HTML/?uri=CELEX:61992CJ0049&from=EN. Accessed 15 December 2020. As is clear from the very terms of Article 85(1) of the Treaty (now Article 81(1) EC), a concerted practice implies, besides undertakings' concerting together, conduct on the market pursuant to those collusive practices, and a relationship of cause and effect between the two. Subject to proof to the contrary, which it is for the economic operators concerned to adduce, there must be a presumption that the undertakings participating in concerting arrangements and remaining active on the market take account of the information exchanged with their competitors when determining their conduct on that market, particularly when they concert together on a regular basis over a long period.

[210]Case C-74/14, Eturas and other vs. Lietuvos Respublikos konkurencijos taryba [2016] OJ C 98/3 ECLI:EU:C:2016:42. Havu and Zupančič (2016).

[211]Roozendaal (2018).

[212]Case C-74/14, Eturas UAB and Others vs. Lietuvos Respublikos konkurencijos taryba, ECLI:EU:C:2016:42 (CJEU 21 January 2016). Sodhi Transport Co. & another vs. State of UP and another, 1986 AIR 1099.

[213]Case T-142/89, Usines Gustave Boël SA vs. Commission of the European Communities, European Court Reports 1995 II-00867.

where commercially sensitive information was exchanged,[214] the onus was on the parties to prove that they had taken sufficient steps to publicly distance themselves from what was discussed in the meetings or they informed authorities of the nature of the meetings.[215] The Competition Act could also apply the reversal of burden of proof standard in order to deal with scenarios arising from hub-and-spoke arrangement.

3.2 *The Predictable Agent Scenario*

The predictable agent scenario refers to a situation where enterprises employ algorithms in such a way that produces a predictable outcome and reacts in a given way to changing market conditions, in the absence of adequate evidence to establish any kind of an agreement between the enterprises.[216] Therefore, the characteristic features of a predictable agent set up would be the presence of a unilateral development or deployment of an algorithm by an enterprise, to accomplish an intended result with the knowledge that there might be other similarly developed algorithms in the market used by its competitors, without any joint understanding to collude. For the purpose of the following analysis, the author assumes the base conditions of algorithmic tacit collusion as posited by Ezrachi and Stucke.[217]

One of the conundrums brought about by the advent of algorithm driven pricing is that it expands the characteristics of the 'oligopoly problem' to any type of digital market. As noted by various scholars, there can be 'conscious parallelism' or 'oligopolistic interdependence' in certain circumstances where enterprises might be able to coordinate their price without colluding in the conventional sense.[218] Due to the high interdependence, it has been theorized that players in an oligopolistic market would invariably attempt to match each other's price.[219] With the algorithms, competitors can constantly monitor each other's price and immediately retaliate without any time lag,[220] if one of the competitors attempt to undercut the price. Further, the ease at which information exchange can be facilitated in the digital market makes regulation of the same next to impossible. Thus, any attempt at reduction of price by once competitor would invariably force other players to imitate the same thus placing all the competitors at a disadvantage with none having any real benefit. This extreme price transparency neutralizes any incentive to compete and

---

[214]The nature of the information being exchanged; (ii) the structure of the market in which the counterparts participate; and (iii) whether the information exchange is likely to improve transparency within this market.

[215]Nicholls (2018).

[216]Nicholls (2018).

[217]Ezrachi and Strucke (2020).

[218]See Posner (2001, pp. 52–53). Also see Rahl (1950).

[219]Green et al. (2014).

[220]Richard A. Posner argued in his 1968 Oligopoly and the Antitrust Laws: A Suggested Approach, that the presence of time lag between the price leader and rest of the oligopolistic players would still afford the former an advantage.

would rather push the players to maintain a supra competitive pricing sustained by a tacit collusion.[221]

The issue with enforcement, however, lies in bringing such a tacit collusion within the sweep of Section 3 of the Competition Act. Like most jurisdictions, not all forms of parallel behavior are prohibited by the Competition Act. Parallelism caused as a product of independent and unilateral actions by the competitors remains to be outside the scope of the Competition Act. As provided in the analysis above for 'action in concert,' parallelism can be prohibited as tacit collusion only when it is possible to establish 'meeting of minds' through plus factors. So far, CCI has been relying on factors such as parallelism in distribution and production, correlation between price change and meeting/communication among the competitors and other similar factors to establish meeting of minds.[222] However, in terms of the change in market dynamics brought about by algorithms, these factors may no longer be indicative of an active conspiracy.[223] Thus, the requirement of establishing meeting of minds poses practical difficulties in effectively tackling algorithmic tacit collusion although the language of Section 3 of the Competition Act is wide enough to cover the same.

In the predictable agent setup, there is conscious parallelism at the human level, where the enterprises deploy their corresponding pricing algorithm being fully aware that their competitors are likely to do the same.[224] The enterprises are able to program (unilaterally) the logic behind the pricing algorithm such that it yields increased profit. In so programming the algorithm, each enterprise knows that a favorable strategy would be to follow the price increase of others and they are also aware that other competitors could opt for a similar program.[225] It could also be the case where all the enterprises use the same algorithm purchased from a third party thereby making the outcome more predictable.[226] Thus, a supra competitive pricing can be sustained through unilateral actions of the enterprises which may only fall under the conventional understanding of conscious parallelism, and if so would fall outside the scope of Section 3 of the Competition Act for failure to establish meeting of minds.

However, a peculiar feature of this setup is the 'knowledge' or 'awareness' component. When the enterprises program the algorithms to match the prices of their competitors, with the knowledge that there is a high likelihood their competitors would do the same and should there be a reciprocal action from its competitors, shouldn't such reciprocal mindset be construed as a meeting of minds. The assumption of awareness or knowledge of the competitors is arguably not misplaced since it

[221] Ezrachi and Stucke (2018).

[222] CCI, MRTP Case: RTPE No. 20 of 2008, All India Tires Dealers Federation vs. Tire Manufacturers; CCI, Case No. 29 of 2010, Builders Association of India vs. Cement Manufacturers' Association.

[223] As such, CCI has been inconsistent in its approach towards plus factors. See supra note 41 and 221.

[224] Ezrachi and Stucke (2018).

[225] Ezrachi and Stucke (2018).

[226] Ezrachi and Stucke (2018).

is a very predictable behavior in a highly transparent digital market. The commonality of awareness among the competitors coupled with the likelihood of reciprocation that is commensurate with an algorithm driven digital market places an expectation in the minds of the enterprises that their competitors would likely act in the same way. This mutual expectation can be read as a 'meeting of minds'. The wide definition of agreement under the Competition Act would, in the opinion of the author, allow room for such an interpretation. This notion has also been characterized as a 'unilateral contract' which would be construed more as an agreement than as individual behavior.[227]

Thus, in an algorithmic driven digital market as described above, owing to the peculiar market conditions and awareness of the enterprises which are commonplace in such a market, India can seriously consider an amendment to introduce a reversal of burden of proof where,[228] instead of presuming the AAEC of such parallel actions, it presumes the existence of meeting of minds. Thus, this proposal stipulates that in the face of a parallel behavior among competitors in a digital market, the DG only needs to establish the AAEC of such parallel behavior, upon which the CCI would presume the existence of the meeting of minds among the competitors. Needless to say, this presumption would be a rebuttable one in accordance with the existing jurisprudence on presumptions[229] and the accused enterprises must be allowed a reasonable opportunity to justify their conduct to be a unilateral business decision motivated by market forces and not just a mindless mirroring of the competitors' pricing to achieve supra-competitive profits.

To further augment the justifications as to the presumption of 'meeting of minds' and the corresponding reversal of burden of proof, it must be pointed out that, unlike the digital eye scenario, the enterprises consciously design the algorithm in such a way that collusion is a very likely and predictable outcome. This aspect on part of the enterprises calls for a more stringent approach in enquiry against algorithmic collusions.

This proposal can be problematic at a first glance. Due to the frequency with which such parallel behavior may occur, some have even observed that a presumption as to underlying communication between the enterprises may not be readily accepted and industrial awareness may not be adequate to substitute meeting of minds.[230] However, the rules of the game that governed the brick and mortar world have significantly changed in the context of digital markets ruled by algorithms, thus necessitating a more radical approach in tackling algorithmic tacit collusion. The proposal must certainly be scrutinized so as to not dampen innovation in the market, which can only be achieved through more deliberation on presuming 'meeting of minds' and ameliorating any adverse side effects of the same. However, such an approach should

[227] Posner (1968, p. 1576).

[228] Such reversal of burden of has already been proposed by various authors in the context of presuming the adverse effects of a collusive act. See Ezrachi and Stucke (2020, p. 258). But such a presumption of AAEC already exists in India. See Section 3(3) of the Competition Act.

[229] Sodhi Transport Co. & another vs. State of UP and another, 1986 AIR 1099.

[230] Ezrachi and Stucke (2020).

not be discarded without giving its due place in the discourse of regulating digital markets.

3.3 The Digital Eye or Self-Learning Scenario

The fourth category of algorithmic collusion identified by Ezrachi and Stucke[231] is their digital eye scenario, here referred to as self-learning scenario. In this scenario, enterprises use self-learning algorithms to maximize their profits or accomplish similar targets. A self-learning algorithm is one where, in addition to the initial inputs entered into it, the algorithm learns from its own experiences. Further, the scenario contemplates that the enterprises, though are aware that tacit collusion could be one of the possible outcomes, do not necessarily intended it.[232] The enterprise using a self-learning algorithm is often only able to set the targets to be accomplished (such as profit maximization) by the algorithm with having little to no control over how the targets are achieved by it. The algorithms, having the ability to learn and improve from its experiences, has the potential to observe the patterns of other pricing algorithm used by the competitors and deem it optimal to coordinate a supra competitive price in a sustainable way. This situation poses unique problems since the self-learning algorithms are able to produce collusive outputs through coordination at an AI level. As OEDC observed in its 2017 report, "[i]t is still not clear how machine learning algorithms may actually reach a collusive outcome."[233] Due to the nature of these self-learning algorithms, the collusive outcome can be achieved with very little inputs from the enterprises, which may be regarded as too indirect or remote to attribute any liability on the enterprises for the collusive act of the algorithm. Thus, an anti-competitive collusion can be achieved in the absence of any kind of agreement or common intent among the competing enterprises.[234]

Unlike the predictable agent set up, where the enterprises knowingly employ an algorithm with complete awareness as to a predictable possibility of a collusive outcome being reached, thereby providing a basis to infer an intent to collude, the digital eye scenario operates in the absence of any such intent, thus rendering any consequential tacit collusion as an unintended by-product. This being the case, it has been viewed that such anti-competitive collusions of self-learning algorithms may escape legal scrutiny.[235]

231 Ezrachi and Stucke (2017b, p. 1782).

232 Ezrachi and Stucke (2017b, p. 1795).

233 OECD (2017).

234 Ezrachi and Stucke (2017b, p. 1783).

235 Ezrachi and Stucke (2017b, p. 1796).

3.3.1 Are Algorithms Colluding in the Sense of Section 3(3) of the Competition Act?

The unique automated nature of self-learning algorithms creates a situation that could potentially be unregulated by the Competition Act in its present existence. When two or more enterprises employ a self-learning algorithm that is programmed to optimize profit, it is possible that these algorithms while considering the various factors to fix prices, may commonly discover conscious parallelism as a sustainable strategy to maintain supra-competitive prices. As noted in the predictable agent set up, it is also possible that the enterprises procured the self-learning algorithm from the same algorithm developer, thereby increasing the likelihood of tacit collusion amongst the algorithms since there would be a lot of similarity in its programming. Further, due to the algorithm's ability to constantly monitor the other algorithms' prices and retaliate in the event of an undercut by one of the competitors, enforcing the parallelism is significantly easier. For the same reasons, the other self-learning algorithms would eventually learn that undercutting the prices is never profitable and would begin to reasonably expect reciprocation in the event of a price increase. Thus, the algorithms, conscious that parallelism would yield supra-competitive profit and reasonably certain that reciprocity is exercised by the other algorithm, would be indulging in an anti-competitive agreement in terms of Section 3(3) of the Competition Act. There is one single requirement not covered: an algorithm is neither an enterprise nor a person.

In India, the requirement of agreement, despite its broad definition, requires that it be entered into by enterprises or persons, both of which have been defined under the Competition Act.[236] Thus, an agreement purely between algorithms without it

[236]'Section 2 (h)of the Competition Act states that "enterprise" means a person or a department of the Government, who or which is, or has been, engaged in any activity, relating to the production, storage, supply, distribution, acquisition or control of articles or goods, or the provision of services, of any kind, or in investment, or in the business of acquiring, holding, underwriting or dealing with shares, debentures or other securities of any other body corporate, either directly or through one or more of its units or divisions or subsidiaries, whether such unit or division or subsidiary is located at the same place where the enterprise is located or at a different place or at different places, but does not include any activity of the Government relatable to the sovereign functions of the Government; Section (L) of the Indian Competition At 2002 states that "person" includes—

(i) an individual;
(ii) a Hindu undivided family;
(iii) a company;
(iv) a firm;
(v) an association of persons or a body of individuals, whether incorporated or not, in India or outside India;
(vi) any corporation established by or under any Central, State or Provincial Act or a Government company as defined in Section 617 of the Companies Act, 1956 (1 of 1956);
(vii) anybody corporate incorporated by or under the laws of a country outside India;
(viii) a co-operative society registered under any law relating to co-operative societies;
(ix) a local authority;
(x) every artificial juridical person, not falling within any of the preceding sub-clauses;

being attributable to the enterprises would not trigger Section 3 of the Competition Act.

Therefore, an amendment in the Competition Act is needed to cover situations of anti-competitive collusions orchestrated by deep learning algorithms. Bearing in mind the peculiarities of the digital market and the ease with which collusion can be affected by use of algorithms, it would be naïve on part of India to hold on to a provision prohibiting anti-competitive agreements that was designed for the brick and mortar markets. An easy approach would be to enforce a complete prohibition on the use of deep learning algorithms since it is near impossible to regulate and control the way they operate. Further, the law in its present form may be inadequate to place any liability on the enterprise that uses such an algorithm. However, such a move would be a step backward for businesses considering that there is a general shift of marketplaces from the brick and mortar world to the digital platforms across all industries. Hence there is a necessity to explore innovative solutions for harmonizing dependency on deep learning algorithms and a need for maintaining pro-competitive equilibrium in the market.

3.3.2 Can the Liability Be Shifted to the Enterprise?

The problem posed by the self-learning algorithms to competition regimes all over the world is novel, unique and evolving. This being the case, any solution devised to allay the challenges posed by the digital eye scenario should also be innovative and adaptable to the dynamic nature of the digital market. An angle worth considering to make the enterprise accountable for the actions of its algorithm would be the principles of agency under contract law. Accordingly, if the algorithm can be said to be an autonomous agent of the enterprise, the enterprise can be made liable for the actions of the agent. However, the biggest hurdle to make this theory practicable is the grant of personhood to the algorithms so that they may qualify as agents of the enterprise.

The essence of the principle of agency is encapsulated by the Latin maxim *qui facit per alium facit* per se, which means 'he who acts through another does the act himself.' Under the Indian Contract Act of 1872 (Contract Act), the law governing agency is covered under Chapter 10.[237] As per the provisions of the Chapter 10, an agent is a person employed to do an act for another or to represent another in dealings

(xi) "practice" includes all activities carried on by the departments of the Central' Government dealing with atomic energy, currency, defence and space.'

[237]Chapter 10 of the Indian Contract Act comprises Section 182 to 238.

with third persons.[238] The Contract Act further describes who may be an agent under Section 184, which imposes additional requirements as to the age and mental soundness of the agent. The term 'person' is not defined under the Contract Act,[239] but the Competition Act provides for a wide definition of 'person.'[240] However, as per the definition an algorithm would not fit in any of the categories mentioned therein, except for the final category of 'artificial juristic person' provided that India considers favorably passing an amendment recognizing self-learning algorithms as an artificial juristic person and as an agent of the enterprise employing it.

The grant of personhood for artificial intelligence (AI) is a debate in itself. With the increase in use of automation in several industries coupled with advancements in AI, jurisdiction across the globe ought to seriously think about its stance on granting personhood to AI to navigate across an array of legal issues concerning the same including determining the liability of their actions and several experts have already theorized the pros and cons for the same.[241] If AI and self-learning algorithms are considered persons, they could be regarded as an agent of the enterprise that employed it and thus make the latter liable for its actions, including violations under competition law.

Section 188 of the Contract Act does raise a concern since it provides that the extent of authority of an agent is 'to do every lawful thing which is necessary in order' to do the act entrusted to it. Therefore, one could argue that the autonomous agent (self-learning algorithm) choosing to unlawfully collude in fixing prices would be outside the scope of the law and thus fail to transfer the liability onto the principal (enterprise). However, the provision was drafted keeping in mind a person capable of knowing what is lawful and unlawful on his/her own, and acting with reasonable care so as to not breach any law. In case of an algorithm, it can only be programmed to abide by the laws. Therefore, care must be taken by the enterprise or the developer to program the algorithms in such a way that it does not violate the provisions of competition act. Failure to program the algorithms accordingly must result in liability. This approach might be regarded as farfetched without more analysis as to the exact way in which such pricing algorithms are designed and the ramifications of granting personhood to such algorithms or deeming them to be agents of enterprises as a legal fiction. However, while treading on unchartered territories of legal conundrums such as the self-learning algorithms, it is necessary that all avenues of solutions are explored. There are other suggestions such as implementing 'algorithm by design' and establishing specialized agencies to monitor and

[238]Section 182 of the Contract Act 1857 states that "agent" and "principal" defined—An "agent" is a person employed to do any act for another, or to represent another in dealings with third persons. The person for whom such act is done, or who is so represented, is called the "principal".

[239]When a term is not defined in a particular legislation the practice is to adopt the definition provided for the term in the General Clauses Act of 1977. The said act defines a person (in Section 2(30)) to include any company or association or body of individuals, whether incorporated or not. However, the author relies on the definition of 'person' in the competition act for the purpose of the present analysis.

[240]See Section 2(L) of the Competition Act.

[241]Chopra and White (2004).

investigate algorithmic collusion in detail. They are discussed in greater detail in the recommendation Section.

4 A Way Forward for the Competition Commission of India

The world is seeing a paradigm shift since the advent of digitization, not only from the technology perspective but from the policy-making perspective, legal perspective, consumer perspective and corporate perspective. With data becoming the only form of 'rivalry' the shift in the world's reliance on data for service optimization has taken new contours to an escalating technopoly. The world hasn't stopped there and the companies have taken all measures to further the use of data by adapting to the new age price determining techniques. The contrive of pricing algorithms has raised serious questions from a competition law perspective and to all jurisdictions alike.

The more sophisticated jurisdictions are already facing the heat, but less mature jurisdictions are yet to encounter such a mammoth task of dealing with competition issues arising from pricing algorithms. The CCI has witnessed investigations in algorithm-driven markets such as the ride sharing service market,[242] platform for hotels and flight markets,[243] and search algorithm market.[244] It cannot be said that India has yet not faced the heat which is ensuing from the anti-competitive practices posed by algorithms. However, the question remains how far the CCI has taken preventive steps to combat issues arising through these algorithms and how far it must go to address the problems that can ensue. The wave of problems posed by such algorithms does not restrict itself to the enforcement issues but obstructs the authorities at the stage of detection itself. The biggest challenge for competition authorities is to detect such anti-competitive practices which are prevalent so discreetly in the market. The authorities will have to rely on technological revolution in their detection mechanism if they want to keep up with the innovative ways of collusion by the enterprises.

India unlike other jurisdictions needs to put in place some general recommendations in place before trying to combat complex anti-trust issues. Since without these general recommendations in place, it would be difficult for CCI to adapt to the complex mechanisms of detecting collusion through algorithms. The author shall place a combination of detection and enforcement recommendations that can be adopted by the CCI.

---

[242]Competition Appeal (AT) No.11 OF 2019.

[243]CCI, Case No. 14 of 2019, Federation of Hotel & Restaurant. Associations of India vs. MakeMyTrip India Pvt. Ltd.

[244]C (2018) 4761, AT.40099—Google Android, Commission Decision of 18 July 2018.

4.1 A Shift in Corporate Governance: Misplaced Antitrust Penalties

Competition policy in India has to be promoted by a combination of compliance obligations on the companies and restructuring the remedial provisions of competition law itself.[245] As per the OECD report 2019 India, apart from USA and China,[246] is the only country which does not have compliance codes or guidelines. Instead they still turn to existing laws for their corporate governance framework and apply 'comply or else' approach.[247] A 'comply or else' approach might be a better approach in a certain institutional framework specifically if it is backed by statutory guidelines.

This argument becomes all the more relevant when we look at antitrust compliance functioning within the companies. The need for a mandatory corporate governance compliance mechanism cannot be overstated, irrespective whether it is for the field of competition law or not.

CCI has released a compliance manual for all enterprises guiding them on what kind of compliance should be in place in the enterprise.[248] However, there is no approved standard for compliance backed by legislation, making the competition law compliance within the companies a mere show. A survey was conducted by the Ernst and Young[249] Fraud Investigation and Dispute Services in the year 2014[250] in which 70% of the 80 odd respondents believed that companies had neither mechanism at the grassroots level for competition law compliance nor control mechanisms. The survey also pointed out that most of the respondents believed that there is a lot of discretionary power with the CCI in determining fines to be levied on defaulting companies and defaulting parties without their being proper guidelines. It further stated the lack of transparency in granting leniency, also plays a major role in reduced detection of anti-competitive activities. The author does not rely on the veracity of the facts since the survey is outdated, however the author still feels the second and third point raised by the survey holds valid.

For the compliance regime to be in place and to be followed, the companies need to be incentivized. The company's incentives are drawn from antitrust sanctions which include potentially large fines in the Indian competition regime. India still does not yet have criminal antitrust sanctions in place. However civil antitrust sanctions are enormous and incorporate the biggest sanction in the form of loss of reputation to the company. The Competition Act provides the remedial measures by penalizing the companies on their turnovers under Section 27 of Competition Act[251] and also

---

[245] Markham (2013).

[246] It has a national corporate governance code that it updated in 2018, it is fully binding, so may instead be understood as mandatory regulation. OECD (2019a).

[247] OECD (2019a).

[248] Competition Commission of India (2017).

[249] Dey and Bhupta (2014).

[250] Ernst & Young (2014).

[251] 'Orders by Commission after inquiry into agreements or abuse of dominant position. — Where after inquiry the Commission finds that any agreement referred to in Section 3 or action of an

impose sanctions on individuals under Section 48 of the Competition Act.[252] The decision-makers (directors)[253] in the company owe a fiduciary duty to the corporation and its shareholders. Failure to discharge their duty shall invite individual sanctions

enterprise in a dominant position, is in contravention of Section 3 or Section 4, as the case may be, it may pass all or any of the following orders, namely: —

(a) direct any enterprise or association of enterprises or person or association of persons, as the case may be, involved in such agreement, or abuse of dominant position, to discontinue and not to re-enter such agreement or discontinue such abuse of dominant position, as the case may be;
(b) impose such penalty, as it may deem fit which shall be not more than ten per cent. of the average of the turnover for the last three preceding financial years, upon each of such person or enterprises which are parties to such agreements or abuse: Provided that in case any agreement referred to in Section 3 has been entered into by any cartel, the Commission shall impose upon each producer, seller, distributor, trader or service provider included in that cartel, a penalty equivalent to three times of the amount of profits made out of such agreement by the cartel or ten per cent. of the average of the turnover of the cartel for the last preceding three financial years, whichever is higher.'

[252] 'Section 48 (1) Where a person committing contravention of any of the provisions of this Act or of any rule, regulation, order made or direction issued thereunder is a company, every person who, at the time the contravention was committed, was in charge of, and was responsible to the company for the conduct of the business of the company, as well as the company, shall be deemed to be guilty of the contravention and shall be liable to be proceeded against and punished accordingly: Provided that nothing contained in this sub-Section shall render any such person liable to any punishment if he proves that the contravention was committed without his knowledge or that he had exercised all due diligence to prevent the commission of such contravention. (2) Notwithstanding anything contained in sub-Section (1), where a contravention of any of the provisions of this Act or of any rule, regulation, order made or direction issued thereunder has been committed by a company and it is proved that the contravention has taken place with the consent or connivance of, or is attributable to any neglect on the part of, any director, manager, secretary or other officer of the company, such director, manager, secretary or other officer shall also be deemed to be guilty of that contravention and shall be liable to be proceeded against and punished accordingly'.

[253] Section 166 of the Companies Act 2002 states that: '(1) Subject to the provisions of this Act, a director of a company shall act in accordance with the articles of the company. (2) A director of a company shall act in good faith in order to promote the objects of the company for the benefit of its members as a whole, and in the best interests of the company, its employees, the shareholders, the

under Section 48 of Competition Act in the same proceedings.[254] The combination of competition law compliance and fiduciary law could help achieve the competition policy objectives.[255]

However, neither of them have been able to achieve the required deterrence and antitrust violations which occur at an unacceptable regularity. The reasons are most obvious. The sanctioning of the company on its turnover 'mis'-places the burden of penalty on the shareholders rather than on the decision makers. Since the penalty is borne by the unaware shareholders, who have no role in setting compliance policies, the sanctioning of the corporation shall not dissuade the senior management from re-engaging in anti-competitive activity and adhering to the compliance policies.

4.2 *What Is Muddled?*

Section 48 read in conjunction with Section 27 of the Competition Act allows the CCI to sanction companies and individuals who were in fiduciary duty or in-charge of company's conduct of business unless they can prove that they were unaware or exercised due-diligence. However, the trend in judgments shows a muddling development. In most of the cartel orders there is a disproportionate penalty spread across the company and the individuals responsible for such anti-competitive activity. A survey carried in an article titled "Scope for Intersection Between Antitrust Laws and Corporate Governance Principles Vis-à-Vis Cartels Deterrence in India," claimed that out of thirty-two cases between 2010 and 2015 under Section 3(3) of the Competition Act, only sixteen cases saw indictment of individuals. CCI was still waiting to pass the order in half of these cases. However, this trend has changed substantially post 2015 and the CCI has become extremely proactive in sanctioning individuals under Section 48 of the Competition Act. The CCI has imposed penalties on individuals

community and for the protection of environment. (3) A director of a company shall exercise his duties with due and reasonable care, skill and diligence and shall exercise independent judgment. (4) A director of a company shall not involve in a situation in which he may have a direct or indirect interest that conflicts, or possibly may conflict, with the interest of the company. (5) A director of a company shall not achieve or attempt to achieve any undue gain or advantage either to himself or to his relatives, partners, or associates and if such director is found guilty of making any undue gain, he shall be liable to pay an amount equal to that gain to the company. (6) A director of a company shall not assign his office and any assignment so made shall be void. (7) If a director of the company contravenes the provisions of this Section such director shall be punishable with fine which shall not be less than Indian Rupees one hundred thousand but which may extend to five lakhs'.

[254] The CCI rejected the argument made by the party in Ministry of Agriculture and Farmers Welfare vs. M/s Mahyco Monsanto Biotech (India) Limited by relying on the COMPAT decision in A.N. Mohana Kurup and Others vs. CCI and Other that the CCI needs to issue a finding on the culpability of the enterprise before initiating the investigation against the persons-in charge and that there needs to be two separate proceedings against the enterprise and the persons-in charge. In essence both the proceedings can be initiated simultaneously.

[255] Ernst & Young (2014).

under Section 48 Competition Act in cases such as the Battery case,[256] BDCA,[257] Sports Broadcasters Case[258] at the same percentage at which the company is charged. However, there is still substantial disproportion on how much penalty is borne by the individual (the actual brain behind the anti-competitive conduct) and by the company who is just a shield for their motive to enter into such wrongful practices and the brunt being faced by the share-holders.

The CCI used the power given under Section 48(2) of the Competition Act[259] to order disassociation with the officers of Kerala Chemists and Druggist Association involved in anti-competitive activity for two years in the Alkeim case CCI has yet not passed any order under Section 48 of the Competition Act terminating a director or an office bearer from his/her position and, as such, the power of the CCI to impose administrative sanctions in this respect remains questionable.[260]

If the practice of disproportionate cost being borne by the companies and the individuals continues to transpire, the corporate governance problem shall worsen and raises three fundamental issues. First, the sanctions are not deterrent enough for the individuals to dissuade from engaging in the anti-competitive activity. Secondly these individuals are the ones who overlook the compliance mandate by the companies, lack of fear amongst them shall impede the compliance adherence. Third, the lack of clarity by the commission on levying penalties or factors affecting grant of leniency, without any detailed guidelines also creates uncertainty on whether the companies will have any advantage for having compliance mechanism in place.

4.2.1 Revisiting Administrative Sanctions

The CCI shall put in place administrative sanctions coupled with civil sanctions to over-come the problem of under-deterrence amongst the senior officials. When collusion is being effected through algorithms the decision-makers or the senior officials of the company are either aware or ought to be aware of such anti-competitive activity and they must be brought under the radar inevitably. The Competition Act is one of the boldest acts in terms of the presumption it raises against every person who

[256]CCI, Suo Motu Case No. 03 of 2017, In Re: Anticompetitive conduct in the Dry-Cell Batteries Market in India.

[257]CCI, Suo Motu Case No. 02 of 2012, Bengal Chemists and Druggists Association.

[258]CCI, Suo Motu Case No. 02 of 2013, In Re: Cartelization by broadcasting service providers by rigging the bids submitted in response to the tenders floated by Sports Broadcasters.

[259]Section 48(2) of the Competition Act states that: '(2) Notwithstanding anything contained in sub-Section (1), where a contravention of any of the provisions of this Act or of any rule, regulation, order made or direction issued thereunder has been committed by a company and it is proved that the contravention has taken place with the consent or connivance of, or is attributable to any neglect on the part of, any director, manager, secretary or other officer of the company, such director, manager, secretary or other officer shall also be deemed to be guilty of that contravention and shall be liable to be proceeded against and punished accordingly.'

[260]CCI, Case No. 28 of 2014, Mr. KP. K. Krishnan vs. M/s Alkem Laboratories and Another Srinivas et al. (2018).

is responsible for conducting the affairs of the company, which has been alleged for behaving anti-competitively. Section 48(1) of the Competition Act raises a presumption against any person who is responsible for conduct contravening the Competition Act. This shall indirectly induce them to put proper compliance measures in place due to the fear of being indicted or being scrutinized for the lack of vigilance. However, this could be a controversial step if it is not backed by proper guidelines stating under what circumstances can the employee ought to have known.

The CCI as suggested in the paper "Scope for Intersection Between Antitrust Laws and Corporate Governance Principles Vis-à-Vis Cartels Deterrence in India" must amend the competition act to include a provision barring the employers from indemnifying the employees' *ex post* or *ex ante* who have been penalized for conducting anti-competitive activity in the market. This amendment is necessary since most of the official/employees indulge in anti-competitive activity on behalf of the employer for the reward in return without the fear of losing money from their pockets. However, the imposition of administrative sanctions shall not be cumbersome on the CCI since the standard to impose such penalties is that of preponderance of probabilities. Moreover, imposition of such penalties does not require expending large resources or manpower and hence can be easily enforced with the existing mechanism in place. However, such amendment might fall foul of transgressing into the Indian Companies Act which deals with the rules pertaining to the functioning of the company. Section 197 of the Indian Companies Act of 2013 (Companies Act) categorically mentions that the company shall carry out insurance to indemnify the managing directors, CEO, CFO, whole-time director or CS of the company if any liability accrues on them with respect to any negligence, breach of duty or breach of trust.[261] However, they shall not be indemnified where they have been proved guilty of the contravention and the premium payable shall be treated as a part of their remuneration. The scope of the Section is expansive as it includes any negligence, breach of trust and duty on the

---

[261] 'Section 197 of the Indian Companies Act 2013 1) The total managerial remuneration payable by a public company, to its directors, including managing director and whole-time director, and its manager in respect of any financial year shall not exceed eleven per cent. of the net profits of that company for that financial year computed in the manner laid down in Section 198 except that the remuneration of the directors shall not be deducted from the gross profits:

Provided that the company in general meeting may, 4[Omitted], authorize the payment of remuneration exceeding eleven per cent. of the net profits of the company, subject to the provisions of Schedule V:

Provided further that, except with the approval of the company in general meeting 5[By a special resolution],—

(i) the remuneration payable to any one managing director; or whole-time director or manager shall not exceed five per cent. of the net profits of the company and if there is more than one such director remuneration shall not exceed ten per cent. of the net profits to all such directors and manager taken together;

(ii) the remuneration payable to directors who are neither managing directors nor whole-time directors shall not exceed,— (A) one per cent. of the net profits of the company, if there is a managing or whole-time director or manager; (B) three per cent. of the net profits in any other case.].'

part of the person in charge and hence includes breach of fiduciary duty and the duty of "ought to know" principle.[262] Section 62 of Competition Act[263] mentions that the provisions of this act shall be in addition to any other law in force and hence instead of bringing in amendment in the competition act, the CCI can make a cross–reference under Section 21(A) of the Competition Act[264] to Companies Act in order to invalidate the indemnification of the directors who have been found to contravene Competition Act.

Further, an amendment must be modelled in lines with §204 of the UK Enterprise Act,[265] wherein CCI could seek director disqualification.[266] Director disqualification for competition breaches has proven to be a great deterrence for officials in jurisdictions like UK and Australia.[267] The CCI has, as has been mentioned above, recently passed an order under Section 48(2) of the Competition Act mandating a company to disassociate itself with two officers who were found contravening the competition law. This order is in nature an administrative sanction. It is a departure from previous decisions where the authorities have never passed disassociation orders. If the decision in the Alkeim case is not overruled, like what happened in the Kerela Cine Exhibitors case,[268] the decision to disassociate could be a welcome step for the future decisions and so for deterrence.

---

[262] Section 48 of the Companies Act 2013 every person who is responsible for conducting the affairs of the company ought to have known of any anti-competitive activity being carried on, on behalf of the company unless they can show otherwise.

[263] The provisions of the Competition Act shall be in addition to, and not in derogation of, the provisions of any other law for the time being in force.

[264] Where in the course of a proceeding before the Commission an issue is raised by any party that any decision which, the Commission has taken during such proceeding or proposes to take, is or would be contrary to any provision of this Act whose implementation is entrusted to a statutory authority, then the Commission may make a reference in respect of such issue to the statutory authority: Provided that the Commission, may, *suo motu*, make such a reference to the statutory authority. (2) On receipt of a reference under sub-Section (1), the statutory authority shall give its opinion, within sixty days of receipt of such reference, to the Commission which shall consider the opinion of the statutory authority, and thereafter give its findings recording reasons there for on the issues referred to in the said opinion.].

[265] Section 204 of the Enterprise Act lists down the factors for disqualification of directors. 'Disqualification for competition infringements: 9ACompetition disqualification order

(1) The court must make a disqualification order against a person if the following two conditions are satisfied in relation to him.
(2) The first condition is that an undertaking which is a company of which he is a director commits a breach of competition law.
(3) The second condition is that the court considers that his conduct as a director makes him unfit to be concerned in the management of a company.'

Available at: http://www.legislation.gov.uk/ukpga/2002/40/Section/204. Accessed 15 December 2020.

[266] See Enterprise Act, 2002, § 204(6). Muralidharan and Deshpande (2016).

[267] Deloitte (2007).

[268] CCI, Case No. 45 of 2012, Kerala Cine Exhibitors Association vs. Kerala Film Exhibitors Association.

The decision Alkeim case could be challenged, though. Ordering disassociation based on the Competition Act may transgresses into the power given of the Indian Companies Act, which is the sole law that can determine the procedure to remove or terminate the directors or officers in charge from the company. The wording under Section 48 of the Competition Act to take "any order as [the CCI] may deem fit" does not, according to the author, give the power the CCI to transgress into the scope of the Indian Companies Act.

The Companies Act 2013 mentions under Schedule V appended to Section 197 that any person found in contravention of the acts and penalized under those acts with imprisonment or a fine exceeding Indian Rupees One Thousand (INR 1,000) shall stand disqualified from being appointed as a whole-time director, managing director or manager of a public company. The schedule mentions the Competition Act and hence any whole-time or managing director or manager who has been penalized under the Competition Act must automatically trigger disqualification under Section 197 of the Companies Act. The scope of Schedule V in Section 197 of the Companies Act is restricted to public companies and hence does not apply to private companies and government companies making the scope of the Section extremely limited.[269]

Despite these considerations, the CCI, under Section 21A of the Competition Act, has the *suo motu* right to make reference to the statutory authority if it is of the opinion that its decision "would be contrary to any provisions of the act whose implementation is entrusted to a statutory authority." In the case under discussion, the CCI can refer to the Central Government for the removal or disqualification of the officer in charge for contravening the Competition Act.

The Central Government has been given wide powers under Section 241 of the Indian Companies Act to initiate a case against any person concerned with the conduct and management of the affairs of the company who has conducted the affairs in a manner prejudicial to the public interest. Section 241(3)(c) of the Indian Companies Act mentions "a company is or has been conducted and managed by such person in a manner which is likely to cause, or has caused, serious injury or damage to the interest of the trade, industry or business to which such company pertains", and hence any person who has contravened the competition act 2002 could be considered to have damaged the interest of the trade, industry or business. The author proposes a clarifying amendment in Section 241 of Indian Companies Act to include any act done in contravention to the Competition Act 2002 to be considered as mismanagement. The central government under Section 241 has the authority to refer the matter to

[269] Section 197(1) The total managerial remuneration payable by a public company, to its directors, including managing director and whole-time director, and its manager in respect of any financial year shall not exceed eleven per cent. of the net profits of that company for that financial year computed in the manner laid down in Section 198 except that the remuneration of the directors shall not be deducted from the gross profits: Provided that the company in general meeting may, authorize the payment of remuneration exceeding eleven per cent of the net profits of the company, subject to the provisions of Schedule V: hence the applicability of Section 197 is limited to public companies. Government companies are specifically excluded. Available at: http://ebook.mca.gov.in/notificationdetail.aspx?acturl=6CoJDC4uKVUR7C9Fl4rZdatyDbeJTqg3XHmN4i4mFb+v2wWhMvQoFsXKgJTHtRr9VmNjj/XQUFc9vZ6tRKIi2gIhxfNI2SOK. Accessed 15 December 2020.

the tribunal under the Companies Act to decide whether the person is fit to hold the office. The decision by the CCI of contravention by an officer in charge under Section 48 of the Competition Act should automatically trigger the cross-reference to Section 241 under the Indian Companies Act.

Unless the amendments coupled with administrative and civil sanctions are not put in place, a full proof deterrence of collusion will become difficult.[270] This shall help, for if the penalties are severe, collusion affected through any means may become unstable.

4.2.2 Lack of Incentives to Apply for Leniency

The second problem is the lack of incentives for the companies or the individuals to whistle blow due to uncertainty of leniency being granted in India under the Lesser Penalty Regulations, 2009.[271] The detection of cartels is a nuisance that is being faced by all jurisdictions alike. However, the other jurisdictions have evidenced an increased detection rate since the inception of the leniency scheme. India, even though has leniency scheme in place since inception it was only recently that India started granting leniency to whistle-blowers. The move is a welcome move but is majorly met with fraught. The reason that can be attributed to the anxiety of application to leniency is due to the unpredictable stand taken by the CCI in the past. It was only in 2017 that the CCI passed its first order granting 75% leniency to Pyramid Electronics in the cartelization case by electronic companies in tenders released by Indian Railways.[272] This was the first case to bring predictability on the factors to be taken in consideration while determining the leniency grant. It was only in the year 2018 that the Commission for the first time in the Indian Zinc-Carbon Dry Cell Batteries[273] case granted one hundred per-cent leniency to Panasonic and further in the case of cartelization by the broadcasting service providers explicitly mentioned the factors of offering leniency with more grit.[274]

However, the CCI still has a long way to go to bring in more predictability in its orders for granting leniency. For instance, it should be explicitly mentioned as to why two parties providing the same information be treated differently.[275] For instance,

[270]The Commerce (Cartels and other matters) Amendment Bill, 2011 amended §80A to reflect a prohibition on body corporate and interconnected bodies, against indemnity of pecuniary penalty for present and former employee, agent, servant and director, vis-à-vis both fines and legal costs. The proposed amendment was adopted in full and is reflected in the Commerce Act, 1986, and any such indemnity granted is declared as void. An indemnity is stated to include "relieving or excusing from liability, whether before or after the liability arises." The Commence Act, 1986, §80A.

[271]The CCI (Lesser Penalty) Regulations, 2009 (No. 4 of 2009).

[272]CCI, Suo motu Case No. 03 of 2014 In Re: Cartelization in respect of tenders floated by Indian Railways for supply of Brushless DC Fans and other electrical items.

[273]CCI, Suo Motu Case No 02 of 2016 Re. Panasonic Corporation, Japan & Others.

[274]CCI, Suo Motu Case No. 02 of 2013 In Re: Cartelization by broadcasting service.

[275]CCI, Suo Motu Case No. 02 of 2013 In Re: Cartelization by broadcasting service.

in the case of Dry-Cell Battery case,[276] the CCI held that the other two applicants did not provide information which could add significant value to the already existing information but both of them were granted leniency of 20 and 30% respectively without assigning the difference in the leniency percentage.[277] Though it could be inferred from the arguments as to why they were treated differently but the commission has to become more reasoned in its approach. The lesser penalty regulations should also make its stand clear on whether if a company is granted leniency, how will the officials who have been alleged be treated. The lesser penalty regulations do not talk explicitly about what would happen to the liability of the official where the company has been granted leniency.[278] Through decisional practice[279] it is evident that the individuals' penalty is reduced at the same percentage as that of the company. However, there needs to be specific guidelines mentioning the same. Unless the sense of predicament amongst the corporations/ individuals on when shall they be granted immunity does not go away, the detection of cartels effected through algorithms or without algorithms shall remain difficult.

The CCI in its compliance manual,[280] has stated steps that have to be taken by the enterprises some of which include explicit statements of compliance by senior officials, training and educating the employees on competition compliance. It has also provided for additional compliance measures to be implemented that "may be considered essential" by the companies,[281] The lack of clarity on 'what' and 'how many' are essential compliance measures and what are non-essential measures has left enterprises disordered on what compliance measures they must have in place which shall be considered by the commission while granting leniency. The misalignment of what commission shall consider essential measures while reviewing leniency applications and what parties might think is essential has made the compliance measures inadequate. The compliance manual mentions in a separate heading 'benefits of competition compliance manual' but fails to mention the grant of leniency as one of the benefits of adhering to all the compliances.[282] The lack of clarity within the commission on how to incentivize the enterprises to adhere has failed the compliance framework. The commission in the Suo Motu case No. 02 of 2013[283] mentioned that if the company had compliance measures in place it would be considered as a mitigating factor while determining the penalty to be levied on them but such compliance measures must be in place before the inquiry is initiated. Any compliance measures

---

[276] CCI, Suo Motu Case No 02 of 2016 Re. Panasonic Corporation, Japan & Others.

[277] CCI, Suo Motu Case No 02 of 2016 Re. Panasonic Corporation, Japan & Others.

[278] Regulation 3 1(A) of the Competition Commission of India (Lesser Penalty) Regulations, 2009 (No. 4 of 2009), Where the applicant is an enterprise, it shall also provide the names of the individuals who have been involved in the cartel on its behalf and for whom lesser penalty is sought by such an enterprise.

[279] CCI, Suo Motu Case No. 02 of 2013 In Re: Cartelization by broadcasting service.

[280] Competition Commission of India (2017).

[281] Competition Commission of India (2017, Chapter 3).

[282] Competition Commission of India (2017, Chapter 5).

[283] CCI, Suo Motu Case No. 02 of 2013, In Re: Cartelization by broadcasting service providers by rigging the bids submitted in response to the tenders floated by Sports Broadcasters.

put in place post the DG's notice shall not be considered a mitigating factor. The Excel crop[284] case also mentions that bona fides by the company will be considered as a mitigating factor while determining the penalty to be levied. However, the commission must come up with certitude[285] the essential compliance measures and the influence of those compliance measures on penalties being levied on companies for their involvement in anti-competitive activity. The commission must come up with a framework to assess whether companies are actually adhering to any of the compliance measures in routine and not only when they are brought under the scanner of anti-competitive activities. If they fail to adhere to the compliance measures or do not have compliance measures in place they shall be penalized without going into the reasons. This approach is called the 'comply or else' approach.[286] This is the model on which Indian Corporate governance is based. However, CCI has not been able to use it for its benefit.

This recommendation to use the 'comply or else' approach could be problematic since it would require a large work-force and shall consume a lot of resources to collect information on companies through random checks or through some form of feedback mechanism. Unless the commission does not use a feedback mechanism, backed by statutory guidelines, the compliance framework shall not achieve its desired purpose. Hence the commission, if it has such resources in place could devise determinative guidelines of compliance measures that must be in place mandatorily. The commission could also be empowered by an amendment to the statute to conduct audits on the compliance mechanisms put in place by the companies.

Alternatively, to avoid the problem of 'one size fits all' a mechanism of 'comply or explain'[287] could be adhered to. However, this governance mechanism requires a dominant role by the regulator for enforcement. For this approach to be successful it depends on how far the companies are willing to be transparent in their operations and a sense of belief that good governance should be the goal. This approach to a great extent depends on how far companies are wanting to adopt such measures which again raises the issue that exists with self-regulation.[288]

The Indian regime on corporate governance has still not reached parity with international standards. The liability of the companies in terms of compliance within their structure is more specifically related to environmental compliances, insider trading, corporate social responsibility, but they yet haven't inculcated the antitrust compliance measures within the company. The other startling problem existing with

---

[284] Excel Crop Care Limited vs. CCI, (2017) 8 SCC 47.

[285] The US Federal Sentencing Compliance Guidelines provide that the fine imposed for antitrust violation may be reduced by the existence of an effective compliance program by the offending organization. See US DOJ Sentencing Guidelines Manual, 2015, § 8B2.1. the Australian Competition and Consumer Commission (ACCC) immunity and co-operation policy provides that in determining the civil penalties for the confessing member of a cartel, the ACCC will factor in whether the corporation has a corporate culture conducive for compliance with antitrust law. Australian Competition and Consumer Commission (2014).

[286] Sarkar (2015).

[287] Sarkar (2015, p. 314).

[288] Sarkar (2015, p. 315).

corporate governance and antitrust liability is the misplaced effect of penalties on the company's turnover and eventually on the shareholders of the companies, leaving the decision-holders scot-free. The solution by Margaret Vestager on Antitrust by Design is an extension of a bigger corporate governance issue. If the companies are induced to have in-built antitrust compliance in their functioning, antitrust by design would automatically follow as a consequence.

4.3 Competition by Design

Margaret Vestager, the EU Commissioner for competition, while addressing the algorithmic collusion in public speeches, has mentioned the reliance on algorithm by design.[289] The CCI could, for example, implement this thought and make it mandatory for the companies to adopt compliance by design while using pricing algorithms. The pricing algorithms must be tuned in such a way that they shall deny any offers to enter into anti-competitive activities. The onus must be on the companies building the algorithms and on the companies using them. The inability to deal with complex technology can no more be a justification for dispiritedness. The competition enforcers must overcome the issues of opacity of algorithms primarily in order to address the issues of detection and infringement.

4.3.1 Algorithmic Transparency

The digital economy demands transparency. India has introduced, for larger public concerns,[290] the concept of disclosure of source code and algorithms in the draft e-commerce policy (draft policy) under clause 4.10.[291] has introduced the concept of disclosure of source code and algorithms. The language used in the draft policy mentions: 'the decisions will need to be explained.' This points towards the mandatory nature of the disclosure of source code or of why certain algorithms are behaving in a certain way. The draft policy, though extremely recent, does not take into account competition law issues that might arise due to the use of algorithms.

---

[289]Vezzoso (2017).

[290]The draft ecommerce policy under clause 4.10 has defined the scope of public concern to include prevention of racial profiling and to protect the constitutional right, the question remains whether the larger public concern could also include within its ambit the market failure due to algorithm.

[291]Clause 4.10 states that in continuation, it is also important for the Government to reserve its right to seek disclosure of source code and algorithms. There will be a greater reliance on AI in decision making in future where parts of the process will become 'AI-fied'. Decisions will need to be explained. There is a need to strike a balance between commercial interests and consumer protection issues, as well as issues of larger public concern, like preventing racial profiling and maintaining constitutionally mandated rights, such as the right to equality.

The government and the CCI must address the problem raised by algorithms' opacity by making it mandatory for companies developing algorithms or using algorithms to disclose why algorithms have made certain decisions and how they have made those decisions. This mandatory disclosure can become a part of the routine where they see a distorted market structure or unfair pricing issues through consumer complaints under the Consumer Protection Act[292] or the Competition Act. Moreover, the commission must put in place self-reporting mechanisms where the companies report on their own algorithms infringing competition law provision. The incentive behind the self-reporting mechanism could be linked with the leniency scheme under Section 46 of Competition Act.[293] The failure to disclose voluntarily could be met with enormous civil penalties. This could aid in dealing with anti-competitive constraints brought about by self-learning algorithms. Under Section 57(1)(a) of the Personal Data Protection Bill,[294] failure to self-report a breach of data by a data fiduciary under Section 25 of the Personal Data Protection Bill can invite penalties up to Indian Rupees Fifty Million (INR 50,000,000) or 2% of the total worldwide turn-over of the preceding year of the company, whichever is higher.[295] Increased sanctions and rightful alignment of sanctions under competition law for collusion may induce individuals and companies to self-report.

4.3.2 Automation of Competition Law

Replicating the provisions of competition law in the computer code could also be a workable option to prevent collusive practices in market using algorithms. How far law provisions can be automated is still inconclusive. As was mentioned by Simonetta Vezzoso in her article "Competition by Design" the human language cannot be equated with computer language which is highly controlled.[296] Rather

---

[292] Available at: https://consumeraffairs.nic.in/sites/default/files/CP%20Act%202019.pdf. Accessed 15 December 2020.

[293] Section 46 of the Competition Act: 'Power to impose lesser penalty- The Commission may, if it is satisfied that any producer, seller, distributor, trader or service provider included in any cartel, which is alleged to have violated Section 3, has made a full and true disclosure in respect of the alleged violations and such disclosure is vital, impose upon such producer, seller, distributor, trader or service provider a lesser penalty as it may deem fit, than leviable under this Act or the rules or the regulations: 75[Provided that lesser penalty shall not be imposed by the Commission in cases where the report of investigation directed under Section 26 has been received before making of such disclosure.] Provided further that lesser penalty shall be imposed by the Commission only in respect of a producer, seller, distributor, trader or service provider included in the cartel, who 76[has] made the full, true and vital disclosures under this Section'.

[294] The Personal Data Protection Bill, 2018 (PDP Bill).

[295] Pursuant to 57(1)(a) of PDP Bill, in the event the data fiduciary contravenes its obligation to take prompt and appropriate action in response to a data security breach under Section 25 of the PDP Bill, such data fiduciary shall be liable to a penalty which may extend to Indian Rupees Fifty Million (INR 50,000,000) or 2% (two percent) of its total worldwide turnover of the preceding financial year, whichever is higher.

[296] Vezzoso (2017).

computer language needs to be more straightforward. The artificial language might not be able to interpret legal provisions like humans do. Hence over-complicated provisions of competition law might not be fit to be replicated in the computer code and might lead to non-compliance. It might be more relevant to prevent practices mentioned under Section 3(3) of the Competition Act which are presumed to have appreciable adverse effect (follow a per se approach) in the market and hence is less complicated in its determination compared to other agreements which need to be weighed for pro-competitive justification and anti-competitive justification. The algorithms can be automated to include practices which have a more straightforward per se approach that they shall not be allowed to carry for instance market allocation, bid rigging, price fixing and output control.[297]

In the fast-evolving digital market ex-post investigation might not be helpful. Therefore, the CCI has to be deploy technology to identify anti-competitive activity ex-ante. Further, the companies can be mandated to prescribe what data shall be taken into consideration by the algorithms while deciding the prices which can restrict the flow of data inducing anti-competitive market outcome.[298] For instance, in the Wall Décor case, the anticompetitive market outcome was a result of data flow.[299] This could have been restricted if the algorithm was designed to not process the data which could result in anti-competitive market outcome. This is the same preventive approach companies have been using while exchanging information since 1990s. The companies proactively deter themselves from exchanging commercially sensitive information that can attract antitrust penalty. Similarly, this preventive approach by companies can be used to feed algorithms not to react or not to process certain data which could be commercially sensitive, in bringing about anticompetitive outcome in the market. However, these approaches in isolation might not meet the intended purpose of subsiding collusion through algorithms. The commission may have to adopt other measures to make the recommendations above extremely useful.

4.3.3 Screening Algorithms

The CCI can move on the lines of EU and adopt the data-driven approach of screening algorithms in order to check for any anti-competitive activity happening on the digital market.[300] The algorithms can be fed to identify patterns of price fixing and distorted

---

[297] Vezzoso (2017).

[298] Vezzoso (2017).

[299] The anticompetitive result in the wall décor case was owing to the data flow that was taken into consideration by the algorithms in making their pricing decisions. The data on the rival's price of posters was collected by the software which was processed and taken into consideration while making the pricing decision. "A data/information model of these algorithms would show the types of data that were part of the system, the relation between data sets/types, the data's quality requirements." Vezzoso (2017).

[300] Screen: a screen is a statistical tool to verify whether collusion likely exists in particular market and its purpose is to flag unlawful behavior through economic and statistical tools. Huber and Imhof (2018, p. 6).

market structure which can further the detection of anti-competitive practices in the market.[301] The screening test approach could be used to conduct structural as well as behavioral tests. For instance, under the structural test approach the screening test can check for market characteristics that makes it conducive to collude and under the behavioral test the screens can check for suspicious market outcomes or deviation from regular behavior of players or in the choices made by them.[302] The screening test has been successfully used by Korea's Fair Trade Commission in detecting bid rigging. They developed a quantitative analysis system, called BRIAS, which could predict the chances of bid-rigging in a market by taking into consideration relevant data that was collected by various public agencies in Korea. The data was in the form of information on number of wins of a particular company, rotation of bids, new participants in the bids, the prices of bids.[303] This technique seems compelling in identifying bid-rigging, however it needs to be seen how well it is developed to capture other type of anti-competitive activities in the market.[304]

4.4 *Market Studies*

The structural test can be made more persuasive by conducting market studies. The recommendation by Ezrachi and Stucke states that the competition authorities should indulge in market studies or sector inquiries. This could help the authorities in identifying unfair practices that are existing in the market even though there is no evidence of coordinated conduct in the market per se. If a market is not functioning well but there are no traces of evidence on collusion, the authorities by conducting frequent market inquires may be able to understand the innovative patterns used by the companies to distort the market. Frequent market inquiries shall help the regulator to understand the characteristics of markets which are more prone to collusion.

The CCI as a part of its advocacy mandate conducts market studies and has conducted sector specific studies including transport, energy, telecommunications etc. In the year 2012 CCI commissioned a study in 6 major onion markets in the country.[305] However, the study was commissioned after the case was closed on alleged anti-competitive practices in the onion market due to a lack of a smoking-gun evidence requirement to prove cartels and also due to lack of clarity with regard to the structure of 'mandi market' in India. However, the authorities found evidence related to some market inefficiency which was suspected to not only relate to the volatility of the market or exogenous factors. It was felt important by the commission to probe into the onion market structure and identify the real cause of market distortion. The

[301] See Buttarelli (2017).

[302] Available at: https://www.learconference.com/wp-content/uploads/2017/07/SlideDecarolisLEAR.pdf. Accessed 15 December 2020.

[303] OECD (2017).

[304] OECD (2017, p. 253).

[305] Chengappa et al. (2012).

study showed that there was collusion in the market of traders of onions and also the bids were rigged.[306] The study helped the CCI to understand the structure of the onion market even though the case was closed and was not taken up after the report. The market study conducted by the CCI allowed them to investigate the market so as to rectify any structural distortion by suggesting remedies.[307] E*x ante* investigations into sectors or markets shall equip the CCI to deal with cases in future with full understanding of the structure of the market. This practice can help the commission in understanding market distortions due to algorithms, if any.[308]

4.5 Specialized Agency

The CCI can build a specialized agency within itself to develop expertise in dealing with digital platforms and the use of algorithms in the digital market in order to speed up the process of investigation and detection. The specialized agency could consist of engineers, IT professionals, data analysts and lawyers in order to understand the technical nature of such markets. The agency dedicated entirely to digital markets can also keep a close check on the working of the digital markets by surveillance and could also keep a track of consumer complaints to see if there are any patterns of anti-competitive behavior or market inefficiency. It could also be given the power to obtain documents or information from companies if they think that there is a distorted market structure. The power to obtain source code of algorithms, as suggested by the draft policy, could be given to this agency, so that they can be proactive in their investigation in order to prevent market failure. Further the agency could be given the power to conduct inquiries over a period of four to five years, in order to understand the patterns in the existing digital market and the functioning of the market. This recommendation is in line with conducting *ex-ante* market studies. It would be conducive if the authorities have an idea of how the market functions to recognize for any anti-competitive activity.[309]

5 Conclusion

For any legal system to withstand the test of time it must be able to adapt to the changing contours of science and society. This is particularly true for Competition Law given the dynamic nature of the markets and its rapid expansion into the digital platforms. The digitization of trade and businesses have without a doubt contributed

---

[306]Chengappa et al. (2012).

[307]Jurisdiction like UK allow the commission to hold market investigations and issue non-binding remedies to improve the market structure. OECD (2017).

[308]OECD (2017, p. 261).

[309]Ezrachi and Stucke (2017a).

to the betterment of commerce and consumer welfare. But the advent of these innovations brings along with it a new set of problems that were not envisaged while the antitrust framework was formulated in India, thereby creating a dire need for timely reforms in its approach to algorithms.

India's response to the emerging problems for algorithmic collusion is still nascent and short-sighted. In terms of the legislation, the Competition Act, 2002 requires significant amendments so as to bring algorithmic collusions within the sweep of Section 3 and to vest the statutory agencies with the necessary powers to effectively investigate collusion on digital platforms. While the Competition Amendment Act, 2020 is certainly a step forward, it has limited itself only to the issue of hub-and-spoke, thereby leaving much to be desired in addressing issues of tacit algorithmic collusions and regulation of self-learning algorithms. Considering the practical impediments in proving the element of 'agreement' in an algorithmic set up, it is also necessary to seriously consider a presumption as to the existence of 'meeting of minds', when parallel conduct has an AAEC in the digital markets. Further, the commission should match the technological influx in the market with its own dedicated digital wing, screening algorithms and periodic market studies to pro-actively detect collusive patterns in the digital markets.

Given the enigmatic nature of the algorithm problem, there may yet be new dimensions to the adverse impact it may have on competition. Therefore, it is imperative that the CCI and NCLAT be mindful of the same and consider a more liberal approach in interpreting the provisions of the Competition Act such that the issues arising out of algorithmic collusions are adequately dealt with. Thus, a coordinated effort by all three organs of the government—the legislature, the executive and the judiciary, is necessary to ensure that the benefits accrued from a strong competitive digital market reach the consumers.

References

Anderson M, Huffman M (2017) The sharing economy meets the Sherman Act: Is UBER a firm, a cartel or something in between? Colum Bus Law Rev 3:859–933

Australian Competition and Consumer Commission (2014) Immunity & cooperation policy for cartel conduct. https://consultation.accc.gov.au/compliance-enforcement/draft-immunity-and-cooperation-policy/supporting_documents/DRAFT%20ACCC%20immunity%20and%20cooperation%20policy%2009%20April%202014%202.pdf. Accessed 15 Dec 2020

Banga R, Das A (eds) (2012) Twenty years of India's liberalization: experiences and lessons. United Nations Conference on Trade and Development, Geneva

Buttarelli G (2017) The Digital Clearinghouse gets to work. European Data Protection Supervisor. https://edps.europa.eu/press-publications/press-news/blog/digital-clearinghouse-gets-work_en. Accessed 15 Dec 2020

Callery C (2011) Should the European Union embrace or exercise Leegin's "rule of reason"? Eur Competition Law Rev 32:42–49

Castillo JC (2019) Who benefits from surge pricing? https://web.stanford.edu/~jccast/JMP_Castillo.pdf. Accessed 15 Dec 2020

Chen L, Mislove A, Wilson C (2015) Peeking beneath the hood of Uber. https://www.ftc.gov/system/files/documents/public_comments/2015/09/00011-97592.pdf. Accessed 15 Dec 2020
Chengappa PG, Manjunatha AV, Dimble V, Shah K (2012) Competitive assessment of onion markets in India. Agricultural Development and Rural Transformation Centre Institute for Social and Economic Change, Bangalore
Chopra S, White L (2004) Artificial agents' personhood in law and philosophy. In: Proceedings of the 16th European Conference on Artificial Intelligence, Valencia, August 22–27, pp 635–639
Comments: The Parke, Davis case: Refusal to deal and the Sherman Act. Duke L.J. 1961(1):120–132
Competition Commission of India (2017) Compliance manual for enterprises. https://www.cci.gov.in/sites/default/files/manual_compliance/manual_booklet.pdf Accessed 15 Dec 2020
Competition & Markets Authority (2018) Pricing algorithms- economic working paper on the use of algorithms to facilitate collusion and personalised pricing https://assets.publishing.service.gov.uk/government/uploads/system/uploads/attachment_data/file/746353/Algorithms_econ_report.pdf. Accessed 15 Dec 2020
Deloitte (2007) The deterrent effect of competition enforcement by the OFT. Office of Fair Trading. https://webarchive.nationalarchives.gov.uk/20140402181127/http://www.oft.gov.uk/shared_oft/reports/Evaluating-OFTs-work/oft962.pdf. Accessed 15 Dec 2020
Demetis DS, Lee AS (2018) When humans using the IT artifact becomes IT using the human artefact. J Assoc Inf Syst 19(10):929–952
Dey S, Bhupta M (2014) Corporate India learns to live with competition law. Business Standard. https://www.business-standard.com/article/opinion/corporate-india-learns-to-live-with-competition-law-114122200003_1.html. Accessed 15 Dec 2020
Ernst & Young (2014) Calibrating the pulse of competition law in India—an EY fraud investigation & dispute services report. Fraud Investigation & Dispute Services Ernst & Young, London
Ezrachi A, Strucke ME (2020) Sustainable and unchallenged algorithmic tacit collusion. Nw J Tech Intel Prop 17(2):217–260
Ezrachi A, Stucke ME (2017a) Artificial intelligence & collusion: when computers inhibit competition. U Ill Law Rev 2017:1775–1810
Ezrachi A, Stucke ME (2017b) Two artificial neural networks meet in an online hub and change the future (of competition, market dynamics and society). https://papers.ssrn.com/sol3/papers.cfm?abstract_id=2949434. Accessed 15 Dec 2020
Ezrachi A, Stucke ME (2018) Sustainable and unchallenged algorithmic tacit collusion. https://papers.ssrn.com/sol3/papers.cfm?abstract_id=3282235. Accessed 15 Dec 2020
Falls CG, Saravia CC (2015) Analyzing incentives and liability in "hub-and-spoke" conspiracies. Cornerstone Research. https://www.cornerstone.com/Publications/Articles/Analyzing-Incentives-and-Liability-in-Hub-and-Spo.pdf. Accessed 15 Dec 2020
Green EJ, Marshall RC, Marx ML (2014) Tacit collusion in oligopoly. In: Blair RD, Sokol DD (eds) Oxford handbook international antitrust economics, vol 2. Oxford University Press, Oxford
Gupta P (2019) Single economic entity and corporate separatedness doctrine: a juxtaposition. https://www.mondaq.com/india/antitrust-eu-competition/788042/single-economic-entity-and-corporate-separatedness-doctrine-a-juxtaposition. Accessed 15 Dec 2020
Havu K, Zupančič N (2016) Case comment: Collusion and online platforms in Eturas. Comp Law Rev 11(2):255–266
Huber M, Imhof D (2018) Machine learning with screens for detecting bid-rigging cartels. https://doc.rero.ch/record/308901?ln=fr. Accessed 15 Dec 2020
Kolasky W, McNeece K (2015) Contingent commissions and the antitrust laws: What can we learn from the In: re Insurance Brokerage Antitrust Litigation? Antitrust Trade Regul Rep 108(2619):1–6
Lee K (2018) Algorithm collusion and its implications for competition law and policy. https://papers.ssrn.com/sol3/papers.cfm?abstract_id=3213296. Accessed 15 Dec 2020
Markham JW (2013) The failure of corporate governance standards and antitrust compliance. S.D. Law Rev 58:499–542

Muralidharan S, Deshpande Ch (2016) Scope for intersection between antitrust laws and corporate governance principles vis-à-vis cartels deterrence in India. NUJS Law Rev 9:93–152

Nicholls R (2018) Algorithm-driven business conduct: competition and collusion. Centre for Law Markets and Regulations. http://unsworks.unsw.edu.au/fapi/datastream/unsworks:52475/bin7174fba5-902f-4331-801c-8f59532b77fb?view=true. Accessed 15 Dec 2020

Nowag J (2018a) When sharing platforms fix sellers' prices, forthcoming in Journal of Antitrust Enforcement 1/2018 (Accepted Version). Lund University Legal Research Paper Series, LundLawCompWP 1/2018. https://ssrn.com/abstract=3217193. Accessed 15 Dec 2020

Nowag J (2018b) When sharing platforms fix sellers' prices. J Antitrust Enf 6(3):382–408

Odudu O (2011) Indirect information exchange: The Constituent Elements of Hub and Spoke Collusion Eur. Comp J 7(2):205–242

OECD (2017) Algorithms and collusion: competition policy in the digital age. http://www.oecd.org/daf/competition/Algorithms-and-colllusion-competition-policy-in-the-digital-age.pdf. Accessed 15 Dec 2020

OECD (2019a) Corporate governance factbook 2019. http://www.oecd.org/corporate/Corporate-Governance-Factbook.pdf. Accessed 15 Dec 2020

OECD (2019b) Roundtable on Hub-and-spoke Arrangements—background note https://one.oecd.org/document/DAF/COMP(2019)14/en/pdf. Accessed 15 Dec 2020

Posner RA (1968) Oligopoly and the antitrust laws: a suggested approach. Stan Law Rev 21:1562–1606

Posner RA (2001) Antitrust law, 2nd edn. The University of Chicago Press, Chicago

Raghavan Committee (2013) Report of high-level committee on competition policy law

Rahl JA (1950) Conspiracy and the anti-trust laws. U Ill Law Rev 44:743–768

Rivas J (2013) Why does Article 101(2) TFEU not list concerted practises? Kluwer Competition Law Blog. http://competitionlawblog.kluwercompetitionlaw.com/2013/04/23/. Accessed 15 Dec 2020

Roozendaal M (2018) Algorithms: teenage troublemakers of EU competition law. European Law Institute

Rutten RL and Buts C (2019) Hub and spoke cartels: incentives, mechanisms and stability. CoRe 3(1):4–16

Sarkar S (2015) The comply-or-explain approach for enforcing governance norms. https://papers.ssrn.com/sol3/papers.cfm?abstract_id=2638252. Accessed 15 Dec 2020

Srinivas K, Rajain D, Venkatakrishnan B (2018) Individual liability in cartel cases. https://www.scconline.com/blog/post/2018/09/08/individual-liability-in-cartel-cases/. Accessed 15 Dec 2020

Urs P, Shroff R (2007) The cement and tyre cartels: what India can learn from the US and EU. Indian Law J 6(2). https://www.indialawjournal.org/archives/volume6/issue-2/article4.html. Accessed 15 Dec 2020

Vestager CM (2016) Big data and competition. Speech at the EDPS-BEUC Conference on Big Data, Brussels, 29 Sept 2016

Vezzoso S (2017) Competition by design. https://ssrn.com/abstract=2986440. Accessed 15 Dec 2020

Wang H, Yang H (2019) Ridesourcing systems: a framework and review. TRANSPORT RES B-METH 129:122–155. https://papers.ssrn.com/sol3/papers.cfm?abstract_id=3375259. Accessed 15 Dec 2020

Whish R, Bailey D (2018) Competition Law, 9th edn. Oxford University Press, Oxford

Algorithmic Hub-and-Spoke Cartels: A Japanese Perspective

Steven Van Uytsel

Abstract The debate on algorithmic collusion has put the hub-and-spoke cartel in the picture. In Japan, a hub-and-spoke cartel, a cartel in which there is a vertical facilitator of horizontal collusion, has long been in existence. *Kansei dango*, bid-rigging on public procurement projects, have been assisted by bureaucrats. The problem with this kind of cartel was that the Japanese Antimonopoly Act (AMA) is not designed to make the vertical facilitator accountable for its cooperation with the cartel. This resulted in a legislative initiative to deal with the bureaucrats participating in the cartel. A similar evolution has been noticeable in relation to trade associations. This triggers the question of how the AMA can respond to situations in which an algorithm enters the role of facilitator. This contribution argues that an easy answer cannot be given. If the implementation of the algorithm is the result of communication between the enterprises participating in the collusion, the unreasonable restraint provision of the AMA, the provision relevant to price fixing, may be applicable. The only caution that remains is whether the algorithm is implemented at enterprises competing with each other. When an algorithm is able to impose a price on enterprises at another level in the market, and there is thus no communication, even indirectly, between competing enterprises, the Japan Fair Trade Commission may shift to the unfair trade practices provision. More specifically, the unfair trade practice of conditional dealing may apply to a situation in which an algorithm fixes the prices of sellers using the algorithm.

Keywords Japanese antimonopoly law · Algorithmic collusion · Cartel · Price fixing · Hub and spoke · Antimonopoly law · Trade association · *Kansei dango* · Accountancy firm · Supplier · Algorithm developer · Uber

---

S. Van Uytsel (✉)
Graduate School of Law, Kyushu University, Fukuoka, Japan
e-mail: uytsel@law.kyushu-u.ac.jp

S. Van Uytsel (ed.), *The Digital Economy and Competition Law in Asia*, Perspectives in Law, Business and Innovation,
https://doi.org/10.1007/978-981-16-0324-2_7

1 Introduction

In her English exposé on the Japanese antimonopoly law, Etsuko Kameoka familiarizes the reader with the concept of a 'vertical cartel.'[1] Even though Kameoka equates the vertical cartel with a vertical agreement in European Union competition law,[2] the context in which she cites the concept is quite different from a mere vertical agreement. Vertical cartels are situated in the realm of *kansei dango*,[3] a practice in which the bureaucracy is acting as a facilitator for the cartel formation between firms bidding for public procurement projects.[4] The *kansei dango* does, in other words, not only reveal a horizontal but also a vertical agreement. The horizontal agreement exists among the competitors submitting the bid and the vertical agreement between the competing firms and the bureaucrats. Despite this complex relationship being catalogued as a cartel, the Act on Prohibition of Private Monopolization and Maintenance of Fair Trade[5] (Antimonopoly Act or AMA) only applies to the horizontal dimension. In other words, the vertical dimension of this bid rigging cartel is not punished under the AMA.[6] Instead, the Japanese legislator has created a separate law, the Act Concerning Elimination and Prevention of Involvement in Bid Rigging (Act on Preventing Bid Rigging),[7] in order to hold bureaucrats liable for their participation in the vertical cartel.

Why does this all matter in a context of an increased use of algorithms in price setting? One of the roles attributed to an algorithm in the framework of price fixing is exactly the coordinating role that the bureaucrats are playing in a *kansei dango*. This role of the algorithm is, depending on the literature consulted, called a hub-and-spoke scenario. Translated to the *kansei dango* scenario, it would mean that the bureaucrats are the hub and the competing enterprises the spokes. If the coordinating behavior of the bureaucrats is punished outside the framework of the AMA, would that also place the algorithm, taking the role of a hub, outside the AMA? Or, should such a view be limited in scope to the hypothetical case in which the role of the bureaucrats is being attributed to an algorithm? This would raise the apt question of how to approach, under the AMA, algorithms engaging in a hub-and-spoke scenario outside the framework of bid rigging. Would it be possible to apply the AMA to such kind of cartels? Or, would these cartels fall outside the reach of the Japan Fair Trade

---

[1] Kameoka (2014, p. 44).

[2] Kameoka (2014, pp. 44–45).

[3] Kameoka (2014, p. 45).

[4] Wakui (2018).

[5] Law No. 54 of 1974, shiteki dokusen no kinshi oyobi kousei torihiki no kakuho ni kan suru houritsu [Law Concerning the Prohibition of Private Monopolies and the Assurance of Fair Trade] (AML). Available at: https://www.jftc.go.jp/en/legislation_gls/amended_ama09/index.html Accessed 15 December 2020.

[6] See infra 4.2 Bureaucrats as the Linchpin of Bid Rigging outside the Scope of the Antimonopoly Law.

[7] Act on Elimination and Prevention of Involvement in Bid Rigging, etc. and Punishments for Acts by Employees that Harm Fairness of Bidding, etc. (Act No. 101 of 2002). Available at: https://www.jftc.go.jp/en/legislation_gls/aepibr_files/aepibr.pdf. Accessed 15 December 2020.

Commission (JFTC)? This chapter purports that an answer to these questions is not easy. The complexity is derived from the historical evolution of the AMA, whereby the interpretation of the original article applicable to cartels required a competitive relationship among the cartel participants. The strict interpretation of communication is another element contributing to the complexity of applying the cartel provision to the hub-and-spoke cartels.

The chapter is structured as follows. Section 2 gives a summary of the debate on the use of algorithms in a hub-and-spoke context. Following this outline, Sect. 3 will situate the difficulty of the AMA in dealing with a hub-and-spoke cartel. This will imply giving a short history on the making of the AMA, followed by an explanation of the article applicable to cartel agreements. Before discussing different algorithmic hub-and-spoke scenarios in relation to the AMA provisions in Sect. 5, Sect. 4 will situate the problem of facilitators of a cartel by looking at how trade associations and bureaucrats are regulated. In Sect. 6, the chapter will conclude that there is still uncertainty to the scope of the AMA partly because no real case exists to clarify its scope in a hub-and-spoke cartel.

2 Algorithmic Hub-and-Spoke Cartels

2.1 Hub-and-Spoke Cartels, the General Context

Ariel Ezrachi and Maurice E. Stucke have developed a taxonomy to converse about algorithmic collusion. The taxonomy is based on the different roles an algorithm can play in the formation and implementation of collusion. Ezrachi and Stucke have identified four different scenarios: messenger, hub-and-spoke, predicable agent and digital eye.[8]

The messenger scenario describes the algorithm taking the role of implementing, monitoring and policing a price fixing agreement that has been discussed and approved by humans.[9] In a hub-and-spoke scenario, a single algorithm will determine the price of firms competing in the same market.[10] Predictable agent exemplifies the scenario in which different algorithms of independent firms predict a similar price

[8]Ezrachi and Stucke (2017, p. 1782). Digital eye has also been termed autonomous machine in an earlier version of the Ezrachi and Stucke's work. Ezrachi and Stucke (2015, p. 7). The Secretariat of the Organization for Economic Co-operation and Development (OECD) merely acknowledges the different roles, but uses different names. The OECD distinguished between monitoring algorithms, parallel algorithms, signaling algorithms, and self-learning algorithms (OECD 2017, pp. 24–32). Niccolò Colombo has still used other terms for the four different roles: classical digital cartel, inadvertent hub-and-spoke, tacit algorithmic collusion and dystopian virtual reality (Colombo 2018, pp. 12–14).

[9]Van Uytsel (2018, p. 157).

[10]Ezrachi and Stucke (2017, p. 1782).

outcome based on the market conditions it can observe.[11] In the digital eye, the algorithm's role is to determine, completely on its own, what the best way is to reach a pre-determined goal, such as profit maximization.[12]

Whereas the application of contemporary competition law to monitoring algorithms is not disputed and the progress in machine learning does not yet allow for the implementation of predictable agent and digital eye, the hub-and-spoke scenario, conceivable in practice, still has unsettled boundaries. Hub-and-spoke cartels "raise delicate questions pertaining to the line between perfectly legal information sharing between trading partners … and situations in which competing undertakings use a common trading partner to facilitate anti-competitive conduct."[13] It is necessary to establish the "the rim around the spokes,"[14] which is the story turning seemingly individual parallel vertical agreements into forbidden horizontal agreements.

The standard is, it seems, not equal in all jurisdictions. The United States (US) puts emphasis on knowledge. The 9th Circuit stated that the tipping point from legal information sharing to illegal anticompetitive conduct could be knowledge. The Court stated that "each defendant knew or had a reason to know of the scope of the conspiracy and … reason to believe that their own benefits were dependent upon the success of the entire venture."[15] In various cases, this knowledge was inferred from communication. The hub communicated to the spokes that it was speaking with other spokes in parallel. More direct communication towards the spokes consisted of treatment to exclude the spoke if the recommended policy would not be implemented. The European Commission has not yet dealt with hub-and-spoke cartels.[16] Within the European Union (EU), the United Kingdom (UK) courts looked at European jurisprudence on information exchange in order to formulate their standards for delineating the rim. Besides the knowledge requirement noticeable in the US, the UK courts also focused on the presence of intent and actual implementation. The information provider must do so with the intent that it is going to be shared by the initial information receiver. The final information receiver must know why and under which circumstances the information was received by the initial information receiver. The final information receiver will use the information in their own price setting on the market.[17] The Organization for Economic Co-operation and Development's (OECD) Background Note—Roundtable on Hub-and-Spoke Arrangements summarizes the difficulties the EU is facing to tackle illegal hub-and-spoke cartels: (1) exchange of information is often oral, (2) intent will have to be inferred from witness statements or circumstantial evidence, (3) difficulty to separate pro- and anti-competitive behavior in negotiations between suppliers and retailers, (4) as it

[11] Van Uytsel (2018, p. 158).

[12] OECD (2017, p. 30).

[13] Tuytschaever (2015, p. 24).

[14] OECD (2019, p. 18).

[15] United States v. Lapier, no 13-30279, 2015 WL 4664689, par. 8 (9th Cir. 7 August 2015).

[16] OECD (2019, p. 20).

[17] OECD (2019, pp. 21–23).

may involve years of negotiations involving several product groups between multiple retailers and products, other cases may be prioritized.[18]

Another important aspect of hub-and-spoke cartels is the position that should be taken towards the hub. The hub, in the end, is an actor in a vertical relationship to the horizontal restriction of competition. Moreover, the hub is not active in the same market as the spokes, the actors that are restricting the competition horizontally. Should a hub therefore be left outside the scope of liability? This is a question that the enforcement authorities had to answer before. What else is a hub than a facilitator of a cartel? In relation to facilitators, the enforcement authorities have already held that the anti-cartel provisions should apply to them in order to guarantee the full effectiveness of the anti-cartel provisions. The US accepts the liability of the facilitator when the "the vertical player was a knowing participant in that agreement and facilitated that scheme."[19] Likewise, European jurisprudence requires an "intention of the facilitator to contribute to the common objectives of the horizontal conspirators, and an awareness of the planned or effected conduct, as well as a willingness to take the risk."[20] Hence, it is not relevant whether the contribution of the hub relates to the economic activity in a relevant market on which a restriction comes about.[21]

2.2 *Algorithms Acting as Hub*

Technological development makes it possible for a computer algorithm to operate the function of a hub. When Ezrachi and Stucke developed this scenario, they set the parameters of what should be understood by an algorithm-driven hub-and-spoke scenario.

Essential to an algorithm-driven hub-and-spoke scenario is that the competitors will use "the same pricing algorithm that stabilizes prices and dampens competition."[22] The use of the same pricing algorithm may be the result of an "intentional attempt to dampen competition," i.e. the "immediate aim is horizontal collusion, and each vertical link is in furtherance of that aim."[23] However, an algorithm-driven hub-and-spoke can also follow from the "unintentional alignment and use of similar algorithms to monitor prices."[24] In both cases, "a single algorithm as a hub would lead to a de facto alignment among rivals that dampens competition."[25]

Based upon the conception that competition can be affected both intentionally and unintentionally, different versions of the algorithm-driven hub-and-spoke scenario

[18]OECD (2019, p. 25).

[19]OECD (2019, p. 26).

[20]OECD (2019, p. 26).

[21]Case C-194/14 P, AC-Treuhand v. Commission EU:C:2015:717, par. 36.

[22]Ezrachi and Stucke (2016, p. 49).

[23]Ezrachi and Stucke (2016, p. 49).

[24]Ezrachi and Stucke (2016, p. 51).

[25]Ezrachi and Stucke (2016, p. 51).

can be conceptualized. First, the algorithm is put in place by a classical hub, meaning a firm in a direct vertical relation to the spokes. Setting up an algorithm to control the price could be formulated by the retailers or could be imposed by the supplier. Second, the algorithm could be employed by a third party with the intention to facilitate collusion between firms on the same level of the market. Most likely, these firms will demand the third party to employ the algorithm. The third party could be of any kind, ranging from a trade association, an accountancy firm, to a price algorithm developer/vendor. Third, a variation of the previous version is presented by the OECD when it stated that the use of a pricing algorithm can be inspired to follow a market leader, "who in turn would be responsible for programming the dynamic pricing algorithm that fixes prices above the competitive level."[26] Fourth, a third party develops a pricing algorithm that is being sold to several competing firms, whether to the supplier or retail side of the market. Fifth, similar to the previous version, but the suppliers or retailers are aware that its price algorithm is being used by several competing firms. Sixth, a third party develops and runs its own pricing mechanism to which other users subscribe to offer their services for the price set by the algorithm of the third party.

When Ezrachi and Stucke elaborated their taxonomy, they were less interested in the first three versions of the hub-and-spoke. These versions are representations of a classical hub-and-spoke. Hence, they should not be controversial in the enforcement of competition law. The situation changes when the latter three versions are considered. It is not clear what the position of competition law should be towards these versions. Ezrachi and Stucke illustrate the fourth and fifth version with a reference to Boomerang Commerce, a vendor of software helping online retailers to optimize their price setting. It is conceivable that the same pricing algorithm of Boomerang is being used by several competing retailers. Despite the decision to use pricing algorithms being made independently, Ezrachi and Stucke are skeptical about the unawareness of the retailers on what is happening in reality.[27] If the retailers need to provide access to their data in order to allow the algorithm to optimize the price setting, retailers must be aware that the data of competing retailers will equally be used when such retailers decide on the same third party vendor. The last version is exemplified with Uber. As "Uber's algorithm determine[s] for hundreds of competing drivers the base price for the trip, *when* to implement a surge price, for *which* areas, for *how long*, and to *what extent*,"[28] the question is raised on whether this business model should be accepted from a competition law perspective. Yet, an answer is not given. In response, Ezrachi and Stucke list elements to take into consideration when looking for an answer. These elements relate to alternatives and market power. In order to determine whether the legal use of an algorithm could tip over in an anticompetitive use, it may be necessary to consider the ability of other firms to keep the prices of the platform under control and, related, the power the platform has obtained in the market. For the latter, Ezrachi and Stucke suggest taking into account the "users'

[26] OECD (2017, p. 27); see also Capobianco and Gonzaga (2017, p. 4).

[27] Ezrachi and Stucke (2016, p. 49).

[28] Ezrachi and Stucke (2016, p. 51).

inability to process complex information, limited switching patterns, usage of apps, and access to platforms."[29]

Of all examples given by Ezrachi and Stucke, an Uber-like pricing algorithm has received the most attention, both in courts and in academic literature. Uber faced a class-action lawsuit in the US for infringing Section 1 of the Sherman Act.[30] Similarly, Uber was investigated in India by the competition authorities.[31] The Luxemburg competition authority had to decide on Webtaxi, a booking platform for taxis in Luxemburg.[32] There is an indication that the US courts are favorable to accepting a price fixing scheme, what can be deducted from the finding that drivers were signing up because the algorithm was providing the same price for all drivers and, if the drivers were really independent, the same price would be against their interest.[33] The Luxemburg competition authority sided with price fixing but argued that it could be set aside by efficiency gains.[34] Julian Nowag, acknowledging case outcomes in the US and Luxemburg, purports that the conceptualization of the EU law provides more flexibility to embrace new technological evolutions than the US law.[35] The Luxemburg outcome, which is also possible in the EU under Article 101(3) of the Treaty of the Functioning of the European Union (TFEU), would be the preferred approach. This approach offers indeed a mechanism to challenge the traditional competition law perspective on price fixing. Subsection 3 of Article 101 TFEU allows for considering consumer benefits in a price fixing scheme,[36] and this to introduce a balance of interests that also Ezrachi and Stucke seem to advocate for.[37]

The situation in Japan is still different. The unique conceptualization of the AMA may prevent a swift application of the law to hub-and-spoke like cartels.

[29]Ezrachi and Stucke (2016, p. 55).

[30]Meyer v. Kalanick, 174 F. Supp. 3d 817 (S.D.N.Y. 2016); Meyer v. Uber Techs., Inc., 868 F.3d 66 (2d Cir. 2017). For a discussion, see Bostoen (2019, pp. 159–160).

[31]For a detailed discussion, see Algorithmic Collusion and Indian Competition Act: Suggestions to Tackle Inadequacies and Naivety [this volume].

[32]Conseil de la Concurrence Grand-Duché de Luxembourg, Case 2018-FO-01, Webtaxi, 7 June 2018. Available at: https://concurrence.public.lu/content/dam/concurrence/fr/decisions/ententes/2018/decision-n-2018-fo-01-du-7-juin-2018-version-non-confidentielle.pdf. Accessed 15 December 2020. For a discussion, see Giannino (2018).

[33]Meyer v. Kalanick, 174 F. Supp. 3d 817 (S.D.N.Y. 2016); Meyer v. Uber Techs., Inc., 868 F.3d 66 (2d Cir. 2017). The case was eventually dealt with in arbitration. Bostoen (2019, p. 160).

[34]Conseil de law Concurrence Grand-Duche de Luxembourg, Case 2018-FO-01, Webtaxi, 7 June 2018.

[35]Nowag (2018, p. 19). On the inflexible approach in the US, see Anderson and Huffman (2017, pp. 907–915).

[36]Nowag (2018, p. 20).

[37]Ezrachi and Stucke (2016, p. 54).

3 Cartels and the Japanese Antimonopoly Law

3.1 A Historical Perspective on the Japanese Antimonopoly Law and Anti-Cartel Enforcement

In an attempt to democratize the Japanese economy, the Allied Powers, in which the United States had the main influence,[38] obliged the Japanese government to elaborate and adopt a competition law.[39] When the first drafts were not in line with the US understanding of what the content of competition law should be,[40] the Supreme Commander of the Allied Powers requested an American lawyer to draft a law.[41] Even though the Japanese government could scrutinize the drafts and suggest changes, the AMA was generally considered to be an amalgam of the different laws regulating competition in the United States[42] supplemented with the refinements elaborated by the courts and administrative agencies.

When Posey T. Kime[43] had to provide a draft competition law for Japan, he almost mechanically transferred the conceptualization of forbidden conduct under the United States' antitrust laws to his draft for the Japanese competition law. Kime suggested that the Japanese competition law should regulate unreasonable restraints of trade, private monopolization and unfair methods of competition. These prohibitions "are designed to prevent excessive concentration of economic power and to eliminate restraints resulting from combination or agreements and other unreasonable restraint of business activities which need not be the product of agreement."[44]

When the AMA was adopted in 1947, it was agreed to have a double approach towards unreasonable restraints of trade. Besides a provision which could be seen as encompassing the entire Section 1 of the Sherman Act, there was also a provision reflecting a particular court interpretation of Section 1 of the Sherman Act, being the per se illegality of certain types of agreements. The former is to be found in Article 3 of the AMA, while the latter was found in the currently abolished Article 4 of the AMA.

---

[38]See Augustine, available at: http://www.columbia.edu/~hds2/BIB95/02occupation_augustine.htm#02. Accessed 15 December 2020.

[39]See, e.g., Gerber (2010, p. 210) and Haley (2001, pp. 1–42).

[40]See Vande Walle (2013a, p. 36).

[41]See Haley (2001, p. 30).

[42]Even though the text is seen to be an amalgam of United States' competition laws, it is not denied that the Japanese bureaucracy had an impact on the content of the actual law. See, e.g., First (2000, p. 1) and Vande Walle (2013a, p. 137).

[43]Posey T. Kime had served two terms at the Indiana State Court of Appeals before he transferred Antitrust Division within the Department of Justice. In this capacity he was asked to lead the newly formed Antitrust Legislation Branch within the Supreme Command of Allied Powers. This Branch was to implement the Edwards Report. Kime headed this Branch for less than one year. Haley (2001, p. 30).

[44]Ariga and Rieke (1964, p. 441).

Article 3 of the AMA stipulates that "[a]n enterprise must not effect private monopolization or unreasonable restraint of trade." The unreasonable restraint of trade prong is further explained in Article 2 (6) of the AMA. This provision specifies that:

> The term "unreasonable restraint of trade" as used in this Act means such business activities, by which any enterprise, by contract, agreement or any other means irrespective of its name, in concert with other enterprises, mutually restrict or conduct their business activities in such a manner as to fix, maintain or increase prices, or to limit production, technology, products, facilities or counterparties, thereby causing, contrary to the public interest, a substantial restraint of competition in any particular field of trade.

Article 3 of the AMA could be regarded as focusing on "general restraints which had an *unreasonably* adverse impact upon competition in the specific line of commerce."[45]

The former Article 4 of the AMA, which was a combined expression of the *per se* rule developed by the United States' (US) courts and the *de minimis non curat lex* principle that was used in US antitrust cases,[46] read as follows:

> No enterprise shall participate in any one of the following types of concerted activities: 1) the establishment, stabilization or enhancement of prices; 2) restrictions on volume of production or that of sales; 3) restrictions on technology, products, markets or customers; 4) restrictions on constructions, or expansions of facilities, or on adoption of new technology or methods of production. The provisions of the preceding paragraph shall not apply in case the effects of such concerted activities on competition within a particular field of trade is negligible.[47]

The spelling out of the *per se* rule in the Japanese AMA is one of the elements that has contributed to the opinion that the Japanese AMA was one of the most stringent competition acts of its time. Such a strict approach was not favored by the Japanese Business Federation, *Keidanren*. It did not bestow the Japanese business community with enough flexibility to cooperate and so gain economic strength.[48] Therefore, *Keidanren* advocated, among others, to abolish Article 4 of the AMA.

Once Japan regained its independence in 1952, *Keidanren* found support for a reform of the AMA among the bureaucrats of Ministry of International Trade and Industry (MITI).[49] It was agreed to abolish Article 4 of the AMA and to divide cartels into two categories: good and bad.[50] Good cartels would be the ones established for addressing a structural overcapacity during a period of recession or for implementing any kind of improvement in the production process. *Keidanren* and MITI agreed that this would be explicitly arranged for in the AMA in the form of a licensing scheme

[45] Ariga and Rieke (1964, p. 453).

[46] Ariga and Rieke (1964, p. 444, n. 22).

[47] Wakui (2018, p. 250).

[48] Vande Walle (2013b, p. 124).

[49] Seita and Tamura (1994, pp. 177–180) (indicating that this mutual support for relaxation of the AML already was a development much earlier than from the period of regaining independence. Also, the US was not necessarily opposed to the relaxation due to the changed socio-political and geographical circumstances).

[50] Schaede (2000, p. 81).

for which the JFTC was responsible.[51] Cartels that were neither a recession cartel or a rationalization cartel, would not necessarily be categorized as bad cartels. For these remaining cartels, the plan was to use the other provision on restraint of trade, Article 3 of the AMA, to judge their lawfulness under the AMA.

3.2 Agreements and Concerted Practices with a Substantial Impact and Conformity with the Public Interest

The abolishment of Article 4 of the AMA meant a loosening of the scope of the AMA towards cartel agreements. A cartel agreement would no longer be declared illegal without looking at the role of the enterprise or the existence of any public policy. Indeed, Article 2(6) of the AMA, which implements unreasonable restraint of trade prong of Article 3 of the AMA, only makes a cartel agreement illegal when it mutually restricts the business activities among competitors and when it is contravening the public policy. The only things that Article 2(6) of the AMA has in common with former Article 4 of the AMA is that neither the form of the agreement nor the insubstantiality in a particular field of trade matters.

To make the anti-cartel law efficient, the AMA has a broad understanding of how enterprises can reach an agreement on price fixing. Article 2(6) of the AMA states that "a contract, an agreement, or any other means irrespective of its name" should be considered when pricing behavior of enterprises is being judged. Crucial in this judgment of whether a contract, an agreement, or any other means irrespective of its name exists, and so the existence of a cartel, is the communication of intention. The communication of intention does not require the explicit exchange of information between the competitors. The Tokyo High Court has stated that it is possible to deduct the communication of intention from all circumstances before and after the price increase. Moreover, communication of intention can even be presumed. Such a presumption can only be made if there has been an interaction between the competitors focusing on competitive sensitive information and the competitors implement a same or similar price increase.

Agreements in the broadest sense on the price are further subject to a substantiality test. The JFTC has the burden to prove that an agreement's restraint is substantial. Since hardcore agreements seldom positively contribute to the economy, the substantiality "may be presumed"[52] and this to lessen the burden of the JFTC. These careful wordings of Masako Wakui stand in contrast with the terminology used by various other Japanese scholars. The creation of a rebuttable presumption that hardcore cartels involve substantial restraints is often referred to as the adoption of a quasi per se rule.[53] Wakui's more careful stance can be explained by her identification of another option for the JFTC to construct a substantial effect. A substantial

[51] Schaede (2000, pp. 81–82).

[52] Wakui (2018, p. 51).

[53] Inoue (2012, p. 58) and Hayashi et al. (2020, p. 47).

effect can be presumed when large companies are involved in the hardcore cartel. To achieve this goal, it is important that the JFTC tweaks the understanding of the relevant product market. This, as will be explained below, is possible since the relevant product market for hardcore cartels is not done by looking at substitutes for the product of which the prices are fixed. Rather, the JFTC has developed a practice to look at the scope of the agreements.[54] By pointing out that the current practice tends to follow the latter approach, Wakui sheds a light on the market share that could be regarded as triggering a substantial effect.[55] The JFTC seems to hold that a market share around and above 80 percent suffices to establish the substantiality requirement. Akira Inoue informs that, based on precedents of the JFTC, it is already safe to conclude that "the combined market share of more than 50 percent can be said to be an indicator of fulfilling 'substantial restraint of competition.'"[56] Below 50 percent would position the enterprises in a safe zone, be it that circumstances surrounding the cartel could still contribute to a finding of a substantial restraint.[57]

The substantial restraint in trade develops in a particular field of trade. Legal scholarship in Japan equals a 'particular field of trade' with the concept of relevant market, be it the product or geographical dimension of the relevant market.[58] Delineating a relevant market for hardcore cartels may sound unconventional. Hardcore cartels are, in many jurisdictions, indeed illegal just by the coming into existence of the agreement. No further analysis, such as to what kind of relevant market the agreements belongs, will be done. That the AMA knows the concept of a relevant market in a provision dealing with hardcore cartels is due to its unusual history. Yet, the presence of the concept in the AMA requires its definition. A relevant market is, in general, determined by demand (supply) substitutability, an exercise in which is examined to what extent customers are willing to substitute one product by another (or a supplier can easily switch to the supply of substitutes). This complex exercise is, however, not done by the JFTC for hardcore cartels. For hardcore cartels, the JFTC limits its task to evaluate the scope of the agreement.[59] (identifying that considerations could be given to "geographical trade patterns, product identity, and the level of function, or distribution, common to the entrepreneurs involved."). In practice, this means that the relevant product market is determined by the product upon which the price is fixed. When the price is fixed for products with high sales volume or for products that are fairly similar, the JFTC further separates the relevant product market according to customers or specific product.[60]

In last order, Article 2(6) of the AMA requires that a restraint needs to be contrary to the public interest in order to be forbidden. Different interpretations have been advanced for the concept of public interest. *Keidanren* advocated to treat public

---

[54] Wakui (2018, p. 53).

[55] Wakui (2018, pp. 90–91).

[56] Inoue (2012, p. 58).

[57] Wakui (2018, p. 91).

[58] Wakui (2018, pp. 52–53) and Ariga and Rieke (1964, p. 446).

[59] Wakui (2018, pp. 53 and 90–91) and Ariga and Rieke (1964, p. 446).

[60] Van Uytsel (2015, pp. 95–96).

interest as a concept encompassing various interests of importance for consumers and the economy.[61] As these interests are not further detailed, this view could create a blanket immunity for all kinds of agreements. Opposite to this view is the opinion that public interest is another way of stating free competition. In practice, this view means that from the moment a restraint of competition has been found, this restraint is also contrary to the public interest.[62] The Japanese Supreme Court, ruling in an Oil Cartel case, has put forward a view somewhere in the middle. After stipulating that public interest in principle means free competition, there could be justifications, the Supreme Court continued, in which retraining competition would be of a higher value than maintaining competition.[63] Lower courts and scholars tend to follow this view, even though it remains unclear what these exceptional circumstances could be to justify a restraint of competition.[64] The Japanese AMA does not include any system similar to Article 101 (3) of the Treaty of the Functioning of the European Union that allows the justification of restraints of competition on well-defined grounds. Neither has a Japanese court formulated such a detailed rule.

3.3 Horizontal Agreements Engaged in by Enterprises in a Competitive Relationship

One of the more peculiar characteristics of Articles 3 and 2(6) of the AMA is the requirement of 'mutually restrict.' Mutually restrict creates the conundrum for how to deal with facilitators of a cartel under the AMA. The conundrum is created by two apparently opposing Tokyo High Court decisions, both of which are still frequently cited in the literature.

The earliest decision on how to deal with facilitators of a cartel, was the Tokyo High Court decision in the Asahi Newspaper Co. case of the 9th of March 1953.[65] In the Asahi Newspaper Co. case, the Tokyo High Court had to decide on a decision of four newspaper publishers to allocate territories to the newspaper publishers' distributors. Based upon the available evidence, it was only possible to prove agreements between the publishers and the distributors. No agreement could be found to place restrictions on the publishers themselves. For the application of former Article 4 of the AMA, the Tokyo High Court held that it was necessary that the business between "independent enterprises in a competitive relationship"[66] must be restrained. Further, the court also stressed that the agreement had to have "common restrictions

[61] Matsushita (1997, p. 172).

[62] Matsushita (1997, p. 172).

[63] Decision of the Supreme Court (Oil Cartel Case), 24 February 1984, Saiko Saibansho Keiji Hanreishu 38(4) 1287.

[64] Wakui (2018, pp. 46–48).

[65] Tokyo High Court (Newspaper Distribution Case), 9 March 1953, 3 Shinketsushu 4.

[66] Wakui (2018, pp. 76–77).

on business activity by mutual agreement."[67] By stating that the concerted practices of former Article 4 of the AMA are essentially the same as unreasonable restraints of trade, the Asahi Newspaper Co. case has influenced the understanding of Article 2(6) of the AMA.

The Tokyo High Court confirmed this position soon after in the Hokkaido Butter Co. case.[68] Also rendered in 1953, the Tokyo High Court held in the Toho-Shintoho case that:

> …unreasonable restraint of trade is formed where independent enterprises in mutual competition jointly impose certain restrictions upon each other and thereby restrain their free business activities. … if mutuality is lacking in the restriction, an unreasonable restraint of trade does not occur.[69]

This interpretation that all participants to the anti-competitive agreement should be aware of and enjoy the effects of such an agreement, has far-fetching consequences. One of the most often cited consequences is that the unreasonable restraint prong of Article 3 of the AMA only applies to horizontal agreements. Vertical agreements, no matter how serious anti-competitive harm they cause, are outside the scope of application.[70] A less cited consequence is the inability to apply the unreasonable restraint prong of Article 3 of the AMA to non-competing enterprises that are playing a role in an anti-competitive agreement.[71] This means, on the one hand, that the JFTC would not be able to punish a facilitator of a price fixing agreement,[72] and, on the other hand, that Article 3 of the AMA would not be applicable to enterprises that have different restrictions.[73]

The JFTC has been consistent in applying Article 3 in combination with Article 2(6) of the AMA to pure horizontal agreement. In pure horizontal agreements, non-competitors would not participate. This view has been upheld for 40 years.[74]

A Tokyo High Court decision of 1993 is said to have changed the position. In the Social Insurance Agency Seal case, the Tokyo High Court had to decide whether a bid rigging scheme in which a non-qualified bidder, Hitachi Information Systems (Hitachi), could be included into an action based on Article 3 of the AMA.[75] In the

---

[67] Wakui (2018, p. 77).

[68] Japan Fair Trade Commission (Hokkaido Butter Co. Case), 18 September 1950, 2 FTC Decision Reports 108.

[69] Tokyo High Court (Toho-Shintoho Case), 7 December 1953, Gyosei Jiken Saiban Reishu 4(12) 3215.

[70] Wakui (2018, pp. 77–78) and Seryo (2004, p. 11).

[71] Wakui (2018, p. 78).

[72] For the absence of a discussion on this issue Wakui (2018, pp. 76–78), Kameoka (2014, pp. 37–56), Inoue (2012, pp. 59–64), and Seryo (2004, pp. 11–12).

[73] Kameoka (2014, pp. 50–51) (giving the example of a cartel member remaining passive). Another example of a different restriction would be if one enterprise would deal in territory A and the other in territory B, despite this being one type of a restriction, i.e. a territorial division.

[74] Wakui (2018, p. 78).

[75] Tokyo High Court (Social Insurance Agency Seal Case), 14 December 1993, 46-III Koto Saibansho Keiji Hanreishu 322.

end, as a non-qualified bidder, Hitachi held that it was not in competitive relationship with the three bidding firms and should therefore not be held liable under Article 3 of the AMA. Furthermore, Hitachi argued that it was not operating its business in the same particular field of trade as the bidding firm. The Tokyo High Court argued that none of these arguments should be considered valid.

The desire to come up with another reasoning than in the Asahi Newspaper Co. case, forced the Tokyo High Court to differentiate that case from the Social Insurance Agency Seal case. The most obvious way out was to differentiate the cases based upon the applicable article. The Court concluded that the 1953 Asahi Newspaper Co. case was based on former Article 4 of the AMA. The Social Insurance Agency Seal case had to be decided based upon Article 3 in combination with Article 2(6) of the AMA. The conceptualization of the latter is slightly different than the former Article 4 of the AMA. Unlike former Article 4 of the AMA, Article 3 in combination with Article 2(6) of the AMA explicitly requires finding a restraint of competition. Therefore, the Court held that it would be awkward to limit the understanding of an enterprise to a competitor. Once this position was taken, the Court could take the following position for the application of Article 2(6) of the AMA.[76] First, enterprises could be active in different fields of trade. Second, there is no need that the enterprises are in the same or similar competitive relationship. Third, mutual restraint does not require a restraint in the same manner. It is sufficient that free business activities of the enterprise are compromised by taking part in the anticompetitive conduct—collusive bidding in this case. Hence, the Court judged that Hitachi is an enterprise "effectively"[77] or "in essence"[78] "in a competitive relationship with the other participants."[79]

The stance taken by the Tokyo High Court in the Social Insurance Agency Seal case has been followed by the JFTC in two bid rigging cases: The Video Machine case and the Okinawa Aluminum Sash case.[80] Moreover, the *Guideline under the Antimonopoly Act concerning Distribution and Trade Practices* adopted language indicating that it is somehow sufficient that the business activities of each of these enterprises are limited (not necessarily in the same way) and that anticompetitive conduct should be directed to the achievement of a common purpose.[81]

Whereas the shift in the understanding of the competitive relationship responds to the critique of several scholars towards the 1953 Asahi Newspaper Co. case and the subsequent interpretation of Article 2(6) of the AMA, Wakui informs that the 1993 Social Insurance Agency Seal case has not been able to extend Article 2(6) of the AMA to vertical agreements. This issue being less important for the issue at

---

[76] Seryo (2004, p. 12).

[77] Wakui (2018, p. 79).

[78] Kameoka (2014, p. 45).

[79] Wakui (2018, p. 79).

[80] Seryo (2004, p. 12) and Kameoka (2014, p. 45).

[81] This is especially reflected in note 2 of the guideline. Available at: https://www.jftc.go.jp/en/legislation_gls/imonopoly_guidelines_files/DistributionSystemsAndBusinessPractices.pdf. Accessed 15 December 2020.

stake, she also mentions that there are still a few scholars arguing that the scope of Article 2(6) of the AMA "should be expanded to include non-horizontal restrictions, which may be necessary to regulate *hub-and-spoke cartel*, in which a non-competitor acts either as a ringleader or as a facilitator."[82] Such an explicit request may be understood against the background that in the Social Insurance Agency Seal case there still is a requirement of a competitive relationship in essence,[83] or as Wakui notes, "the defendant [needs to be] somehow engaged in business relating to the relevant product."[84]

The demand for an explicit statement on what the position of Article 2(6) of the AMA should be towards hub-and-spoke cartels could also be justified by the fact that two categories of facilitators are regulated either by another article in the AMA or by a law outside the AMA. These two actors are trade associations and bureaucrats.

4 'In Competition with' in a Broader Antimonopoly Law Perspective

4.1 Trade Associations Regulated Separately in the Antimonopoly Law

Trade associations are a classical example of how a third party is being used to facilitate the creation of a cartel. It has been documented that trade association meetings function as a cover up for illegal cartel meetings. Compliance manuals stress the need for having clear guidelines on the participation of trade association meetings, just because the danger of crossing the line between legal and illegal conduct is thin. Just because of their potential of engaging in murky behavior, trade associations are considered to be within the ambit of competition law. This is no different in Japan, be it that a separate provision deals with trade associations. Article 8 of the AMA set the parameters of what trade associations are allowed to do.

The creation of a separate provision for trade associations is not the result of the original drafting of the AMA. In fact, trade associations were not part of the 1947 version of the AMA.[85] The absence of any reference to trade associations, though, worried the Supreme Command of the Allied Powers (SCAP). SCAP feared that the AMA would not be sufficient to deal with the resurrection of associations controlling a whole industry. The main reason for this concern was the evolution of the *Glorious Bouren*, a trade association set up during the Meiji period to control the output of the cotton spinning industry. When SCAP ordered the *Glorious Bouren* to dissolve

[82] Wakui (2018, p. 80).

[83] Kameoka (2014, p. 45).

[84] Wakui (2018, p. 80).

[85] Wakui (2018, p. 104) and Schaede (2000, p. 76). Trade associations were regulated under the Trade Associations Law.

in 1947, a new association was set one year later with the same members and the same staff. As this was certainly not the only example, SCAP announced a law to limit the activities of trade associations.[86] The Trade Association Law was adopted by the Japanese parliament, the Diet, in 1948.[87] This law put the trade associations, broadly understood as "group of two or more businessmen who gather to further their joint business interests,"[88] under the control of the JFTC. The trade associations saw their activities limited to, among others, the exchange of technical information and negotiations with labor unions.[89] Similar to former Article 4 of the AMA, all price fixing facilitated by the trade associations were declared *per se* illegal. Another prohibition was to "inappropriately influence the government or bureaucrats."[90]

When revising the AMA in 1953, the content of the Trade Association Law was transferred to the AMA. As mentioned above, Article 8 of the AMA forbids trade associations to engage in any of the following activities:

i. substantially restraining competition in any particular field of trade;
ii. entering into an international agreement or an international contract as provided in Article 6;
iii. limiting the present or future number of enterprise in any particular field of business;
iv. unjustly restricting the functions or activities of the constituent enterprise (meaning an enterprise who is a member of the trade association; the same applies hereinafter);
v. inducing an enterprise to employ such an act as falls under unfair trade practices.

Guidelines Concerning the Activities of Trade Associations under the Antimonopoly Act (Trade Association Guidelines)[91] were developed in 1979 and updated in 1995. Based on these Guidelines, Schaede summarizes what is forbidden for the trade associations:

> …trade associations must not establish restrictions on price, quantity, investments, market access, or access to technology. Neither can they engage in *dangô* (bid rigging), formulate quality restrictions, set exclusive standards, exchange critical information, formulate binding management guidance for their members, or exclude nonmembers from business. In short, associations must not restrict the functions and business activities of firms in their markets in any way.[92]

The trade association provision has been used a few times. One of the cases shows the trade association taking the role of a facilitator of a cartel. This case, the Kumamoto

[86] Schaede (2000, pp. 76–77).
[87] Schaede (2000, p. 77).
[88] Schaede (2000, p. 77).
[89] For more details on the content of the law, Schaede (2000, p. 77).
[90] Schaede (2000, p. 77).
[91] Available at: https://www.jftc.go.jp/en/legislation_gls/imonopoly_guidelines_files/tradeassociation.pdf. Accessed 15 December 2020.
[92] Schaede (2000, p. 126).

Taxi Association case, involved an agreement to raise the price among 60 independent taxi companies in Kumamoto and ten surrounding cities.[93] When a few taxi companies and individual taxi drivers refused to take part, the cartel participants turned to their joint taxi ticket vendor. This vendor, technically speaking outside the cartel, was asked not to sell vouchers to the taxi companies and individual drivers resisting the price-hike. Hence, these companies and drivers were excluded from a pool of 2000 government and business organizations that were eligible to use these vouchers. After the JFTC advised to terminate the exclusion of some taxi companies and individual taxi drivers from the voucher system, the facilitator of the cartel withdrew the exclusion.

The question could be raised whether Article 8 of the AMA is necessary for dealing with the Kumamoto Taxi Association case. Ariga and Rieke have opined that Article 8 of the AMA is required for trade associations that are not engaged in "an entrepreneurial activity."[94] However, one could argue that selling the vouchers is a commercial activity, turning the association into an enterprise. Hence, Article 8 of the AMA could only be justified by arguing that not all trade associations develop commercial activities. Schaede, though, tempers the optimism in this regard. Not all non-commercial activities of trade associations are taken seriously by the JFTC and thus the impression is given that some of the activities do not infringe Article 8 of the AMA, the extra provision on trade associations.[95]

Schaede exemplifies this by referring to information exchange. Even though information sharing on the price is considered as an infringement in the Trade Association Guidelines,[96] Schaede refers to four elements to argue that information sharing in general is not seriously taken into consideration by the JFTC. First, even though trade association meetings are frequently and thus often exchange information, the JFTC has barely taken any action towards trade associations.[97] Second, trade associations, often at the initiative of the responsible ministries, "gather and publish data on the industry, including data on prices and possibly costs."[98] Third, trade associations are allowed to publish data as long as it is not possible to recognize the data of individual enterprises.[99] In other words, the data of all enterprises need to be aggregated. Fourth, the Trade Association Guidelines explicitly shift the responsibility back to the enterprises by stating that the enterprises are infringing upon the law if pricing decisions are based on price information published by trade associations.[100]

The extra provision on trade associations within the AMA could be seen as an *accident de route*. However, when the role of the trade associations in cartel formation

---

[93] Cited by Schaede (2000, p. 127).

[94] Ariga and Rieke (1964, p. 468).

[95] Schaede (2000, pp. 126–128).

[96] Available at: https://www.jftc.go.jp/en/legislation_gls/imonopoly_guidelines_files/tradeassociation.pdf. Accessed 15 December 2020.

[97] Schaede (2000, p. 128).

[98] Schaede (2000, p. 128).

[99] Schaede (2000, p. 128).

[100] Schaede (2000, p. 128).

is considered, it could be argued that such a provision was necessary because not all trade associations engage in entrepreneurial activities. Such trade associations would not have fallen under Article 3 of the AMA. Despite the justification for the extra provision, one cannot escape the conclusion that it has barely been used.

4.2 Bureaucrats as the Linchpin of Bid Rigging Outside the Scope of the Antimonopoly Law

Another example of how the help of third parties proved to be difficult for the AMA to regulate is *kansei dango* or bid rigging in public procurement projects. Usually, bid rigging is an agreement among competitors to fix who will submit the winning big and/or the price of the winning bid. In Japan, however, bid rigging has had often an extra dimension. The extra dimension was created by the participation of bureaucrats.[101] The interests of bureaucrats to help in setting up and running a bid rigging scheme has been explained by the presence of the *amakudari* system.[102] This system allowed for sending bureaucrats that could not be promoted inside the bureaucratic system to take up a high position in the private sector. In return for offering positions, the private sector firms were assisted by the bureaucrats to organize bid rigging schemes to inflate the prices of the public procurement projects.

The bureaucrats were an essential part of the bid rigging scheme. In Japan, bureaucrats had the discretion to choose between two different types of procurement.[103] According to the Public Accounts Law,[104] central and local governments as well as other public entities can choose between an open tendering system and a designated or selective tendering system.[105] Even though the open tendering system is the general rule with the designated or selective tendering system as the exception, the latter has become the primary government procurement system in Japan until the late 1990s.[106] Unlike the open tendering system, in which all qualified parties can submit their bids, the designated or selective tendering system entails that the contracting agency designates or selects a fixed number of firms qualified to bid. In

[101] Van Uytsel (2017) and Woodall (1996).

[102] Usui and Colignon (2003).

[103] A third tendering system, the limited (single) tendering system will not be covered in this paper. This tendering system is limited to (1) conditions of extreme urgency due to time constraints; (2) cases in which no firms have participated in an open or selective tendering system; (3) cases in which the successful tenderer failed to conclude the contract; (4) cases that only one particular supplier can offer the goods or services due to legal restraints; (5) in other cases where the order so provides. For a full explanation, Kusonoki (2007, p. 527).

[104] Kaikei hou [Accounts Law], Law No. 35 of 1947, last amended by Law No. 53 of 2006 (Accounts Law).

[105] Accounts Law, Articles 29-3(1) and 29-3(3).

[106] It is only after the Saitama Saturday Club case that the government took the open tendering as the default. See Vande Walle (2012, p. 21).

both systems, the contract will then be awarded to the firm submitting the lowest responsible tender.[107]

The discretion within the procurement procedure allowed the bureaucrats to create stability in a relationship among competitors, in which the trust is otherwise vulnerable. There are two reasons why the discretion within the procurement system can offer stability. First, the bidding firms are certain that outside firms will not be able to participate in the bidding process. Second, there is no risk of one of the bidding firm to cheat on the agreement as this firm will risk not to be selected for any of the next rounds of public procurement.

It is obvious that the bureaucrats, not engaging even in business activities, are not in competition with the enterprises aiming to rig a bid. Because of this, Wakui purports, Article 2(6) of the AMA cannot apply.[108] This does not mean that bureaucrats are completely outside the scope of the AMA. The criminal provisions of the AMA, unlike with the administrative sanctions (cease-and-desist order or surcharge), apply to any person, and not just to an enterprise engaging in anti-competitive conduct. Based on the Articles 89(1) and 95(1) of the AMA, both the employees of an enterprise and a government official may be prosecuted for infringing upon the AMA. However, the JFTC has used barely its discretion to refer a cartel to the Prosecutor's Office for a criminal investigation.[109]

Leaving aside the existing provisions in the criminal law,[110] the "missing element in the [AMA] was remedied by the enactment of the Act on the Elimination and Prevention of Involvement in Bid Rigging, etc., and the Punishments for Acts by Employees that Harm Fairness of Bidding."[111] This Act on Preventing Bid Rigging gives the power to the JFTC to inform the head of the procuring office and demand for the implementation of improvement measures. Upon receiving the demand of the JFTC, the head of the procurement office has also the obligation to investigate the involvement of bureaucrats. If their involvement is proven, he also has to determine whether the offending bureaucrats are liable for damages and should be subject to disciplinary actions.

The legislative evolution, basically fortifying Wakui's conclusion of the non-applicability of the AMA to the bureaucrats, partly confirms the 1953 Tokyo High Court decision on the role of facilitators of anti-competitive conduct. Following the reasoning of Kameoka, who denotes the *kansei dango* as a vertical cartel, the AMA cannot be applied because the presence of the bureaucrats in the cartel disturbs the horizontal nature of the agreement. She states that the "negotiations among bidders are horizontal, the agreement between the public officer and the bidding firms is regarded as vertical."[112] Does this conclusion conflict with the 1993 Tokyo High

---

[107] Umeda (2010) and Kusonoki (2007, pp. 526–527).

[108] Wakui (2018, p. 43).

[109] Wakui (2018, p. 43).

[110] Article 96(6) of the Criminal Code in Japan criminalizes bid rigging. However, due to the severity of the sanction and the social stigma attached to it, the Criminal Code provision is not used.

[111] Wakui (2018, p. 45).

[112] Kameoka (2014, p. 45).

Court decision on facilitators? Probably not. At the end, as has been indicated by Wakui,[113] the bureaucrats are not engaging in a business activity at all. Hence, they can even not be "in essence"[114] competitors of each other.

5 Algorithms as the Facilitator of a Cartel and the Antimonopoly Law

5.1 Trade Associations, Bureaucrats, and Algorithms as a Hub

The involvement of third parties in the construction of an unreasonable restraint of trade has posed serious problems for the enforcement of the AMA. The earliest identified problem was with trade associations. When the AMA was just enacted in 1947, SCAP were worried that the term enterprise was not broad enough to catch trade associations. Indeed, the AMA only focused on enterprises and not, like in the European competition legislation, decisions by associations of enterprises. The adoption of an extra law, the Trade Association Law of 1948, was the result. Competition issues related to trade associations were dealt with under the Trade Association Law until the law was incorporated in the AMA in 1953. Ever since, trade associations were held accountable under Article 8 of the AMA. However, the JFTC's application of Article 8 of the AMA could pose problems for effectively catching a hub-and-spoke cartel.

Trade associations are placed above its members and enterprises that are active in the same business sector. These enterprises, being competitors of each other, could share price sensitive information with the trade association. The trade association, in turn, could pass that information to the other members and so create a situation in which each member, aware of what is happening in the sector, could fix the prices. In this scenario, the trade association is acting as the hub. The trade association is collecting the information and steering the other members, competitors of each other, in their effort to collude. No direct communication occurs among the members.

To apply Article 8 of the AMA to the above-mentioned scenario, it is required that the flow of information is the result of a decision within the trade association. In the absence of a formal decision, the flow of information needs to be perceived by the members as a decision of the trade association. In other words, the information should be recognized as something that should be followed. The latter seems to stress compliance with the information received. To speak of a hub-and-spoke cartel, it is required that the trade association has shown an intention to be part of the cartel and that the members recognize the intention as binding and thus implement.

---

[113] Wakui (2018, p. 43).

[114] Kameoka (2014, p. 45).

When we expand the scenario to include an algorithm, it could be conceived that the trade association receives information from its members, analyzes that information by using an algorithm and then communicates to each individual member a price. No direct communication occurs among the members. As long as the process of information sharing, in which the algorithm plays a central role, reflects a decision of the trade association and the members implement the result of the information sharing, Article 8 of the AMA could be applied to the trade association.

The final decision to apply Article 8 of the AMA rests with the JFTC. Even though the Supreme Court has decided that Article 8 of the AMA could be applied in combination with Articles 3 and 2(6) of the AMA, the JFTC has never applied both articles in combination. If a situation were to occur in which both the hub and the spokes are infringing upon the law, it is to be seen whether the JFTC will focus its enforcement on the spokes and limit its action to the hub to issuing an informal request to not be involved.

More than trade associations, bureaucrats have proven to be a facilitator in cartel formation in Japan. The bureaucrats are not reached by Articles 3 and 2(6) of the AMA. Neither is the public procurement office considered as an enterprise. To catch these facilitators, another law has been created. Even if these facilitators would shift to an algorithm, the situation would not change. The adoption of an algorithm will not make the bureaucrats liable under the AMA. Most likely, their decision to shift human actions facilitating a bid rigging scheme to an algorithm, will still keep the bureaucrats liable under the Act Preventing Bid Rigging.

5.2 *Algorithms not Employed by Trade Associations and Bureaucrats as a Hub*

Outside the scope of trade associations and bureaucrats, algorithms could be put into operation by a supplier, a price leader, an accountancy firm, retailers separately from each other, or a software operator. The first three operators of an algorithm reflect a classical hub-and-spoke cartel, while the latter two operators of an algorithm exemplify the algorithmic hub and spoke elaborated by Ezrachi and Stucke.

When a hub-and-spoke cartel that is being operated by a supplier facilitates a price fixing scheme among retailers,[115] the flow of information goes from the retailers to the supplier. The supplier makes that information available to the other retailers. Instead of leaving this to a human being, the supplier could install an algorithm to collect information from the retailers, process it, and then steer the conduct of the retailers. To set up this kind of price fixing scheme, it is not necessary that the retailers share information directly with each other. All information exchange could run through the supplier and subsequently the algorithm. Direct communication between the horizontal parties to the price fixing scheme is not required. An argument could

[115] If it were a way to guarantee the same price among retailers, we would be dealing with retail price maintenance and not a hub-and-spoke cartel.

be made that, as long as the horizontal partners reacted towards the information received through the hub with the implementation of the same or similar conduct, Articles 3 and 2(6) of the AMA could apply. In the end, there was an exchange of sensitive information followed by an implementation in the price setting. Of course, the implementation reveals that there is an underlying understanding among the retailers what the purpose is of the information exchange. The question is whether the hub could be held liable. The hub, who is a supplier, is not a direct competitor of the retailers. The hub is, however, active in the same product market. Is this enough to argue that the hub is 'in essence' a competitor of the retailers? Without a clear statement of the JFTC a definite answer cannot be given.

The situation would be different if the supplier is substituted by a price leader. In the OECD conceptualized scenario, a cartel only exists among horizontally competing firms. Among these firms, one firm will act as a price leader and carry the burden of "programming the dynamic pricing algorithm that fixes the price above the competitive level."[116] Once the price has been set, the price will be collected by the algorithm that is running across the competitors. The collected price will then be the basis for setting the price at the respective competitors. All elements to constitute an unreasonable restraint of trade are present. Sensitive information is being exchanged and a same or similar action is implemented. Moreover, the hub of the conspiracy is active in the same product market, due to which both the hub and the spokes could be held liable.

Another variant of the previous scenarios is that the role of the hub will be fulfilled by an accountancy firm. If information is exchanged in order to run an algorithm at the accountancy firm to decide the price of the respective competitors and this exchange is being followed by an implementation of the same or similar conduct, the problem will be to hold the accountancy firm liable for running the algorithm that controls the price fixing. In the end, the accountancy firm is by far in essence a competitor of the price fixers. At best, the JFTC will be able to take an action against the horizontally competing firms that have been part of the illegal price fixing.

What then with the scenarios for which Ezrachi and Stucke warn in case an algorithm is going to act as a hub?[117] In the first scenario, the same algorithm will be sold to and used by various firms that are each other's competitors. Unlike in the scenarios described above, the hub is not assembling information from the competing firms, it only has a relationship to the firm it belongs to. It is possible that the use of the same algorithm will lead to the same price setting. Unless the use of the same algorithm has been the result of communication among the competing firms, it is hard to argue that the unwitting use of the same algorithm could be caught by the AMA. Would it change if the firm is aware that competitors have purchased the same algorithm? For example, the firm could learn from the algorithm producer or vendor that the same algorithm has been sold to competing firms. Since this kind of knowledge does not constitute an exchange of sensitive information, the application of the AMA would be difficult to defend.

[116]OECD (2017, p. 27); see also Capobianco and Gonzaga (2017, p. 4).

[117]For the hub-and-spoke scenarios, see Ezrachi and Stucke (2016, pp. 47–50).

The last algorithmic hub and spoke scenario for which Ezrachi and Stucke caution is the scenario in which a firm develops and operates an algorithm that sets the price for enterprises that subscribe to the use of that algorithm.[118] The popular example in this context is Uber. The complexity for applying Articles 3 and 2(6) of the AMA to this scenario is to prove the presence of communication between parties that could be considered active in the same market. If we build the scenario around Uber, we know that Uber runs an algorithm to collect information on available drivers and customers. Based on that information, the algorithm determines the price. The communication from the driver to the algorithm is his availability at a certain spot. The customer communicates his request for a ride to the algorithm. The algorithm communicates a price to both the customer and the driver. There is no communication between the drivers. However, their communication with the algorithm has an influence on the price, and so does the request for a ride by the customer. Is the communication that one is available as a driver sensitive information? In the end, the information provided is not more than conveying the message that he has 'opened his store.' In an online setting, where price setting can be made dependent on many more parameters than in an offline situation, this may be different. The more shops open the lower the price will be, or vice versa. But the algorithm does more. The algorithm stipulates that a driver in a similar situation will demand the same price from the customer. There is no communication at all about this aspect. This is decided by the algorithm. Hence, can we speak of communication about the price between competing drivers? The situation resembles more a unilateral imposition of a price to be asked for a service offered by an enterprise in a different level of the market.

Mark Anderson and Max Huffman on the one hand and Julian Nowag on the other hand have shed light on the imposition of a price on an enterprise in another level of the market.[119] They have discussed whether resale price maintenance could be applied. Resale price maintenance has specific application requirements. One of the requirements is the transfer of a product from one level of the production or distribution chain to the other. When applied to Uber, all authors agree that the business scheme of Uber does not involve the sales of a product to the drivers which they subsequently sell to the riders. Since the AMA also presupposes the sale of goods to apply its provision on resale price maintenance, it will also be for the same reason as in the US and the EU that Articles 19 and 2(9)(iv) of the AMA cannot be applied to the Uber business scheme.[120]

How then to qualify the price imposed by Uber on the drivers? With its rich diversity on unfair trade practices, the provisions that the JFTC applies to vertical agreements and unilateral conduct, the AMA has some backup provisions that can apply in case the resale price maintenance provision cannot. One of these provisions is Article 2(9)(vi) of the AMA, which gives the JFTC the power to designate practices that should be considered as unfair. One of these designations is codified in the

[118] Ezrachi and Stucke (2016, pp. 50–52).

[119] Nowag (2018, p. 19) and Anderson and Huffman (2017, pp. 907–915).

[120] Wakui (2018, p. 181).

General Designation last revised in 2009 (2009 General Designation).[121] Paragraph 12 of the 2009 General Designation is probably the most relevant for discussing algorithms that set a price for enterprises at different levels of the market.

Paragraph 12 of the 2009 General Designation designates conditional dealings as an unfair trade practice. Conditional dealings are unjust restrictions of trade that do not amount to a resale price maintenance (Article 2(9) of the AMA) and exclusive dealing (Paragraph 11 of the 2009 General Designation). One example of restrictions for which this Paragraph 12 of the 2009 General Designation is restrictions on price. Most of the restrictions on pricing that the JFTC has condemned, are restrictions in which a "supplier eliminates price competition amongst its retailers."[122] More recently, the JFTC sought to apply this provision to parity clauses, which means that a platform demands its sellers not to set the price on other platforms lower. In doing so, the price charged across the platforms tend to be the same.

The designation on conditional dealing has two weaknesses. The JFTC is not able to levy a surcharge, which is an administrative fine taking away the profits made during the infringement of the AMA, for infringing Paragraph 12 of the 2009 General Designation. The AMA only gives the power to the JFTC to issue a cease and desist order for infringements of the designations under the 2009 General Designation.[123] Further, such a cease and desist order only follows when a notification has been given to the enterprise under investigation. Many enterprises respond to this notification.[124] As a consequence, the JFTC has barely had the chance to elaborate on the application modalities of this provision. In recent history, for example, the JFTC had the opportunity to provide its view on the parity clause, but since Amazon changed its behavior subsequent the notification, the JFTC closed the investigation without explaining Paragraph 12 of the 2009 General Designation.[125] Therefore, to know whether the designation of conditional dealing could reach the business scheme presented by Uber, and whether the JFTC would even consider justifications for this business scheme, may not be for the near future. Of course, before the JFTC can give its view on Uber and its algorithm, both have to be present in Japan. Uber only entered Japan in 2020 by partnering with existing taxi companies.[126] It can thus be

---

[121] Designation of Unfair Trade Practices (Fair Trade Commission Public Notice No. 15 of June 18, 1982 as revised in 2009). Available at: https://www.jftc.go.jp/en/legislation_gls/unfairtradepractices.html. Accessed 15 December 2020.

[122] Wakui (2018, p. 191).

[123] Wakui (2018, p. 140). It is also stipulated that only the unfair trade practices qualified in the AML can be subject to a surcharge. For a short description of the problem in this book, Regulating Competition between Digital Platforms: The Japan Fair Trade Commission's Preference for Unfair Trade Practices [this volume].

[124] Regulating Competition between Digital Platforms: The Japan Fair Trade Commission's Preference for Unfair Trade Practices [this volume]. The process of notification has recently been changed to a commitment procedure.

[125] Regulating Competition between Digital Platforms: The Japan Fair Trade Commission's Preference for Unfair Trade Practices [this volume].

[126] Available at: https://www.japantimes.co.jp/news/2020/07/03/business/corporate-business/uber-starts-in-tokyo/. Accessed 15 December 2020.

presumed that the algorithm functions slightly different than what we have seen so far across the world.

6 Conclusion

The Japanese AMA has had a complex relationship with facilitators of a cartel. The earliest example is the help given by trade associations. Japan, still under the governance of SCAP, realized this problem and drafted a law to address the role of trade associations in a competitive setting. This law was later transferred to the AMA. A similar development occurred when bureaucrats started to facilitate bid rigging for public procurement projects. Rather than dealing with the whole bid rigging scheme under the AMA, it was decided that only the bid rigging enterprises could be held liable under the AMA. For the bureaucrats, the legislator adopted a new law.

With the arrival of algorithms, there has been a renewed interest in cartel facilitators. To what extent can an algorithm be held accountable as a facilitator of a cartel? As long as the algorithms are used as tools by the trade associations and bureaucrats, there is no doubt that little will change to the current legal scheme. The relevant laws remain applicable to deal with these situations.

The main issue arises, though, when trade associations and bureaucrats are not involved. This chapter has identified that the algorithm can be put in place by a supplier, a leading price setter among the competing firms, or an accountancy firm. However, for the enterprises to be liable as a hub, it is required that there is a competitive relationship between the hub and the spokes. It is obvious that this relationship is present in case the hub is a leading price setter among the competing firms and is absent in case the hub is an accountancy firm. When the hub is a supplier, the issue is open for discussion as all are active in relation to the same product. Algorithms would not change the situation. In the end, the algorithms are a mere tool in the hands of any of these enterprises.

More controversial is when the algorithm is acting as a hub. From the two scenarios we have discussed, we have concluded that it is only possible to bring the algorithm under the AMA if there has been communication among the competing firms to employ the same algorithm. As long as the application of the same algorithm by competitors is a coincidence, the AMA would not apply. If the hub is being operated by an enterprise different from the competiting spokes, we have argued that, due to the lack of communication between the spokes, the unfair trade practice of conditional dealing may be applied to an algorithm forcing its spokes to ask the same price. This approach is in line with how the JFTC has been dealing with hub-and-spoke cartels outside the framework of trade associations and bureaucrats as cartel facilitators.

Acknowledgements This chapter has received support of the project Artificial Intelligence, Price Setting Strategies and Antitrust Law: Towards a Regulatory Framework, a Grants-in-Aid for Scientific Research (C) with No. 18K01300.

References

Anderson M, Huffman M (2017) The sharing economy meets the Sherman Act: is UBER a firm, a cartel or something in between? C Bus Law Rev 2017(3):859–933

Ariga M, Rieke LV (1964) The Antimonopoly Law of Japan and its enforcement. Wash L Rev 9(3):437–478

Augustine MR, A research guide to research on the Allied occupation of Japan. http://www.columbia.edu/~hds2/BIB95/02occupation_augustine.htm. Accessed 15 December 2020

Bostoen F (2019) Competition law in the peer-to-peer economy. In: Devolder B (ed) The platform economy: Unraveling the legal status of online intermediaries. Intersentia, Cambridge, pp 143–172

Colombo N (2018) Virtual competition: human liability vis-à-vis artificial intelligence's anticompetitive behaviours. Eur Compet Regul Law Rev 2(1):11–23

Capobianco A, Gonzaga P (2017) Algorithms and competition: friends or foes. Compet Policy Int—Antitrust Chron 1(2):1–6. https://www.competitionpolicyinternational.com/wp-content/uploads/2017/08/CPI-Capobianco-Gonzaga.pdf. Accessed 15 Dec 2020

Ezrachi A, Stucke ME (2015) Artificial intelligence & collusion: When computers inhibit competition. Working Paper CCLP (L) 40. https://www.law.ox.ac.uk/sites/files/oxlaw/cclpl40.pdf. Accessed 15 Dec 2020

Ezrachi A, Stucke ME (2016) Virtual competition: the promise and perils of the algorithm-driven economy. Harvard University Press, Cambridge

Ezrachi and Stucke (2017) Artificial intelligence & collusion: when computers inhibit competition. Univ Ill Law Rev 5:1775–1801

First H (2000) Antitrust in Japan: the original intent. Pac Rim Law & Policy J 9:1–71

Gerber D (2010) Global competition: law, markets, and globalization. Oxford University Press, Oxford

Giannino M (2018) Webtaxi: the Luxembourg Competition Authority exempts an algorithmic price-fixing arrangement on efficiency grounds. https://www.lexxion.eu/en/coreblogpost/webtaxi-the-luxembourg-competition-authority-exempts-an-algorithmic-price-fixing-arrangement-on-efficiency-grounds/. Accessed 15 Dec 2020

Haley J (2001) Antitrust in Germany and Japan: the first fifty years, 1947–1998. University of Washington Press, Seattle

Hayashi S, Wu K, Ma X (2020) The Japanese competition law in its own way: a historical review of the AMA and its characteristic. In: Van Uytsel S, Hayashi S, Haley JO (eds) Research handbook on Asian competition law. Edward Elgar, Cheltenham, pp 44–64

Inoue A (2012) Antitrust enforcement in Japan: history, rhetoric and law of the Antimonopoly Act. Dai-Ichi Hoki, Tokyo

Kameoka E (2014) Competition law and policy in Japan and the EU. Edward Elgar, Cheltenham

Kusonoki S (2007) Japan's government procurement regimes for public works: a comparative introduction. Brook J Int'l L 32:523–552

Matsushita M (1997) The antimonopoly law of Japan. In: Richardson JD, Graham EM (eds) Global competition policy. Institute for International Economics, Washington, DC, pp 151–198

Nowag J (2018) When sharing platforms fix sellers' prices. https://papers.ssrn.com/sol3/papers.cfm?abstract_id=3217193. Accessed 15 Dec 2020

OECD (2017) Algorithms and collusion—background note by the Secretariat. DAF/Comp(2017)4. https://one.oecd.org/document/DAF/COMP(2017)4/en/pdf. Accessed 15 Dec 2020

OECD (2019) Hub-and-spoke arrangements—note by BIAC. DAF/COMP/WD(2019)112. https://one.oecd.org/document/DAF/COMP/WD(2019)112/en/pdf. Accessed 15 December 2020

Schaede U (2000) Cooperative capitalism: Self-regulation, trade associations, and the antimonopoly law in Japan. Oxford University Press, Oxford

Seita AY, Tamura J (1994) Historical background of Japan's antimonopoly law. Univ Ill Law Rev 1:115–185

Seryo S (2004) Cartel and bid rigging. https://www.jftc.go.jp/eacpf/05/jicatext/aug31.pdf. Accessed 15 Dec 2020

Tuytschaever F (2015) Cartels and proof of cartels: private practitioner's perspective. In: Wijckmans F, Tuytschaever F (eds) Horizontal agreements and cartels in EU competition law. Oxford University Press, Oxford, pp 7–33

Umeda S (2010) Government procurement law and policy: Japan. https://www.loc.gov/law/help/govt-procurement-law/japan.php#_ftn24. Accessed 15 Dec 2020

Usui Ch, Colignon RA (2003) Amakudari: the hidden fabric of Japan's economy. Cornell University Press, New York

Vande Walle S (2012) The Saitama Saturday Club case: political meddling, public opinion, and antitrust enforcement in Japan at a turning point. https://papers.ssrn.com/sol3/papers.cfm?abstract_id=2132658. Accessed 15 Dec 2020

Vande Walle S (2013a) Private antitrust litigation in the European Union and Japan. Maklu, Antwerpen

Vande Walle S (2013b) Competition and competition law in Japan: between scepticism and embrace. In: Dowdle MW, Gillespie J, Maher I (eds) Asian capitalism and the regulation of competition: towards a regulatory geography of global competition law. Cambridge University Press, Cambridge, pp 123–143

Van Uytsel S (2015) Anti-cartel enforcement in Japan: does leniency make the difference? In: Beaton-Well C, Tan Ch (eds) The leniency religion, anti-cartel enforcement in a contemporary age. Hart Publishing, Oxford, pp 81–107

Van Uytsel S (2017) Am I a bid rigger: how bureaucrats came within the focus of regulating bid-rigging in Japan. Presentation at the Asian Competition Forum (December 11–12, Hong Kong). https://asiancompetitionforum.com/new-page. Accessed 15 Dec 2020 (link disconnected as of 22 April 2021)

Van Uytsel S (2018) Artificial intelligence and collusion: A literature overview. In: Corrales M, Fenwick M, Forgó N (eds) Robotics, AI and the future of law. Springer, Singapore, pp 155–182

Wakui M (2008) Antimonopoly law: competition law and policy in Japan. Arima Publishing, Suffolk

Wakui M (2018) Antimonopoly law: competition law and policy in Japan. Independently Published

Woodall B (1996) Japan under construction: corruption, politics, and public works. University of California Press, Berkeley

Index

S. Van Uytsel (ed.), *The Digital Economy and Competition Law in Asia*, Perspectives in Law, Business and Innovation,
https://doi.org/10.1007/978-981-16-0324-2

D

E

F

G

H

I

J

K

The manufacturer's authorised representative in the EU is Springer Nature Customer Service Centre GmbH, Europaplatz 3, 69115 Heidelberg, Germany. If you have any concerns regarding our products, please contact ProductSafety@springernature.com

Printed and bound by CPI Group (UK) Ltd, Croydon, CR0 4YY

30/09/2026

02225330-0006